JOURNAL FOR THE STUDY OF THE OLD TESTAMENT SUPPLEMENT SERIES

63

Editors
David J A Clines
Philip R Davies

JSOT Press
Sheffield

SHILOH

A Biblical City in
Tradition and History

Donald G. Schley

Journal for the Study of the Old Testament
Supplement Series 63

DS
110
.S26
S3
1989

For Jan

Copyright © 1989 Sheffield Academic Press

Published by JSOT Press
JSOT Press is an imprint of
Sheffield Academic Press Ltd
The University of Sheffield
343 Fulwood Road
Sheffield S10 3BP
England

Printed in Great Britain
by Billing & Sons Ltd
Worcester

British Library Cataloguing in Publication Data

Schley, Donald G.
    Shiloh: A biblical city in tradition
    and history
    I. Title   II. Series
    221.9'5

    ISSN 0309-0787
    ISBN 1-85075-161-7

CONTENTS

ABBREVIATIONS

AJA	*American Journal of Archaeology*
ANET	*Ancient Near Eastern Texts* (ed. J.B. Pritchard)
BA	*Biblical Archaeologist*
BAR	*Biblical Archaeological Review*
BASOR	*Bulletin of the American Schools of Oriental Research*
CBQ	*Catholic Biblical Quarterly*
EAEHL	*Encyclopaedia of Archaeological Excavations in the Holy Land* (Jerusalem: Israel Exploration Society)
EI	*Eretz Israel* (Jerusalem: Israel Exploration Society)
EncJud	*Encyclopaedia Judaica*
HBD	*Harper's Bible Dictionary* (New York: Harper & Row, 1974, 1985)
HUCA	*Hebrew Union College Annual*
IDB(S)	*Interpreter's Dictionary of the Bible (Supplement)*
IEJ	*Israel Exploration Journal*
IJH	*Israelite and Judean History* (ed. J.H. Hayes & J.M. Miller)
JbDT	*Jahrbücher für Deutsche Theologie*
JBL	*Journal of Biblical Literature*
JNES	*Journal of Near Eastern Studies*
JPOS	*Journal of the Palestine Oriental Society*
JSOT	*Journal for the Study of the Old Testament*
JSS	*Journal of Semitic Studies*
JTS	*Journal of Theological Studies*
KS	A. Alt, *Kleine Schriften zur Geschichte des Volkes Israel* (3 vols.; 4th edn, München: Beck, 1968)
NedTT	*Nederlandse Theologische Tijdschrift*
NKZ	*Neue Kirchliche Zeitschrift*
OTS	*Oudtestamentische Studiën*
PEFQS	*Palestine Exploration Fund Quarterly Statement*
PEQ	*Palestine Exploration Quarterly*
QDAP	*Quarterly of the Department of Antiquities of Palestine*
SAT	*Die Schriften des Alten Testaments* (ed. H. Gressmann, et al.)
Sem	*Semitica*
TWAT	*Theologisches Wörterbuch zum Alten Testament*
VT(S)	*Vetus Testamentum (Supplement)*
ZDPV	*Zeitschrift des deutschen Palästina-Vereins*

PREFACE

This work was originally presented to the faculty of Emory University in August, 1986, as a dissertation under the title, 'The Traditions and History of Biblical Shiloh'. From its inception the project was intended to provide a thorough critical review of the historical issues involving the ancient Ephraimite sanctuary. My personal goal was to establish a fresh basis for the discussion of Shiloh's role in Israelite history and religion, especially in view of the numerous unspoken assumptions which have accrued to this debate during the last several generations. Therefore, the research was undertaken from a *forschungsgeschichtlich* perspective, with special emphasis on the origins of the modern debate in the contradictory positions taken on the subject by Ewald and Graf in the middle of the nineteenth century. And it is noteworthy that the present discussion has not really moved beyond the place it was 130 years ago.

Nevertheless, the aim of this work is not primarily the delineation of the history of the debate. Rather, the *Forschungsgeschichte* which dominates the first half of the book is meant to establish an informed basis for evaluating the evidence of the second half, which is critical and interpretative, and which focuses upon the biblical text. Thus the argument seeks to move from an understanding of the historical debate to a fresh evaluation of the evidence, which is somewhat free from uncritical assumptions about the course of Shiloh's history and its significance for the history and religion of ancient Israel.

Especial thanks are due John H. Hayes for his constant interest in and criticism of this work, from beginning to end, and to Max Miller for encouraging me in the development of certain of the more novel ideas which appear in these pages. A debt of gratitude is also owed to the faculties of Old Testament and Assyriology of the University of Göttingen for their dedication in teaching me classical biblical criticism, and for their willingness to discuss with me departures from, or new venues within that tradition. Finally, I am indebted to my wife, Jan, for her ten years of sacrifice in support of my research and education, which alone has made this book possible. This work is dedicated to her.

D.G. Schley
30 October 1987

Chapter 1

SHILOH IN NINETEENTH-CENTURY
OLD TESTAMENT CRITICISM: FROM DE WETTE
TO THE RISE OF THE NEW DOCUMENTARY HYPOTHESIS

1.1 *The Importance of Shiloh in the Critical Discussion*

Although the biblical city of Shiloh was hardly the central focus of
Old Testament criticism in the nineteenth century, scholars of that
era almost always discussed Shiloh in connection with the problems
of the nature of early Israelite worship and the centralization of the
cult. On the one hand, Shiloh during the pre-monarchic period was
associated with the traditions of the wilderness cultus. Not only was
the tent shrine located at Shiloh (Josh. 18.1; 19.51b; 22.19, 29; 1 Sam.
2.22b; Ps. 78.60, 67), but the other major features of the priestly
cultus were found there as well: the camp (Josh. 18.9; Judg. 21.12);
the ark (1 Sam. 3.3; 4.4-6; 14.18); the priesthood of Aaron (Josh.
19.51b; 21.1-2; 22.12-13, 30-32; 24.33; 1 Samuel 1-4); the altar (Josh.
22.9-34); and the *'ēphôd* (1 Sam. 14.3). On the other hand, Shiloh
appears only once in texts pertaining to this period in connection
with the tradition of strict cultic centralization: in Josh. 22.9-34, the
Israelites call upon the Transjordanian tribes to explain a seemingly
schismatic altar erected by those groups in the territory of the Jordan
upon their return from the conquest of Palestine. Elsewhere,
however, Shiloh is found alongside other apparently legitimate
Yahwistic shrines in the pre-monarchic period (esp. Mizpah and
Bethel: Judg. 20-21). During the period of the monarchy, Shiloh
plays a less important role. In 1 Kings 11-15, Shiloh is the domicile
of the prophet Ahijah, who first anoints Jeroboam as king over the
northern tribes, yet later condemns that king for the erection of the
shrines at Dan and Bethel. Ps. 78.60-72 and Jer. 7.12-15, moreover,
represent Shiloh as the spiritual predecessor to Jerusalem. Jeremiah
designates Shiloh as 'the place where Yahweh caused his name to
dwell at first', employing a specifically deuteronomic formula. The

eclipse of Shiloh by Jerusalem in conjunction with the rise of the Davidic monarchy appears to lie behind the oracle in Gen. 49.10-12 as well.

The main reason for Shiloh's importance in the debate over the centralization of the cult was as follows. In the law of Deuteronomy 12, a single, central place of worship is prescribed for the Israelites. That law, however, never actually designated a site for the sanctuary, though most scholars since W.M.L. de Wette have assumed that the centralization law in Deuteronomy referred to Jerusalem. The priestly laws of Exodus–Numbers, similarly, did not give any command regarding the place of worship in a specific, geographic sense. Worship in the priestly code centered instead on the wilderness camp of the Israelites. In this context, worship and sacrifice were to be carried out at a specific institution: the tent sanctuary, alternately designated the *'ōhel-mô'ēd* (the 'tent of meeting') or the *miškan-Yhwh* (the 'dwelling-place of Yahweh'), usually translated 'the tabernacle of Yahweh'. According to Lev. 17.1-9, the only legitimate place of sacrifice for the Israelites in the wilderness was this tent shrine. Apart from the ambivalence of the designation of the tent shrine, this institution all but disappears from the historical books following the Israelite conquest of Canaan. When there is mention of this shrine, it is nearly always in connection with Shiloh. The only exceptions are a single reference in 1 Kgs. 8.4, where the tent of meeting is brought up with the ark of the covenant into the temple in Jerusalem, and two references in 2 Chron. 1.2, 6. In the latter texts, which parallel that in 1 Kgs 8.4, the tent of meeting is brought from the great high place of Gibeon to Jerusalem. 1 Chron. 21.29, and 2 Chron. 1.5 contain further notes on the tabernacle of Yahweh, which roughly parallel those in 1 Kings. Thus, Shiloh is the only place associated with the tent shrine before the reigns of David and Solomon.

During the nineteenth century, then, it was possible to use the biblical traditions about Shiloh *either* (a) to demonstrate the absence of a knowledge of the Mosaic law restricting the worship of Yahweh to a single sanctuary prior to the establishment of the temple in Jerusalem, and down into the later years of the Judean monarchy (when the reforms of Josiah were put into effect), *or* (b) to claim continuity between the cultic regulations of the Pentateuch and the early pre-monarchic and settlement periods. In either case, scholars were obliged to cite those particular passages which seemed to support their respective cases, while simultaneously explaining away the various passages which cast doubt upon their positions. The role of Shiloh in the early history of Israel was therefore an important topic in the discussion of the centralization of worship in pre-monarchic Israel.

Nonetheless, Shiloh did not attract sufficient interest in scholarly circles to become the subject of a separate controversy. Instead, the question of Shiloh's status in Israel's early period nearly always arose in the context of the larger literary-critical and historical issues regarding the relationship of pentateuchal law to the narratives of the historical books, particularly as this problem related to the centralization of the cult. Consequently, scholarly opinion concerning Shiloh was usually formulated in treatments of these larger issues. Only Karl Heinrich Graf saw fit to prepare a separate treatment on Shiloh: in 1855 he published a little-known Latin monograph on the temple at Shiloh, which encompassed most of the major issues that subsequently occupied scholars with regard to Shiloh.[1] Otherwise, Shiloh continued to play an important tangential role in the Old Testament criticism of the nineteenth century.

1.2 De Wette and his Successors

1.2.1 De Wette

The scholar who more than any other influenced the course of the nineteenth-century debate over the relationship of pentateuchal law to the narratives of the historical books was W.M.L. de Wette. Although one might think first of Julius Wellhausen,[2] Wellhausen's influence came at the end of the century and contributed above all to the consensus on pentateuchal sources which emerged during the last quarter of the nineteenth and the first quarter of the twentieth centuries. It was de Wette's work, however, which introduced the basic argumentative framework upon which later scholars such as Gramberg, Vatke, Graf, and Wellhausen would develop and build. In fact, de Wette's *Beiträge zur Einleitung in das Alte Testament*,[3] first published as a supplement to Vater's *Commentar über den Pentateuch*, established the terms of debate on the authenticity of the pentateuchal law, and the relationship of that law to the narratives of the historical books, from that time down to the present.

De Wette's most salient contribution to this debate was the way he posed the question of the reliability of the pentateuchal claim that the Law came from Moses. De Wette addressed this problem by juxtaposing and then comparing the materials of the pentateuchal narratives with those of the Old Testament historical books. From this arrangement of the evidence he argued that the characteristic feature of pentateuchal law was the prescription of a single, central place of worship, with a ritual law administered by a monolithic, hierarchical priesthood. In contrast to these key Mosaic prescriptions, the books of Judges–2 Kings reflected a situation where no such centralized worship or cultic hierarchy could be found.[4] Instead of a single central sanctuary,[5] de Wette pointed out that three main sanctuaries appear in the book of Judges: Mizpah (Judg. 11.11; 20.1; 21.1, 5, 8), Bethel (20.18, 26; 21.2-4), and Shiloh (Judg. 18.31; 21.12, 16-24).[6] Moreover, priestly rights and authority seemed to have resided with the heads of families and clans, and sacrifice could take place when and wherever the patriarch of the group chose.[7] Where evidence of priesthood was found, the particular priesthood was not expressly levitical, and was more often irregular, as in the case of the priesthood at Dan (Judg. 18.30), that of Micah in the Ephraimite hill country (Judg. 17), that of the house of Eli at Shiloh (1 Sam. 1-4), or that of Samuel, who was not a Levite, but rather a child simply dedicated to the deity through the free vow of its mother. Thus, de Wette argued, the narratives of the historical books were devoid of any knowledge of Mosaic law. That law accordingly had to be ascribed to a period in Israelite history later than the composition of the books of the former prophets.

Thus, de Wette's approach to the problem of the relationship of pentateuchal law to the narratives of the historical books treated Shiloh as one of many holy places at which the Israelites worshipped Yahweh in the time before Josiah's reign.[8] Overall, de Wette's views on the history of the Israelite cultus can be summarized as follows. Until the construction of the temple in Jerusalem under Solomon, there had been no thought of a national holy place where worship of Yahweh was to be carried out to the exclusion of all other sanctuaries. The Mosaic law, in fact, was not set into force until the time of Josiah.[9] All traces of cultic centralization to be found in the historical books were interpolations from later periods, and therefore useless for the reconstruction of the earlier periods of Israel's cultic history. Institutions such as the 'tent of meeting', which had assumed a central role in the pentateuchal narratives, were ideal retrojections (*Rückprojezierungen*) from the time of the monarchy.[10] The tent of meeting, which in the historical books is associated only with Shiloh until the capture of the ark of Yahweh by the Philistines (1 Sam. 4), and thereafter only with Gibeon and later Jerusalem, was a fictional conception based on the model of the Solomonic temple.[11] If there was any factual basis to this institution, it was to be found only in the brief reference in Exod. 33.7-11 to Moses' pitching of a simple tent outside of the camp which he then named the 'tent of meeting'. Of the famed Mosaic tabernacle (the *miškān* or dwelling-place) only the tent of meeting as depicted in Exod. 33.7-11 might preserve the memory of some historical reality.[12]

De Wette gave a more detailed treatment of the specific history of Shiloh in his *Lehrbuch der hebräisch-jüdischen Archaeologie*.[13] In this work he argued that the tent of meeting became historically uncertain after the time of Joshua, and that no certain trace of its whereabouts appeared until the time of David. De Wette sought possible locations for this shrine at Mizpah in Gilead (Judg. 21.11), Shiloh (1 Sam. 1-3), Mizpah in Benjamin (Judg. 20.1; 21.1, 5, 8), Bethel (Judg. 20.28; 21.2), Gilgal (Judg. 3.19; 1 Sam. 7.16; 11.15; 13.8, 11; 25.21, 33), Nob (1 Sam. 21.1-9; 22.9ff.), and Hebron (2 Sam. 5.3; 15.7), all of which he considered to be uncertain. This treatment might at first appear to contradict the view expressed by de Wette in his earlier *Beiträge*. However, de Wette's treatment of the tent shrine in his *Lehrbuch* reflected his already stated view that the *'ōhel-mô'ēd* might have been historical as it appeared in Exod. 33.7-11, but certainly not as it was depicted in Exodus 26-27.

In addition, de Wette treated previous explanations of the disappearance of the tent shrine in the later historical narratives. Several earlier attempts had been made to interpret Mizpah and Bethel as appelative nouns for Shiloh.[14] These same arguments had been taken up by certain biblical scholars as a means of explaining the apparent discrepancy between the demand for a single, central shrine in Deuteronomy 12, and the presence of multiple Yahwistic shrines in the books of Judges-2 Kings. The sacral role of Bethel and Mizpah in Judges 20-21, where Shiloh also appeared as the site of the camp (Judg. 21.12) and the yearly feast of Yahweh (Judg. 21.19), necessitated some explanation for this apparent contradiction to

pentateuchal law. But de Wette dismissed these arguments as
arbitrary, noting instead that the biblical writers themselves had
taken pains to distinguish these various shrines. A case in point is the
exact description of Shiloh's geographic location found in Judg.
21.19. These careful directions come immediately after several
references to Bethel and Mizpah, which are given no further
clarification, as if both writer and audience knew their locations.
Consequently, Bethel and Mizpah were not alternate designations
for Shiloh, but rather, completely different locations.[15] Of equal
importance was de Wette's treatment of the note in Maimonides to
the effect that 'after the death of Eli, the dwelling at Shiloh was
destroyed (or deserted?), and they went to Nob, and built there a
sanctuary'.[16] Maimonides' conclusion was later to play an important
role in the debate over the destruction of Shiloh. It is, in fact, the
earliest known mention of a destruction of Shiloh in connection with
the disaster at Aphek. De Wette ascribed this tradition to mere
caprice (*Willkür*), and further discounted the reference to the tent of
meeting at Gibeon in the Chronicles.[17]

De Wette's major contribution to the historical discussion came in
the form of the questions he raised about the relationship of the
narratives of the historical books to the laws of the Pentateuch,
rather than in the form of definitive answers. Yet the prominence
Shiloh had assumed in the discussion of the centralization issue in de
Wette's treatment was one which it would occupy throughout the
rest of that century and on into the next.

1.2.2 *Winer*

De Wette's groundbreaking work did not, however, establish a
consensus in the academic world of the early nineteenth century.
Thus, Georg Benedikt Winer's *Biblisches Realwörterbuch*, first
published in 1820, described Shiloh as the 'seat of the tabernacle and
of the national cultus from Joshua to Eli'.[18]

Nevertheless, Winer, in his treatment of the tabernacle,[19] supported
de Wette's conclusion that the pentateuchal image of the tabernacle
was actually a retrojection of the Jerusalem temple:

> One must therefore accept that the saga of that cultic tent was
> fantastically embellished, so that out of a simple, portable
> sanctuary a magnificent, idealized palace—a fairy castle—emerged
> in the tradition.[20]

Winer thus accepted the historicity of the tent of meeting, not as the tent sanctuary was depicted in the Exodus 26-27, 35-40, but as it appeared in Exod. 33.7-11. Later scholars such as Graf and Wellhausen adopted de Wette's view of the tent shrine, but went further than either de Wette or Winer and consigned the tent sanctuary entirely to the realm of fiction.

1.2.3 *Gramberg*

The publication of C.P.W. Gramberg's *Kritische Geschichte der Religionsideen des Alten Testaments* in 1829 continued many of the positions first advanced by de Wette.[21] Thus Gramberg maintained de Wette's view of the tent of meeting, contrasting the simple tent of Exod. 33.7-11 with the tabernacle or *Prachtzelt* of Exodus 26-27, 35-40, which he regarded as mythical.[22] Gramberg also took the narrative of Joshua 22 to be a fictional creation by an editor seeking to demonstrate that the laws of Moses were in force already at the time of Joshua.[23] Gramberg further shared de Wette's contempt for the books of Chronicles as an historical source[24] and asserted the innocence of the historical books with regard to Mosaic law and the centralization of the cultus. Consequently Gramberg accepted the necessity of assigning to the pentateuchal law a later date of composition than the books of Joshua–2 Kings. As a corollary to this principle, Gramberg agreed with de Wette's insight that those passages in the historical books in which the forms of the Mosaic cultus were present, such as Joshua 22, had to be dated to the latest period of Israelite history.

Nevertheless, Gramberg maintained certain significant differences with de Wette. He explained, for example, the confusing reference to variant sanctuaries in the later chapters of the book of Judges in terms of the idea that the tent of meeting had been at Shiloh during the pre-monarchic period. At the same time, Gramberg rejected as dependent upon the narratives Judges those passages in Joshua which alone would have made such a view tenable (e.g. Josh. 18.1-10; 19.51; 21.2; 22.9, 28-29).[25] Conversely, Gramberg argued that the *bēt-hā'ĕlōhîm* at Shiloh in Judg. 18.31 was in fact a reference to the tent of meeting,[26] and also took the reference to Bethel in Judg. 20.10, 26 as referring to the *bēt-hā'ĕlōhîm* in Shiloh, while at the same time interpreting Bethel in Judg. 21.2 loosely as 'the dwelling-place of God'. These arguments presaged those of later, more conservative scholars, who sought to defend the authenticity of the Mosaic cultus in the early period of Israel's history.[27]

In a somewhat different fashion, Gramberg interpreted the *hêkal-Yhwh* and the *nēr-'Ĕlōhîm* in 1 Samuel 1–4 as Solomonic anachronisms and argued that the writer had here interpolated his own view of the temple of Solomon. The only sanctuary at Shiloh, according to Gramberg, had been the tent of meeting.[28] Gramberg further argued that after the capture of the ark by the Philistines, the tent of meeting and the ark had been separated. With the return of the ark, that cult object had continued to be transported into battle (1 Sam. 14.18), while the tent remained at Shiloh where it was no longer venerated.[29]

Whereas Gramberg's general critical assumptions corresponded to those of de Wette, the details of his work revealed a piecemeal approach which did not fully incorporate de Wette's views. Indeed, many of the arguments advanced by Gramberg concerning the tent of meeting at Shiloh in the period of the Judges and the appellative use of *bēt-hā'ĕlōhîm* and *bēt-'ēl* for that sanctuary, which de Wette himself had refuted, were taken up anew by later opponents of de Wette's work. These arguments were used particularly in attempts to defuse de Wette's case against the existence of a single national shrine in the pre-monarchic period.[30]

1.2.4 *Vatke*

The next vigorous proponent of views similar to those of de Wette was Wilhelm Vatke. Vatke's *Biblische Theologie*, published in 1835,[31] further developed de Wette's arguments regarding the emergence of the Mosaic cultus at the end of Israel's history. In this connection, Vatke argued that the unity of the people of Israel and the centralization of the cult as expressed in Exodus–Numbers could only have occurred as the result of a cultural unification of the people at a later date.[32] Vatke also shared de Wette's view that multiple sanctuaries had been in use in Israel before the elevation of Jerusalem under David and Solomon.

At the same time, Vatke maintained certain of the positions first propounded by Gramberg, which would be used in later attempts to undercut de Wette's case against the antiquity of pentateuchal law. With regard to the sanctuary at Shiloh, Vatke contended that *bēt-'ēl* and *bēt-hā'ĕlōhîm* each referred to the 'dwelling-place of God'. These terms had designated not actual temple buildings, but rather, tent-like structures, or mobile sanctuaries; only Ba'al had been worshipped in a temple proper. Vatke did not mean to challenge de Wette's observations at this point, but rather, to draw a sharp distinction between the nomadic cultus of the Israelites and the sedentary, cultured worship of Ba'al.[34] Vatke further considered the use of women in the menial service of the cult, as described in Exod. 38.8 and mentioned in 1 Sam. 2.22b, to have been an early custom; only later had these women been replaced by the Levites.[35] Of these views, the appelative significance of *bēt-'ēl* and *bēt-hā'ĕlōhîm* for the tent sanctuary was taken up by more conservative scholars seeking to harmonize the manifold references to various cultic sites in the pre-monarchic period with the deuteronomic prescriptions for a single, central sanctuary.[36]

As in the work of Gramberg and de Wette, Shiloh played only a peripheral role in Vatke's treatment of Israelite religion, while simultaneously taking a central place in the debate over the centralization of the cult. Despite Vatke's continuation and development of de Wette's insights, a new consensus was about to emerge which would nearly smother the historical considerations which they had raised concerning the nature of cult and worship in the early history of Israel.

1.2.5 *Robinson and Smith's Biblical Researches*

Before embarking upon a treatment of this new trend in scholarship, it is important to remark upon a small but vital step taken in the recovery of the history of biblical Shiloh. In 1838, Edward Robinson, professor of biblical literature at Union Theological Seminary in New York, traveled to Palestine with Eli Smith, a colleague who had a command of Arabic. Robinson and Smith criss-crossed Palestine, recording the local Arabic place-names, including those of uninhabited ruins. On the basis of this research, Robinson and Smith were able for the first time to draw correlations between biblical place-names and the modern Arabic place-names of Palestine.[37] Among the sites identified in this manner was a ruin in the central Palestinian hills called in Arabic *Tell Seilun*. Robinson and Smith saw that this Arabic name corresponded to the Hebrew *šilōh/šîlô* or Shiloh.[38]

Heretofore, the approximate location of Shiloh had been known only through the *Onomastikon* of Eusebius, and through the directions to the site given in Judg. 21.19. Robinson and Smith were now able to make a precise determination of the geographic situation of Shiloh on the basis of the Arabic, which appeared to have preserved the ancient Semitic name known through the Hebrew Bible. The work of Robinson and Smith thus brought the recovery of the history of biblical Shiloh one step closer to realization.

1.3 *The Reaction to the Work of de Wette, Gramberg, and Vatke*

1.3.1 *Hengstenberg*

A year after Robinson and Smith made their journey, Ernst Wilhelm Hengstenberg of the University of Berlin published his comprehensive critique of the analysis of the pentateuchal cultus which de Wette, Gramberg, and Vatke had developed.[39] Hengstenberg's work hardly disproved de Wette's theories, but it did set the stage for a more conservative consensus which lasted nearly half a century. In general, Hengstenberg argued that the Mosaic origin of the law of the Pentateuch was authentic. He attempted to prove that pentateuchal law had been in force in the early period of Israelite history by showing that there was evidence for the practice of these laws in the books of Joshua, Judges and Samuel.

Hengstenberg began his work by attacking the historical premise on which de Wette had based his analysis. Behind de Wette's critique of the Mosaic origins of the law lay two key factors: the evident incongruity between the stipulations of Mosaic law and the actual history of Israel as depicted in Joshua–2 Kings, and the historical assumption that the Israelites, having been provided by Moses with sensible forms of worship, and a priesthood to guarantee popular obedience to that worship, would never have turned to proscribed forms of religion. The biblical account led one to believe, however, that not only were the Israelites always ready to turn away from the Yahwistic cult, but that the priests were most often the leaders of the apostasy. Accordingly, the Israelites' propensity to turn to forms of worship condemned in pentateuchal law demonstrated the simple and non-hierocratic nature of their religion.[40] In fact, neither law nor cult had existed at an early date, and the conflict between the worship of Yahweh and idolatry had arisen only much later, perhaps under Assyrian influence.

Hengstenberg, on the other hand, maintained that the biblical account was based on a more realistic view of human nature than that of de Wette. He argued that the laws of the Pentateuch, with their strict emphasis on sin and repentence and on Yahweh's holiness, would have posed severe hardships for a people living in close contact with the fertility cults of Canaan, which stressed the power of nature and nature deities, and catered to human pleasure and sensuality.[41]

Hengstenberg followed this attack on de Wette's critical presuppositions with a point-by-point treatment of the specific biblical passages upon which de Wette had built his arguments. Much of the tone of this part of Hengstenberg's work was apologetic, however, which fact led to a rejection of much of his scholarship. Scholars such as Ewald, who were similarly opposed to the views of de Wette and his colleagues and yet were committed to a critical reconstruction of pentateuchal sources which took seriously the Mosaic origins of the Yahwistic cultus, dismissed Hengstenberg as uncritical.[42] Nevertheless, it is precisely because Hengstenberg's work was widely perceived to have been apologetic, and lacking in critical merit, that one must examine his treatment of certain of these positions, especially those having to do with Shiloh.

To begin, Hengstenberg denied that any discrepancy existed between the establishment of the central sanctuary at Shiloh (Josh. 18.1; 22.9-34) according to pentateuchal law (Lev. 17; Deut. 12) and the apparent freedom of worship and sacrifice elsewhere in Joshua (Josh. 24) and Judges (e.g. Judg. 6; 20, 21). In Joshua's raising of the great stone 'under the oak in the sanctuary of Yahweh' at Shechem (Josh. 24) the word *miqdāš* referred not to a building per se, but rather to a *holy place*. A breach of the law would have taken place only if Joshua had *sacrificed* there. As it was, Joshua merely sought out a venerated holy site for the setting aside of the foreign gods.[43] Hengstenberg further contended that in the narrative of Judges, any site of the appearance of the deity was considered to have been a 'holy place', and the person witnessing such an appearance was *pro tempore* priest.[44] Thus, Gideon's altar at 'Ophrah (Judg. 6) would have constituted a breach of the law only if Gideon had erected a permanent cultus.[45] Hengstenberg raised similar objections to treating the other holy places in Judges as breaches of the centralization law. Mizpah (Judg. 20.1) had not been chosen as a holy site, but for its proximity to Gibeah.[46] Bethel, likewise, was not a proper holy place, or sanctuary, but only the temporary seat of the ark during the war against Gibeah and the Benjaminites; the true seat of both the ark and the tent of meeting had been Shiloh.[47]

Hengstenberg sought not only to demonstrate that the narratives of Joshua–2 Kings did not *contradict* the laws of the Pentateuch, but that these narratives offered positive evidence for the practice of those laws as well. His first step was to show that there had been a central shrine during the pre-monarchic period. To this end Hengstenberg argued from the references to Shiloh in Joshua 18–22 that Shiloh had been the central shrine of the Mosaic cultus in the pre-monarchic period.[48] He further supported this claim on the basis of the cryptic statement by the wandering Levite in Judg. 19.18: *wĕ'et-bēt Yhwh 'ănî hōlēk*, which he translated, 'and I frequent the house of God'.[49] Hengstenberg used this statement as a proof for the existence of a single national shrine at the time in which this story was set. Hengstenberg cited the reference to the *bēt-hā'ĕlōhîm bĕšilōh* ('the house of God at Shiloh', Judg. 18.31) as further proof of the existence of a single, central shrine at Shiloh during Israel's early history.[50]

Hengstenberg raised the additional argument that Shiloh had been the site of the celebration of the Passover feast immediately following the war with Benjamin (Judg. 21.19). Moreover, he claimed that all the great feasts had been celebrated there.[51] In this connection, Hengstenberg concluded that the *ḥag-Yhwh* ('the feast of Yahweh, Judg. 21.19) referred specifically to the Passover. He appealed to the phrase *miyyāmîm yāmîmāh* (lit. 'from days to days', usually understood as 'yearly, annually') in the same verse to corroborate this thesis, since the same usage occurred in conjunction with the prescriptions for the Passover in Exod. 13.10. Similarly, Hengstenberg interpreted the dancing of the maidens in Judg. 21.21 in parallel with the dancing of maidens led by Miriam in Exod. 15.20. He then used this interpretation as additional evidence for the celebration of the Passover during the period of the Judges, claiming that the song of Mirian was set within the seven days' Passover celebration.[52] Finally, Hengstenberg cited the use of *miyyāmîm yāmîmāh* in 1 Sam. 1.2[52] as additional evidence that this yearly feast had been celebrated at Shiloh.[54]

The most important passage in Hengstenberg's argument for a central shrine at Shiloh in the pre-monarchical period, however, was 1 Samuel 1–3.[55] The references to the *bēt-Yhwh* ('the house of

Yahweh', 1 Sam. 1.7, 24; 3.15), the *hêkal-Yhwh* ('the temple of Yahweh', 1 Sam. 1.9; 3.3), and the tent of meeting (1 Sam. 2.22) all pointed to Shiloh as the exclusive national shrine. Hengstenberg cited the important passages in Psalm 78 and Jer. 7.12 and 26.6 in support of his argument, and further noted, on the basis of Jer. 7.12, that the Shilonite sanctuary had been destroyed in the war with the Philistines. The city itself, however, had continued down through the monarchical period; Jeremiah's prophecy had only meant to point to the destruction of the temple in Jerusalem.[56]

Hengstenberg's work concerning the national shrine in pre-monarchical Israel was crucial to the formation of the mid-century consensus. Most, if not all, of the arguments called forth by successive conservative scholars who held the view that there was a central Israelite sanctuary according to Mosaic law in the period before the dominance of Jerusalem were to be found in rudimentary form in Hengstenberg's defense of the authenticity of the Pentateuch. Nevertheless, his work did not exert the decisive influence on Old Testament scholarship in the middle of the nineteenth century. That honor fell to the Göttinger Orientalist, Heinrich Ewald.

1.3.2 *Ewald*

In 1845, only six years after the appearance of Hengstenberg's defence of the authenticity of the Pentateuch, Ewald published the first edition of his *Geschichte des Volkes Israel*, in seven volumes.[57] This work, unlike that of Hengstenberg, could not be faulted as 'apologetic'. On the contrary, Ewald's treatment was highly 'critical': it included a five-stage supplementary theory of pentateuchal growth and was the first comprehensive attempt by a modern critical scholar to present a systematic reconstruction of Israelite history.[58]

To begin, Ewald adopted some of the more radical positions put forth by de Wette, attributing the preponderance of the imagery associated with the tent of meeting and the tabernacle in Exodus 25–31, 35–40 to the influence of the Solomonic temple upon the pentateuchal prescriptions, although he also regarded the Solomonic temple as having been built according to the model of the sacral tent.[59] Ewald also considered Deuteronomy to be the latest addition to the Hexateuch, as de Wette had done, and attributed to its author the final revision of the Hexateuch as a whole.[60]

Conversely, Ewald maintained the early provenance of much of the material which de Wette had wanted to relegate to the later period of Israelite history,[61] and advocated a 'supplementary hypothesis' in contrast to de Wette's 'fragmentary hypothesis'. Thus, while much of the description of the tabernacle had to be attributed to the experience of the Jerusalem temple, the tent shrine itself had been real, in a way that de Wette hardly would have conceded:

> Now the sacred Tabernacle of Moses had long been recognised as the great central point of the religion and constitution of the people, and the Ark of the Covenant had just received an accession of glory by its reception in Solomon's Temple, built after the model of the Tabernacle; and therefore ... the author starts from that visible sanctuary and describes how it was executed, with all its contents and appurtenances, after the divine model shown to Moses by Jahweh (Ex. xxv-xxxi), and was to be built by human hands upon the earth that it might be entered by the priests in their robes of office, or by Moses, and the sacred rites be performed in it (Ex. xxxv-xl).[62]

Another important point on which Ewald differed markedly from de Wette was in the interpretation of the history of Israel following the conquest of Canaan. De Wette had seen national unity as something which had been achieved only in the period of the monarchy. The disorder and disunity reflected in the book of Judges had been the dominant characteristic of Israelite life before the establishment of the monarchy.

In this connection, Hengstenberg had already challenged de Wette's position with respect to the unity of the cult, and Ewald's critique followed a similar tack, though in a more developed form. Ewald had a high regard for the relationship between tradition and actual history, and on this basis he argued for the authenticity of the traditions of Israel's apostasy from orthodox Yahwism in Palestine soon after the Israelites had entered the Promised Land (cf. Judg. 2.6-13). Ewald used the figure of the wandering Levite in Judges 17–18 to illustrate his thesis,[63] and he related these traditions to the scattering of Levi and Simeon (Gen. 49.5-7). Above all, the dispersion of the Levites and the *unsittlich* founding of the Danite priesthood by a Levite (Judg. 18.30) seemed to Ewald to offer certain evidence of a radical decline of the Mosaic religion after the settlement of the Israelites in Palestine.[64] As further evidence of this decline, Ewald cited the corruption of the sons of both Eli and

Samuel (1 Sam. 2.12-17, 22; 8.1-3), which had made necessary the emergence of a new institution to replace that of judgeship.[65] While the monarchy had emerged from a period of anarchy, then, it only succeeded in restoring a former unity which had been lost through the moral and institutional decline during the time of the judges.

Ewald also put forth a different interpretation of the priesthood than that of de Wette. De Wette had argued that the pre-monarchical cultic life had been characterized not by an established priesthood and priestly regulations, but by the reign of freedom:

> As with the patriarchs and the Homeric Greeks, God's open sky was his temple, every mealtime a sacrifice, every auspicious or strange occasion a sacral festival, and every prophet, king and family head without further ado priest.[66]

De Wette had relied heavily upon the narratives in Judges and Samuel to make this point.[67] Ewald, however, accepted the historical authenticity of the Aaronic line, and argued that Eli was portrayed as the proper high priest in 1 Samuel according to pentateuchal law, despite the fact that the later genealogies in the Chronicles overlooked him entirely (1 Chron. 6.3-15; 24.1-5).[68]

Ewald's treatment of Shiloh differed still more radically from that of de Wette. According to Ewald's reconstruction, Shiloh had been the central shrine of the Israelite tribal confederacy during the pre-monarchical period. Joshua had established Shiloh as Israel's central sanctuary when he had had the ark brought there from the camp at Gilgal.[69] Ewald supported this view by referring to Ps. 78.60-72 and Jer. 7.12-15, which Hengstenberg had already drawn into the discussion.[70] No other city, Ewald noted, was ever set on equal footing with Jerusalem in the biblical traditions.[71]

To be sure, Shiloh had been important to the tribes for its central location, but that importance, just as that of Gilgal, did not go back to patriarchal times. There had been many other places stemming from the pre- or post-Mosaic periods which claimed a certain sanctity, and where altars were to be found. Such a shrine was at Bethel.[72] Further examples of sanctuaries stemming from the pre-settlement period were Shechem,[73] Gilgal,[74] and Mizpah.[75] Bethel had not been chosen as the central shrine, however, because it had remained a Canaanite stronghold until long after Joshua's death. Shechem, for its part, had stood as the center of temporal power, but not as the center of the cult.

Yet Shiloh had not remained the central sanctuary. The place seemed to have lost all further significance after the death of Eli, and there was no continuing high priest. Furthermore, the tent sanctuary was found elsewhere following Eli's death, notably at Gibeon (2 Chron. 1.3, 13). Ewald's appeal to the Chronicles stood in striking contrast to de Wette's open contempt for these books as historical sources.[76] Ewald concluded from this evidence that the Philistines must have sacked and destroyed Shiloh after capturing the ark, just as Hengstenberg had supposed. The failure of the Israelites to carry the ark back to Shiloh following its return from exile in Philistia seemed to Ewald to confirm this theory. After the disaster at Ebenezer, Shiloh had been rebuilt and reinhabited only very slowly, as was the case with many ancient cities. The tent sanctuary itself survived the calamity, and was transferred first to Nob, and later to Gibeon (1 Chron. 16.39; 21.29).[77] Indeed, it is essentially Ewald's formulation of the theory of a destruction of Shiloh in the mid-eleventh century which has survived to dominate the discussion of biblical Shiloh down to the present.

The publication of Ewald's *Geschichte* in 1845 came at a critical juncture in the discussion of the origins of Israel and the reliability of the biblical traditions. Ewald revised and republished this work in two successive editions over the next two decades.[78] Through the *Geschichte*, and his own academic stature, Ewald exerted tremendous influence upon Old Testament scholarship. He had put de Wette's critique to rest, at least for a time, and confirmed a generation of scholarship in which the pentateuchal traditions were given a high degree of historical credence.

In addition to the decisive role Ewald played in the wider discussion of Old Testament criticism in the mid-nineteenth century, the Göttinger Orientalist also had a profound influence on the subsequent debate over Shiloh. First of all, Ewald was the first scholar to work into a cohesive form the historical arguments supporting the theory that Shiloh had been destroyed after the Israelite defeat at Ebenezer. Moreover, he was the first to pull together all the various texts in the Hebrew Bible which could support this view and which have since become the key points of reference in the modern discussion of Shiloh. Furthermore, Ewald was the first biblical historian to construct a *critical* synthesis of Israel's history which took seriously the idea of Israel as a cultic community with a central sanctuary in the pre-monarchical era. In the twentieth century, this banner was carried most ably by Martin Noth, who also developed another idea first proposed by Ewald: that of the sacral twelve-tribe league.[79] Thus, Ewald not only dominated the mid-nineteenth century formulation of the issues with regard to the place of Shiloh in the history of Israel, he was an important harbinger for the course the debate would take in the succeeding century.

1.3.3 *Saalschütz, Das mosäische Recht*

Ewald's *Geschichte* was followed by a number of less ambitious but nonetheless detailed works which dealt with Shiloh in some respect. *Das mosäische Recht*, by J.L. Saalschütz, appeared in 1846.[80] In his introductory remarks, Saalschütz took issue with de Wette's view that pentateuchal law had been largely the product of later composition. He adduced several reasons for his conclusion. First, the objections raised to the Mosaic authorship of the Torah by de Wette concerned the details, but not the totality of the Law, although Saalschütz admitted the correctness of many of the observations on which de Wette's claims had been based[81] and even suggested a later redaction of the Mosaic law by prophets or priests. Saalschütz also noted that the Pentateuch knew nothing of a king outside the book of Deuteronomy, and on the other hand contained not a hint of an important motif in the historical books, that Yahweh was the true king of Israel (cf. 1 Sam. 8.7-9). Finally, Saalschütz sought to explain the fragmentary composition of some of the laws by arguing that the law had been written by Moses, not as a coherent system, but as a piecemeal composition over a period of forty years. Thus, he sought to refute the evidence cited by de Wette to assail the theory of Mosaic authorship.

On the other hand, Saalschütz was not an apologist for Mosaic authorship of the Pentateuch. On the contrary, he held that only the *law* was 'Mosaic', and that the Pentateuch itself was a literary creation by a later hand, or *hands*.[82] Saalschütz also admitted to the presence of many historical anachronisms in the Pentateuch, such as the repeated reference to the 'land of Canaan'. He thought it the task of the exegete to examine supposed 'contradictions' to see whether these could be explained by the work of the final redactor. When it was not possible to understand a contradiction by consideration of the work of the final redactor, then the contradiction had to be seen as an indication of the holiness afforded these documents at a later time.[83]

As far as the central sanctuary was concerned, Saalschütz argued that the historical existence of the tent sanctuary was not a central concern of his study, which above all sought to elucidate the laws in theoretical form, regardless of the period in which they had come into existence. On the other hand, he took issue with critics such as Bahr, who argued that the depiction of the tent shrine in the Pentateuch was unbelievable simply because the modern mind found the amount of precious metals in the possession of the Hebrews to be unbelievable.[84] However, Saalschütz also argued that there was in the Pentateuch no stipulation regarding worship at the tent sanctuary after the settlement: only the cultic paraphernalia—the ark, the tablets, the shewbread table, and the golden lamps—had been part of the permanent cultus. Thus, he anticipated an argument employed later by Bleek, von Haneberg, and finally Kaufmann, in distinguishing between the nature of the central sanctuary before and after the settlement.[85]

1.3.4 *Riehm*

In a vein similar to that of Saalschütz, Eduard Riehm published *Die Gesetzgebung Mosis im Lande Moab* in 1854.[86] Riehm claimed substantial agreement with Ewald in his treatment of Deuteronomy, though he denied any slavish dependence upon the Orientalist from Göttingen. Riehm, as de Wette and Ewald, held Deuteronomy to be the latest book of the Pentateuch. And while Riehm considered de Wette's work important mainly for having provoked critical discussion of Deuteronomy, he did not think that de Wette's criticism offered much in itself. He found Hengstenberg's work, rather, to be the most useful treatment of Mosaic law.[87]

Riehm's most important contribution in connection with the discussion of biblical Shiloh was the direct challenge he raised to de Wette's treatment of the centralization issue. In treating 'the place where Yahweh will cause his name to dwell', Riehm noted that this deuteronomic concept was one of a firm geographic location, and that this concept occurred in the Bible in connection with only two places: Shiloh and Jerusalem. He further pointed out that cultic centralization in Deuteronomy had a perspective different from a similar theme present in the other pentateuchal traditions: in Deuteronomy the centralization of the cult was conceived in terms of a fixed geographic locus; elsewhere the Pentateuch knew only the tent, and gave no hint of the non-transferrable place of worship known to Deuteronomy.[88] This line of argument was a development upon that already advanced by Saalschütz, who had distinguished between the cultus before and after the settlement, and between the laws of Deuteronomy and those in the rest of the Pentateuch. These distinctions are fair, since Deuteronomy really does presuppose a cultic order different from that in Genesis–Numbers. It is no accident that subsequent scholars have raised similar issues in arguing for the antiquity of the priestly cultus.

1.3.5 *Graf, De Templo Silonensi*

Although the middle of the nineteenth century was dominated primarily by conservative treatments of biblical history, there was at least one important writer who carried on the line of criticism laid down by de Wette. This was Karl Heinrich Graf, a student of Eduard Reuss of Strasbourg.[89] Graf's initial contribution to the discussion of Shiloh in the history of Israel came in the form of a small latin monograph, *De Templo Silonensi, commentatio ad illustrandum locum Iud. 18.30,31*, which he published in 1855. Graf's monograph was in fact the first major treatment concentrating on Shiloh to be produced by a critical biblical scholar.

In this treatment, Graf advanced several points made originally by de Wette. First, he denied that Shiloh had ever functioned as a central sanctuary. The concept of a single, central Yahwistic sanctuary had not existed in Israel until the time of Josiah. Second, Graf contended that the tent of meeting had been no more than a late fiction modelled on the Solomonic temple. He used the references to Shiloh in 1 Samuel 1–3, where the sanctuary there was designated a *hêkāl*—a technical term for 'temple'—to support this point. Similarly, Graf denied the authenticity of the references to the tent of meeting at Gibeon in Chronicles, contending that the Chronicler had invented this information to explain how there had come to be *two* high priests in the days of David and Solomon.[90] For Graf, just as for de Wette, the narratives pertaining to Shiloh in Judges 17–18 served to provide further proof that the period before the monarchy knew no central sanctuary, either in the sense of the deuteronomic or of the priestly traditions.

Graf also made two crucial suggestions of his own. First, he argued that there had been no tent sanctuary at Shiloh, simply a permanent temple structure.[91] Second, this temple had continued in existence until the Assyrian deportation of the northern kingdom. The desolation of Shiloh to which Jer. 7.12-15; 26.6-9 referred was the result of this event, rather than a consequence of the defeat described in 1 Samuel 4. Graf reached this conclusion by reading Judg. 18.31 in parallel with Judg. 18.30, and using the phrase, *'ad-yôm gĕlôt hā'āreṣ* (v. 30) to explain the parallel expression *kol-yĕmê hĕyôt bēt-hā'ĕlōhîm bĕšilōh* (v. 31).[92] Graf's claim that there had been no tent sanctuary at Shiloh was the subject of burning debate during the next two decades. This issue was finally decided in Graf's favor, at least temporarily, after Wellhausen's work had destroyed the conservative consensus of the mid-nineteenth century. The second of Graf's observations, that the Shiloh sanctuary had not been destroyed, but had continued in existence down to the fall of the northern kingdom, came to define the counterpole to Ewald's hypothesis that Shiloh had been destroyed as a result of the disaster at Ebenezer. Nonetheless, Graf's treatment of Shiloh received little immediate comment, though the more conservative scholars of the age found it necessary to refute at least some of his claims, and Graf himself appears to have accepted Ewald's theory towards the end of his life.[93]

1.3.6 Saalschütz, Archaeologie der Hebräer

In the same year that Graf published his monograph on Shiloh, Saalschütz published his second major work: *Die Archaelogie der Hebräer*.[94] Here Saalschütz entered some additional arguments into the discussion which would prove important in the ensuing years, and some which would continue to be used more than a century later. First of all, he argued that the term *bēt-'ēl* did not at first designate a building, but only a place of veneration or worship, an argument for which he found support in the story of Jacob's dream (Gen. 28).[95] This argument contradicted Graf's claim that the term *bēt-'ēl* or *bēt-hā'ĕlōhîm* referred to a fixed building, though Saalschütz gave no indication that he was attempting to refute Graf at this point.[96] Another argument advanced by Saalschütz, which exercised more long-term influence than that concerning the meaning of *bēt-'ēl*, was his assertion that the tent sanctuary had not had a permanent location in the Promised Land, but had instead been moved from place to place.[97] He mentioned both Bethel (Judg. 20.27-28) and Shiloh (1 Sam. 1.3; 3.1; 14.3) in this connection and argued that this protable sanctuary had served as the central place of worship until the time of Solomon. Wherever the tent had been set up, *representative* worship had been carried out by the priests, who offered daily sacrifice in the name of the whole people. Elsewhere, however, individuals had been free to consecrate their own sacrifices.[98] In a significant development upon his earlier treatment,[99] Saalschütz argued that the ritual law of Leviticus and Numbers had been in force only during the wilderness period, and that the limitation of all sacrifice to the altar in the tent sanctuary had ceased with the entry of the Israelites into Palestine.[100] This change had taken place, according to Saalschütz, because the possibility of such centralized worship had ended when the Israelites had dispersed throughout Palestine. Thus, the prohibition on sacrifice apart from the tent sanctuary and its altar was replaced by permission for the free enjoyment of meat, which no longer counted as a sacrificial meal (Deut. 12.15-16).[101]

The difference between Saalschütz's approach and that of de Wette was as follows. De Wette did not regard the period of the wilderness wanderings as historically verifiable, and much of it he frankly regarded as 'mythical', or at best the retrojection of later institutions, customs, and practices into an earlier time. De Wette therefore found no reason to discuss the relevance of the laws of the priestly code in Leviticus and Numbers to life *in the camp* versus life *in the Promised Land*. Saalschütz, having rejected de Wette's view of the wilderness period, sought a critical reconstruction which took seriously a substantial degree of historicity for the Mosaic period and its institutions, which he then sought to reconcile with the data in the historical books. It was precisely this difference in outlook between de Wette and Saalschütz—the former rejecting the historicity of the pentateuchal traditions regarding the early centralization of the cultic institutions because of perceived incongruities with the testimony of the traditions of the historical books, the latter seeking to understand these inconsistencies in light of the peculiarities of the pentateuchal institutions and the conditions present among the people—on which the entire debate over the centralization of Israel's cultic institutions has turned through several subsequent generations of Old Testament scholarship.

In summary, Saalschütz's treatment of the issue of the centralization of the cult in his second work departed from his earlier treatment. His initial treatment of Mosaic law had hardly broached the problem of the central sanctuary in the Pentateuch vis-à-vis the historical books. In his second volume, however, he advanced the theory that the tent shrine had served as a portable central sanctuary, and that the priestly laws of centralization centered exclusively on life in the camp. Thus, the erection of the tent of meeting at Shiloh had not been one of the major steps toward centralization, as had been assumed in rabbinic tradition (*m. Zebah.* 14.4-8; *Meg.* 1.11). The change between Saalschütz's first and second books was the result of his effort to explain the apparent contradictions in the text via the critical interpretation of the text itself, rather than through traditional clarifications.

1.3.7 *Keil*

Karl Friedrich Keil published his *Handbuch der biblischen Archaeologie* in two volumes, in 1858 and 1859 respectively.[102] Keil was a conservative scholar who paid close attention to the philological aspects of exegesis, and whose historical reconstruction closely followed the biblical narratives. Thus, in treating the history of the tent sanctuary, Keil argued that the Israelites had first erected the tabernacle at Shiloh, and that Shiloh had remained the one legitimate cultic site until the time of Eli.[103] Therefore, the tent sanctuary had been transferred, first to Nob, and later to Gibeon, while the tent erected by David for the ark was different from the tabernacle. In fact, the ark had had no firm locus, and was often carried into battle. During the war with Benjaminites, the ark had been kept at Bethel, where it had remained so long that an altar was also erected there.[104] However, Keil made no further effort to deal with the other places of sacrifice mentioned in the Bible in the pre-monarchic period.

Keil made two other observations pertinent to the cultic site at Shiloh. First, he argued that the priesthood of Eli had been the first instance of a priest from the line of Ithamar succeeding to the position of high priest, a post which, according to the pentateuchal sources, should have remained in the line of Eleazar.[105] Second, Keil attributed the simultaneity of the priesthood of Abiathar and Zadok to the existence of two sanctuaries—one at Gibeon, and one at

Jerusalem, from the time that David had erected the tent for the ark on Mt Zion.[106] This last observation carried with it a certain degree of irony, since it had been Graf's contention that the existence of two sanctuaries was a convenient fiction meant to explain the presence of two ruling high priests under David and Solomon.[107]

1.3.8 *Bleek*

Every scholarly consensus, it seems, comes to be exemplified in a single representative work, and the definitive statement of the mid-century consensus on the problem of the Pentateuch and the historical books of the Old Testament was published in Friedrich Bleek's *Einleitung in das Alte Testament* in 1860.[108] Bleek was the only scholar besides Ewald during this period to attempt a consistent and critical refutation of de Wette's critique. With regard to the Pentateuch itself, Bleek brought out several examples of laws and law collections which made no sense outside of their given setting in the wilderness camp. Thus, he argued, the pentateuchal sources did not present an anachronistic hierarchical priesthood, but only Aaron and his sons. At the same time, Bleek accepted de Wette's argument that there was no certain evidence in the later historical literature that the deuteronomic law of the central sanctuary had ever been in force— not merely in the time preceding the building of the Jerusalem temple, but for a considerable time therafter. With de Wette, Bleek acknowledged that not only had idolaters worshiped at the high places and local shrines, but the most zealous servants of Yahweh! The laws of sacrifice in Leviticus 17 did not have as their object the central place of worship of Deuteronomy 12, but rather, the *door of the tent of meeting*. Moreover, the differentiation of sacrificial animals on the basis of those slaughtered *in the camp*, and those slaughtered *outside the camp* made no sense outside the setting of the camp. When one considered Jerusalem as the actual locus of the central shrine, the incongruity between Leviticus 17 and Deuteronomy 12 became all the more apparent.[109] Bleek resolved this problem in the practice of the law by noting that the law of Leviticus 17 did not merely forbid sacrifice at a place other than the tabernacle: it specifically banned the slaughtering and butchering of *any animals at any other place*, whether within or without the camp. All that was to be slaughtered was to be slaughtered at the *door of the tent of meeting* and consumed as a thank offering before Yahweh, after the blood had been poured out upon the altar and the fat burned. Such a regulation could not possibly have been written for application to a later time, when the people were dispersed in the land. Even less could someone of a later time have envisioned this law as applying to life after the conquest and settlement. Such a law could have been written only for life in the camp.[110] Other Mosaic laws had been occasioned by specific occurrences and were thus tied to specific narrative traditions.[111] These two classes of laws—those written for the camp, and those occasioned by specific occurrences and therefore imbedded in the narrative tradition—constituted the original core of Mosaic law.[112]

Therefore Bleek, like Ewald, accepted critical methods, and acknowledged the division of the Pentateuch into various literary strata. However, he did not accept de Wette's arguments for the late dating and fictional nature of the Mosaic law *in toto*. Rather, Bleek sought to demonstrate that many of the laws of the Pentateuch were best understood from the standpoint of the narratives in which they occurred.

Bleek's treatment of the biblical passages pertaining to Shiloh also reflected his critical outlook with regard to the Pentateuch. Thus, he regarded the Shiloh references in Joshua 18–19 as belonging to the Elohistic *Grundschrift* of the Hexateuch.[113] Joshua 22, which recounted the Reubenites' building of an altar at a place other than Shiloh, Bleek regarded as belonging to a later age, owing to its similarity to the view of centralization in Deuteronomy 12. Nowhere else in the historical books had the Israelites displayed such zeal in suppressing the offering of sacrifices at various altars.[114] Deuteronomy itself had been inserted into the hexateuchal framework as the last step in the redaction of these narratives, and this final redaction had included substantial changes to the book of Joshua.[115]

Certain passages in the book of Judges pertaining to Shiloh also received important treatment from Bleek. The *bēt-hā'ĕlōhîm* in Judg. 18.31b he interpreted as the tent of meeting with the ark, and the phrase *'ad-yôm gĕlôt-hā'āreṣ* ('until the day of the captivity of the land', Judg. 18.30) he altered to read *'ad-yôm gĕlôt-hā'ărôn* ('until the captivity of the ark'). From these modifications, Bleek argued that the references in Judg. 18.30, 31 were no later than the time of the Yahwistic-Elohistic composition of these narratives, which were pre-deuteronomic.[116]

Bleek's treatment of Shiloh came to an end with his treatment of Judges. Owing largely to his rejection of de Wette's terms of discussion on the issue of centralization, Bleek had reached conclusions which differed radically from those of de Wette. While accepting the lateness of the tradition of geographic centralization of the cult, as formulated by de Wette, Bleek had denied the applicability of this tradition to the pentateuchal materials outside Deuteronomy.

With regard to Shiloh, Bleek did not offer especially new or revolutionary ideas. His importance in the history of the debate over Shiloh lay, rather, with his treatment of the issue of cultic centralization. Bleek's analysis of this issue had weighty implications for the place of Shiloh in the history of the religion of Israel, since it demonstrated that the place of Shiloh in Israelite history could be separated from the centralization issue altogether. Thus, Bleek argued for the authenticity of the hexateuchal traditions, but denied the Mosaic origin of the deuteronomic tradition. By this means, he was able to avoid the problems of scholars such as Hengstenberg, who had treated the hexateuchal laws as a monolith.

1.3.9 *Küper*
In 1866, C. Küper published his work, *Das Priesterthum des alten Bundes*.[117] Küper followed Keil's treatment and showed further dependence upon Hengstenberg and Ewald, regarding Shiloh as the central sanctuary in the pre-monarchic period,[118] while admitting the separation of the ark from the tabernacle during this time. Küper further argued for a decline of the theocratic order during the period of the Judges.[119] Thus, Küper recognized the existence of multiple places of sacrifice prior to the erection of the temple in Jerusalem, and like Ewald explained these practices in terms of an era of social decay.

1.3.10 *Graf, Die geschichtlichen Bücher des Alten Testaments, and 'Zur Geschichte des Stammes Levi'*
In 1866, Graf's *Die geschichtlichen Bücher des Alten Testaments* appeared in print.[119] Like his earlier monograph on Shiloh, Graf's new work challenged the critical consensus that the priestly laws of the Hexateuch formed the authentic basis of subsequent Israelite history and society as depicted in the historical books of the Old Testament. Further, Graf formulated for the first time the theory of

pentateuchal composition which came to be known as the New Documentary Hypothesis. Graf's theory continued the main lines of criticism laid down by de Wette, in that he maintained the late and unhistorical character of the materials in the Pentateuch which came to be designated 'priestly', in his skepticism regarding the historical worth of the books of Chronicles, and in his insistence that the centralization of the cult was the key to ordering and dating the pentateuchal sources.[120]

Although Graf wrote little directly pertaining to Shiloh in this work, he argued vehemently that those passages which made Shiloh the pre-monarchical central sanctuary were late and inauthentic.[121] Graf's work did not meet with ready acceptance, though it did lay the foundation for a new consensus which would emerge over the next twenty years.[122] Ewald's third edition of the *Geschichte des Volkes Israel* appeared in 1866 and the conservative consensus continued to dominate Old Testament studies in Europe. The failure of Graf's work to reach a wide audience, in fact, was largely the result of the widespread influence exerted by scholars such as Ewald.

Graf's last major contribution to the debate over biblical Shiloh was an article on the history of the tribe of Levi which he published at the end of the decade, and in which he altered some of the positions he had taken earlier.[123] While Graf reiterated his view that the tent of meeting at Gibeon was a late fiction by the Chronicler to explain the presence of two high priests under David,[124] he pulled back from his earlier arguments about the continuation of the Shiloh sanctuary until the fall of the northern kingdom. Instead, he argued in agreement with Ewald:

> The house of God at Shiloh—where the ark had stood for several centuries during the period of the Judges, where the sacrifices for the collective tribes of Israel were brought and where the assembly of the people gathered—is depicted as a temple in the traditions of Samuel . . . Therefore, the destruction or desertion [of Shiloh], at the time when the Philistines stripped the tribe of Ephraim of all its power and won supreme dominion [over Palestine], is placed by Jeremiah on the same footing as the destruction which he foretells for the temple in Jerusalem (Jer. 7.12, 14; 26.6, 9).[125]

In this new work, Graf advanced the same arguments in favour of a destruction (or abandonment) of Shiloh following the Philistine victory at Aphek, which he once had so strenuously opposed. He even claimed that the ark had been returned to Shiloh after its release by the Philistines because 'dort weder Tempel noch Priesterschaft mehr war'.[126] Conversely, Graf stood by his original claim that a temple rather than a tent shrine had stood at Shiloh. At the same time Graf argued that Eli and his line had been authentic descendants of Aaron, who had been deposed from this status at a later date because of the ascendancy of the line of Zadok, and that the Aaronites had had their original home in the Ephraimite hill country.[127]

Graf's last publication thus retracted his earlier objections to the theory that Shiloh had been destroyed in the mid-eleventh century. His previous observations on the consistent parallelism between the destruction/abandonment of Shiloh on the one hand, and the exile of the northern kingdom on the other, were thus forgotten. Not until the publication of Frants Buhl's *Geographie des alten Palästinas*[128] would anyone formulate a position on the history of Shiloh which relied upon the evidence originally adduced by Graf.

1.3.11 *Von Haneberg*

Following the publication of the third edition of Ewald's *Geschichte*, other scholars continued to write in support of the reigning consensus on the Mosaic origin of pentateuchal law and institutions. One of these, Dan. Bonifacius von Haneberg, abbot of the Benedictine monastery of St. Boniface in Munich, in 1869 published the second and largely revised edition of his earlier work, *Das Handbuch der biblischen Alterthumskunde*, entitled *Die religiösen Alterthümer der Bibel*.[129]

Von Haneberg not only continued much of the same line of argument as that established by Hengstenberg, he also brought together many observations made by other scholars and added a few interesting insights of his own. To begin with, von Haneberg accepted the plurality of sancturaies during the period of the Judges and sought to explain this apparent inconsistency with deuteronomic law by maintaining, as Hengstenberg had done, that a prophet such as Samuel had had the authority to designate—temporarily—a particular site of sacrifice.[130] Von Haneberg coupled this view with the claim that after the erection of the tabernacle at Shiloh, Shiloh had become the central sanctuary of the land.[131] Gradually, after the tent sanctuary had fallen into disuse, it had been replaced with a building. During the years that the tabernacle had stood at Shiloh, moreover, the worship at the high places had been prohibited.[132] By the time of David, the old portable sanctuary had become no more than a relic.[133] Shiloh itself had been abandoned after the capture of the ark,[134] when the ark and tent had been separated. The high place at Gibeon, with its altar, and that at Jerusalem during the reigns of David and Solomon, reflected the rivalry between the two priestly houses of Ithamar and Eleazar, to which the erection of the temple had put an end.[135] The tabernacle, ark, and other furnishings, including the bronze altar at Gibeon, had been brought into the temple by Solomon to be kept there as relics.[136] According to von Haneberg, it was nonsensical to think that 1 Kgs 8.3-9 described the actual erection of the tent shrine within the temple.[137]

In making these claims, von Haneberg was at pains to refute the recent treatment by Graf, which he cited as a newer exponent of an older, though rejected critical view to the effect that the tabernacle and the narratives surrounding it belonged in the realm of legend rather than history.[138] The confusion as to the legitimate place of worship first arose, according to von Haneberg, after the loss of the ark, when both Gibeon and Nob became places of sacrifice. Indeed, Gibeon had only become 'the great high place' on account of the presence of the tent there.[139]

While von Haneberg had made some interesting observations, he was unable to give a clear picture of the relationships of the various cultic places to the one central place of worship. On the one hand, he had depended upon the Talmudic tradition first cited by Saalschütz that the erection of the tent sanctuary at Shiloh had been accompanied by the setting into force of the prohibition on multiple places of worship. On the other hand, this position undercut von Haneberg's initial acknowledgment of a plurality of holy places. While von Haneberg was therefore unable to offer a convincing synthesis, his own observation that 1 Kgs 8.3-9 recalled the depositing of the ark and the tent of meeting in the temple as *reliquiae* raised an important consideration in weighing the historicity of the tradition of the tent of meeting in the pre-monarchic cult.

1.3.12 *Wellhausen, Der Text der Bücher Samuelis*

The next important work to be published after that of von Haneberg was Wellhausen's *Der Text der Bücher Samuelis*.[140] Although technical in nature, this work offered a continuation of the type of approach found in de Wette's critique of the Mosaic origins of the pentateuchal cult. Thus, for example, Wellhausen argued that the reference to the sexual relations between sons of Eli and the women who served at the door of the tent of meeting in 1 Sam. 2.22b was a late secondary addition to the present text.[141] Not only were there no other allusions to the tent shrine in these chapters, but the sanctuary otherwise depicted at Shiloh in 1 Samuel was a temple, not the tabernacle, a view reminiscent of Graf's position. Furthermore, it was absurd to believe such a report regarding the sons of Eli, because 'the philandering with the serving women of the temple squares poorly with the obviously princely status of these priests'. Wellhausen held 1 Sam. 2.22b to be dependent upon Exod. 38.8, the only other mention of women in the service of the ritual cult in the Old Testament, and he attributed its presence in this passage to an attempt by the Pharisees to make the Sadducean priesthood look bad. While he considered the omission of this verse in the LXX to speak decisively against its veracity, Wellhausen reported that Josephus, who had been sympathetic to the Sadducees, also knew of this scandal. Thus, Wellhausen was compelled to consider the possibility that this small reference had existed already in the Urtext. Nonetheless, he rejected the originality of the reference to the tent of meeting in 1 Sam. 2.22b on literary grounds, in apparent agreement with Graf's view that the tent of meeting itself was an unhistorical reflection on the Jerusalem temple.

1.3.13 *Oehler*

If Wellhausen's book was the first wind of a major change in the reigning consensus, the acceptance of the Mosaic origins of pentateuchal laws and institutions continued in no small way. G.F. Oehler published his *Theologie des Alten Testaments* in 1873.[142] Oehler worked from essentially the same perspective as Ewald. He accepted the theological order of the Pentatuech as chronologically primary to the rest of Israelite history and treated the period of the Judges as one of the decline of theological order.[143] Oehler also argued that the centralization law of Deuteronomy 12 had not been enforceable after the conquest and settlement of the Promised land.[144]

Oehler maintained that the pre-monarchic center of worship had been Shiloh, where the tabernacle had been set up; he cited Josh. 18.1; 19.51; Judg. 18.31; 1 Samuel 1-2 in support of this position and compared Ps. 78.60 and Jer. 7.12 with these passages. Oehler further argued that Shiloh had been the site of the great feasts during the time of the Judges.[145] He cited Judg. 21.19 and 1 Sam. 1.3 in support of this view, and contended that regular sacrifices had been offered at Shiloh (1 Sam. 2.12-17). Oehler also appealed to arguments first raised by Hengstenberg to by-pass some of de Wette's arguments regarding the multiplicity of sanctuaries in the pre-monarchic period. Thus, the patriarchal custom of erecting an altar at any site where the deity had appeared had continued into the settlement period. Other apparent exceptions to the exclusive character of the tent sanctuary had arisen only in time of war: when the ark was brought up to battle, it had been set up *in the camp* and sacrifices were offered there.[146] That there had only been one ark and one tent shrine confirmed for Oehler the unity of the pre-monarchic cult.

Shiloh had ceased to be the central sanctuary following the capture of the ark and the disarming of the Israelites in the aftermath of the battle of Ebenezer. In the wake of this defeat, the tabernacle was transferred to Nob where the 'levitical' cult continued uninterrupted. The loss of the ark and the shift in the locus of the central shrine, however, brought an end to centralized worship. Consequently, Ramah, Bethel, and Gilgal became places of sacrifice.[147] Thus, the disaster at Ebenezer effected the first interruption of the Mosaic cult. Later on, the tabernacle was erected at Gibean, but under David the *miškan-Yhwh* on Mt Zion became the new center of the cult.

In conclusion, Oehler's reconstruction of the history of Israelite religion up to the erection of the temple on Mt Zion was based on the premise that the Mosaic cult of the wilderness period had continued uninterrupted down to the loss of the ark to the Philistines. At that time, the one central sanctuary had been supplanted by a number of holy places where sacrifice had been permitted. Oehler's work thus continued the line of argument developed by Hengstenberg and did not make a significant independent contribution to the historical debate with regard to the history of the cultus. Above all, Oehler failed to come to grips with the evidential basis of de Wette's position: that independent Yahwistic shrines had existed not only in the period immediately prior to the ascendency of Jerusalem, but from the earliest days of the settlement until far into the period of the monarchy.

1.3.14 *Köhler*

The last major work to advocate the historicity of Mosaic institutions in the early history of Israel prior to the revolution occasioned by Wellhausen's *Geschichte Israels* was A. Köhler's *Lehrbuch der biblischen Geschichte des Alten Testamentes.*[148] Köhler followed his immediate predecessors. He agreed with von Haneberg that the tent shrine had not continued intact from the time of Moses until the building of the temple in Jerusalem. Instead, the tabernacle had needed periodic renewal.[149] At the same time, Köhler considered Shiloh to have been the only uncontested center of the legitimate Yahwistic cultus from the time of the conquest on.[150]

Perhaps the most important aspect of Köhler's work, however, was his attempt to answer the critiques leveled by de Wette, Graf, and most immediately, Wellhausen. Köhler offered some counter-arguments to de Wette's position concerning multiple holy places prior to the monarchy. Thus he argued for the LXX reading of Josh. 24.25, where the sanctuary in question was the one in Shiloh, not Shechem.[151] Moreover, Köhler attempted to refute Wellhausen's treatment of 1 Sam. 2.22b, arguing that Josephus' knowledge of this controversial note showed that the LXX translators had deliberately dropped this reading. Köhler again raised the long-standing objections to Graf's contention that the terms *bēt-'ēl* and *bēt-hā'ĕlōhîm* necessarily referred to a building.[152] Köhler cited Exod. 23.19; 34.26; Josh. 6.24; 2 Sam. 12.20; Pss. 5.8; 23.6; 27.4; 52.10; 55.15 as evidence that these terms could refer to a tent. More important in this connection was his appeal to 2 Kgs 23.7, where *bayit* clearly refers to something woven, not to a building, as Graf had insisted. Finally, Köhler adduced 2 Sam. 7.5-6, where Nathan says that no temple had been erected to Yahweh before the time of David. Köhler also attempted to explain away the references to 'doorposts' at the temple at Shiloh (1 Sam. 1.9) and 'doors' (1 Sam. 3.15) as well as to the *hêkal-Yhwh* (1 Sam. 1.9; 3.3), where Samuel is depicted as sleeping (1 Sam. 3.3).

Köhler's work therefore fell into the same class as so much of the work produced by the nineteenth-century advocates of the Mosaic origins of the Pentateuch: i.e. while he offered many good observations, Köhler had failed to grasp the real strength of the critique raised by de Wette. De Wette had worked with broad patterns of evidence within the biblical narratives, and no piecemeal refutation of particular details, which failed to deal with the overall picture, could successfully challenge his work. Much less could attempts to depict the sanctuary in 1 Samuel 1–3 as purely a tent shrine be taken seriously.

Köhler's work was not the last to be published from the perspective of the mid-century consensus. Still, it was the last before the publication of Wellhausen's decisive re-formulation of de Wette's critique of the pentateuchal cultus. While Wellhausen did not experience immediate and universal acclaim, his work did spell the end of the consensus which had stood so long, and in which his own teacher, Heinrich Ewald, had played the leading role.

Chapter 2

THE WELLHAUSIAN REVOLUTION AND ITS CRITICS

2.1 *The Emergence of a New Consensus*

The consensus with regard to the composition of the Pentateuch and the history of Israel which had been formulated by Old Testament scholars in the mid-nineteenth century had encountered its first serious opposition with the publication of Graf's *Die geschichtlichen Bücher des Aten Testaments* in 1866.[1] At the same time, a young Dutch scholar by the name of Abraham Kuenen, who had been influenced by Graf, was publishing a major work along similar lines. Kuenen's first work was his *Historisch-Kritisch Onderzoek naar het ontstaan en Boeken des Ouden Verbonds*, published in three volumes between 1861 and 1865.[2] Kuenen published a further treatment along these same lines in his *De Godsdienst van Israel*, in 1869 and 1870,[3] as well as numerous special studies which appeared from the late 1860s down into the 1880s in the journal *Theologisch Tijdschrift*.[4]

The work of Kuenen, like that of his older contemporary Graf, had strong affinities with the lines of criticism laid down by de Wette, Gramberg, and Vatke earlier in the century. The representatives of the mid-century consensus had agreed that the materials in the Pentateuch ascribed to the *Grundschrift*—those materials which would later be designated as *priestly*—formed the oldest stratum of tradition. Kuenen, however, advocated the argument, first formulated by de Wette and continued by Gramberg and Vatke, that these materials actually belonged to the latest layer of pentateuchal sources, and represented in reality a late fantastic depiction of Israel's origins from the standpoint of the culture and institutions of post-exilic Israel. Following the work of Colenso in England, Kuenen went farther than Graf, who had argued for the lateness of the laws of the *Grundschrift*, while maintaining the antiquity of the narrative traditions of this body of writings.[5]

The next work of importance to be published from the Grafian perspective was that of August Kayser, who, like Graf, had been a student of Reuss in Strasbourg. Kayser's *Das vorexilische Buch der Urgeschichte Israels und seine Erweiterungen*, in which he argued that the Priestly Codex had been unknown to any of the pre-exilic and early exilic writers of the Old Testament, appeared in 1874.[6] Kayser's work was followed by that of Bernhard Duhm of Göttingen. In 1875, Duhm released his *Die Theologie der Propheten als Grundlage für die innere Entwicklungsgeschichte der israelitischen Religion*, where he attacked the critical consensus that Israel's religion had gone through successive Mosaic, prophetic, and finally, Judaic stages. While Duhm had worked independently of the school of Graf, he made a signal contribution to that line of argument, contending that the religion of Israel had to be understood in light of the theology of the prophetic movement, and that the legal tradition of Judaism had its origins in the post-exilic community.[7]

2.2 *Julius Wellhausen*

By the middle of the 1870s, then, the beginnings of a considerable case had arisen against the generally accepted view that the law and institutions of the Pentateuch stemmed from Moses, yet that view remained fairly intact. Almost a decade and a half after Kuenen's *Historisch-Kritisch Onderzoek* had appeared, however, another young Göttingen scholar, Julius Wellhausen, published a series of articles in the *Jahrbücher für deutsche Theologie*, which dealt with the composition of the Hexateuch and of the historical books of the Old Testament.[8] These articles comprised a number of special studies which focused on key passages in the interpretation and dating of the pentateuchal sources. In 1878 Wellhausen published a much more ambitious volume under the title of *Geschichte Israels*.[9] This volume constituted a full-blown attack on the reigning consensus—'die herrschende Meinung'—which Wellhausen's teacher Ewald had been so instrumental in formulating. Above all, Wellhausen's *Geschichte Israels* was a scathing critique of the historicity of the *Grundschrift*—the priestly document—of the Pentateuch, aimed at proving that these materials, both narrative and legal, stemmed from post-exilic Judaism. Wellhausen's work also attacked the historical validity of the books of Chronicles, especially as far as Chronicles seemed to lend weight to those scattered references in the books of Samuel and Kings which pointed to the existence of the Mosaic cult at the time of the monarchy. This same polemic lay at the basis of Wellhausen's revision of the fourth edition of Bleek's *Einleitung*, which also appeared in 1878.

The effect of this massive and schematically consistent attack on the earlier consensus for the discussion of Shiloh was immediately apparent. First of all, any connection between Shiloh and the tent of meeting was ended for those scholars who accepted Wellhausen's reconstruction, because this institution was seen as a late fiction modeled on the Solomonic temple. Moreover, Graf's arguments that Shiloh had been the site of an actual temple prevailed. Earlier attempts to understand the problem of tent versus temple at Shiloh on the basis of Talmudic and Mishnaic tradition became moot.[10] Furthermore, Shiloh could no longer be considered the pre-monarchic central holy place, since there had been no cultic centralization before the reign of King Josiah and his reform. Just as de Wette had contended three quarters of a century earlier, Shiloh was treated as one of the many pre-monarchic sanctuaries which were to be found in Israel. Any special status which had accrued to Shiloh had been derived from the ark, which had been kept there independent of any tent shrine (cf. 1 Sam. 1-4).[11] Through the prophet Samuel, Shiloh had also been the center for the movement which had led to the establishment of the monarchy.[12] The succession of central holy sites from Shiloh, to Nob, to Gibeon, and finally to Jerusalem, was to be dismissed.[13]

Indeed, Wellhausen's entire treatment of Shiloh and the tent of meeting was tied to his pivotal contention that the priestly source of the Hexateuch presupposed centralization, and was therefore post-deuteronomic. Rather than the site of the central sanctuary, Shiloh became for Wellhausen the paradigm for the local independent sanctuary, administered by a local family of priests. He contrasted the autonomous cult at Shiloh to the ordered cultic inheritance of priestly office in P. Nonetheless, Wellhausen was compelled to admit that Shiloh represented an unusual 'type' of sanctuary, in that the Elide priesthood there had assumed the role of powerful, highly regarded officials at a major *public* sanctuary. Other sanctuaries, such as that of Micah in Ephraim (Judg. 17-18), Gideon at Ophrah (Judg. 8.27), and that of Abinadab at Kiriath-Jearim (2 Sam. 6.3-4), had been in private hands.[14]

Consequently, Eli, the priest of Yahweh at Shiloh, was not a representative of the Aaronite priesthood. Instead, the Elides formed a hereditary priesthood in their own right, just as many other families had. The proof that the Aaronite priesthood had not been normative at an early stage in Israel's history, Wellhausen found in Judg. 18.30, where Jonathan, the son of Gershom, the son of Moses, is named as the founder of the priesthood of Dan. According to Wellhausen, the Elides had traced their ancestry back to Moses as well. The Aaronite line was only a late invention by the Zadokite priesthood in Jerusalem, to justify the pre-eminence of their line over that of the Levites. In Wellhausen's view, the Levites had been the traditional priests of the ancient sanctuaries of the countryside. They had traced their ancestry back to Moses, the founder of the cult, and as such the original priest.[15]

In only one respect did Wellhausen maintain a degree of continuity with his teacher on the subject of Shiloh. Concerning the destruction of Shiloh following the capture of the ark at the battle of Aphek, he assumed Ewald's position *ipso facto*.[16] Of this event Wellhausen wrote:

> The consequences of this defeat were disastrous: the power of Joseph was broken, and the Philistines knew how to exploit their victory. They subjugated not only the plain of Jezreel and the abutting chain of hills to the south, but also the actual stronghold of the land, the Ephraimite hill country. They destroyed the ancient sanctuary at Shiloh, and the priestly family there fled southward and settled in Nob, in the tribal territory of Benjamin. The Philistines even extended their rule over Benjamin: in Gibeah there was a Philistine governor.[17]

That Wellhausen took this position was probably due to the influence of Ewald upon his pupil. In most other respects, however, Wellhausen set forth the lines of criticism laid down by de Wette, Vatke and Graf with vigor and effect.

The work of Graf, Wellhausen, and Kuenen was neither immediately nor universally accepted, despite the effort expended by those scholars to drive home their synthesis. The Mosaic origins of pentateuchal law, in fact, continued to receive support. Eduard Riehm, a representative scholar of the earlier consensus, published the *Handwörterbuch des biblischen Altertums* in 1884. This work maintained the older view of the historicity of the tent of meeting, its erection at Shiloh, and the continuation of Shiloh as the main pre-monarchic cultic site,[18] and continued earlier arguments that the references to the 'house of Yahweh' in 1 Samuel had to be read in light of Judg. 18.31, and meant, in fact, the tent shrine.[19]

Above all, Riehm's *Handwörterbuch* stressed the continuity of Mosaic cultic institutions into the pre-monarchical and monarchical periods of Israelite history, and it was at this very point that the school fo Graf, Kuenen, and Wellhausen had taken exception to the older consensus. Over the next twenty years, however, increasing support accrued to this new school of thought, while the older consensus faded into insignificance. Its adherents gradually died off, while those scholars who did not embrace the new consensus, such as Dillmann, Kittel, and Baudissin, sought to establish independent lines of criticism.

2.3 *The Scholars of the Wellhausian School*

Many, mostly younger scholars gradually lent their weight to the position which had been staked out by Graf, Kuenen, and Wellhausen concerning the composition of the Pentateuch. Eventually this new 'school' came to dominate Old Testament studies until it approached a critical orthodoxy. The lively debate over biblical Shiloh, which had been carried on since the time of de Wette, eventually was replaced by a general agreement on Wellhausen's view that Shiloh had been the site of a Yahwistic temple, that this sanctuary had risen to prominence on the eve of the monarchy, and that it had been destroyed by the Philistines in the wake of the Israelite defeat at Ebenezer. This reconstruction was accepted by scholars such as Reuss, Maybaum, Stade, Cornill, Budde, Smend, Benzinger, Nowack, Guthe, Dibelius, Meyer, and König. Even those who dissented from the emerging accord on the pentateuchal sources adopted the broad outlines of Wellhausen's reconstruction of the history of Shiloh, which came to be treated as a matter of historical fact. Nevertheless, many of the very scholars who lent their weight to this consensus on Shiloh's history offered their own divergent insights on the subject.

2.3.1 *Budde and Stade*
Karl Budde of Giessen, a student of Wellhausen, deviated from his teacher's position only insofar as he regarded the epithet 'true priest'

of 1 Sam. 2.27-36 to have designated Samuel originally, and only later to have been applied to Zadok.[20] Bernhard Stade, also of Giessen, moved beyond the position of Wellhausen and Budde. Whereas Wellhausen had accepted 1 Samuel 1-3 as historically reliable and considered only the song of Hanna (1 Sam. 2.1-10) and the prophecy in 2.27-36 to have been later additions to the Samuel-Eli narratives,[21] Stade argued that 1 Samuel 1-3 was not historically reliable in its entirety, and as a whole derived from the time of Josiah.[22] Moreover, the prophesied catastrophe in 2.27-36 was not the disaster at Ebenezer, as Wellhausen had assumed, but the bloodbath at Nob, where Saul had exterminated the last of the Elide line. Another theory advanced by Stade was that the ark had contained not stone tablets, but rather, 'holy stones', perhaps meteorites.[23] Finally, Stade argued that the Shilonite temple was the oldest Israelite temple, and had been built to house the ark, which had been a war-related palladium of the tribe of Joseph, or of the Josephide tribe of Benjamin.[24]

2.3.2 *Smend*

Another scholar to deviate somewhat from Wellhausen's view was Rudolf Smend. Smend accepted most of Wellhausen's reconstruction but differed at two crucial points. First, while he considered Aaron to have been little more than a literary double for Moses, he felt that the connection between Aaron and the golden calf in Exodus 32 proved that Aaron was the legitimate patriarch of the North Israelite priesthood.[25] Smend also gave credence to the authenticity of the tent sanctuary, arguing that Yahwistic worship had been quite simple at its inception, and that temples such as Solomon's in Jerusalem had been built according to foreign models, which would not have been tolerated at an earlier day.[26] In spite of these notable differences with Wellhausen's synthesis, Smend considered the Shilonite priesthood to have been Mosaic, deriving from Eliezer, the son of Moses (Exod. 18.4), whose pedigree had later been altered to make him a son of Aaron, through the priesthood of Phineas.[27] The ancestral inheritance of this priesthood was located at Gibeath-Phineas in the Ephraimite hill country, and the priests of this line formed the hereditary priesthood of the ark.[28] Smend's lead on the antiquity of the tent shrine may have been followed to some degree by Guthe, who regarded the tent of meeting as a melding of the later features of the

Solomonic temple with the memories of the ancient desert shrine.[29] This view was similar to that taken earlier by Ewald.[30]

2.3.3 *Dibelius*

The most interesting treatment given to the subject of Shiloh after Smend was that of Martin Dibelius, who later made his mark as a scholar of the New Testament. In his first monograph,[31] Dibelius contended that the ark was not a desert cult-object, but a Yahwistic cult-object which had been captured by the Israelites in Canaan. Similarly, the sanctuary at Shiloh had been taken over from the Canaanites by the tribe of Joseph, since temples were a feature of settled, rather than nomadic, culture.[32] The Shilonite sanctuary subsequently achieved great importance as the 'chief sanctuary', owing to its status as the main sanctuary of Joseph, the most powerful of all the tribes. As the chief cult-object of Joseph, the ark served as a war palladium, and was housed in the temple at Shiloh. At the disaster of Ebenezer, where the ark was captured by the Philistines, the power of Joseph was broken and the temple at Shiloh destroyed. The Philistines were subsequently able to extend their sway over the central hill country of Ephraim.[33] Dibelius's reconstruction did not differ from Wellhausen's with regard to the fate of the Shiloh temple, but he went considerably beyond any previous writer in fleshing out the place of the ark as a Josephide cult-object. Of perhaps greater significance was Dibelius's denial of the historical connection between Samuel and the Elide priesthood in Shiloh (1 Sam. 1-3).[34] This connection was artificial, according to Dibelius, as was demonstrated by the fact that Samuel was never depicted later as *priest at Shiloh*, but as the *seer at Ramah*.[35] Another, and in some respects similar, suggestion had been put forth earlier by Benzinger, who considered the connection between the Shilonite priesthood and that of Nob to be of fictional origin.[36]

2.3.4 *Meyer*

A final treatment which deserves mention is that of Eduard Meyer.[37] Meyer, too, accepted the broad outlines of the Wellhausian synthesis, but his reconstruction was eclectically composed. In accord with Wellhausen, Meyer argued that the Elide priesthood had originally traced its descent from Moses, and that it had only later 'corrected' this tradition, and linked the line to that of Aaron, who became the figure of the 'true priest'. This 'correction' had allowed the cult in Jerusalem, i.e. the house of Zadok, to claim their line as the sole legitimate representative of the true Yahwistic religion.[38] Meyer relied on older sources in contending that Aaron was a *personification of the ark*.[39] He also continued Smend's argument that the holy tent belonged to the origins of Israel's Yahwistic faith, but he tied the tradition of the tent shrine to the cultic center at Kadesh.[40] The tent, in fact, had been the most important Israelite cult object. It may have contained an altar, and certainly housed the holy lots. From it the law was read before the assembled people, and a 'man of God' within gave divine oracles.[41] The ark Meyer identified with the god Yahweh Sebaoth at Shiloh, which he considered to have been separate from the cult of the holy tent[42] But contrary to Dibelius, Meyer associated the ark with Israel's nomadic origins.[43] Only when the ark had been set up at Shiloh had it become identified with the settled farming life, and its god had become an agricultural deity.[44] The ark and tent were combined into a single cultus in Jerusalem for the first time under David.

The generation of scholars which had been so heavily influenced by the Graf-Wellhausen hypothesis thus offered a variety of views regarding biblical Shiloh, all of which, however, stayed within the broad outlines of Wellhausen's reconstruction. One significant deviation from Wellhausen's views was the argument made first by Smend, and taken up later by Stade and Meyer, that the tent shrine actually derived from the wilderness period. Smend was also responsible for arguing that the line of Aaron was the legitimate priestly line of the northern tribes. Another bone of contention in the overall discussion was the ark, its origin and its relationship to the Israelite tribes. Further disparities remained as well, such as the historical relationship between Eli and Samuel, and the genealogical connection between the priesthood of Shiloh and that of Nob. Otherwise, the Wellhausian revolution issued in a strong consensus regarding the Shiloh priesthood and sanctuary, especially among those scholars whose work identified them with that school.

2.4 *The Critics of the Graf-Wellhausen Hypothesis*

Despite the impressive gains made by the Graf-Wellhausen hypothesis in the years immediately following Wellhausen's publication of his *Geschichte Israels*, significant opposition to his reconstruction continued to emerge. There were two main sources of this resistance: the older scholars who had helped formulate the mid-century consensus, and younger scholars who continued to raise critical objections to both the premises and conclusions of the Graf-Wellhausen school. The views of these older scholars were superseded in importance, however, by the critiques leveled by younger men such as August Dillmann, Franz Delitzsch, and Rudolf Kittel. Critical medial stances in the debate were taken by Wolf Wilhelm Grafen Baudissin and August Klostermann. Opposition to the theories of Graf, Kuenen and Wellhausen regarding the pentateuchal sources even continued down into the next century, and found new support in the works of Otto Proksch and Paul Karge. The majority of the scholars who opposed the Graf-Wellhausen hypothesis, however, gradually died off without leaving any lasting legacy. Indeed, only Procksch, whose work had barely been noticed in his own day, left a sizeable impression on the succeeding generation.[45] Thus, by the time Gunkel and Gressmannn published their *Schriften des Alten Testaments*, the Grafian theory of pentateuchal origins was all but an established orthodoxy, and scholars could consider that they stood on the firm footing of the established results of one era of scholarship, and on the verge of a new one.[46] In fact, as early as 1899, the British scholar Addis had expressed the opinion that the Graf-Wellhausen hypothesis must be the basis of all future discussion.[47] Nonetheless, the scholars who opposed the treatment of Israelite history promulgated by the new consensus often were careful exegetes. Their insights consequently deserve review, more especially as there was still an open debate, albeit a polarized one, when they wrote.

2.4.1 *Dillmann*

The foremost of the critics of the school of Graf, Kuenen, and Wellhausen was August Dillmann, whose views were laid down in his two commentaries, the one on Exodus and Leviticus,[48] the other on Numbers, Deuteronomy, and Joshua.[49] Although there is neither time nor space here to review Dillmann's work in its entirety, its main features must be noted. First, he advocated the composition of the hexateuchal documents in the order PEJD (in his scheme, ABCD), in which J had been dependent upon E. Dillmann did not regard D as an original law-code, but as a parenetic plea for, and interpretation of older extant laws, notably those of E, J and P. The division of Deuteronomy 12–26 from the rest of the book he considered fallacious, since the parenetic language and style of the 'framework' passages were consistent throughout the book. In more general terms, Dillmann argued that the extra-biblical evidence from the ancient Near East demonstrated the antiquity of the priestly order in Israel, a view subsequently advanced by Kittel and eventually borne out by the work of Dussaud in this century (see below, 3.1). Dillmann also insisted that only *a coincidence* of literary *and* historical criteria could determine the existence of a source behind the present form of the text, and that it was incorrect to use one to explain the other, as Wellhausen, so Dillmann argued, was especially wont to do.

With regard to biblical Shiloh, Dillmann's work on the tent of meeting was especially important. The tent of meeting, he argued, had been the 'place of the presence of God' according to E and P (cf. Exod. 33.7-11; Num. 11.16, 24-25; 12.16),[50] but was unknown to D.[51] The laws of Deuteronomy, moreover, were based on those of the other three sources. The centralization law in Deuteronomy 12, for instance, was based on Lev. 17.7-11. In general, Deuteronomy had reproduced the more ancient priestly regulation, then modified it according to the needs of that later time.[52] On the other hand, Dillmann recognized the idea of 'the place where Yahweh will cause his name to dwell' as peculiar to Deuteronomy. In so doing, he opposed the view of Delitzsch and Kleinert that 'the place where Yahweh would cause his name to dwell' referred to the successive sites where the tabernacles had been erected as directed by Yahweh through a prophet.[53] At the same time, Dillmann argued that the tent of meeting had originated in the period of Israel's wilderness wanderings, a point which had been recognized by some of the most notable representatives of the new consensus.[54]

Dillmann's views of the priesthood also had a bearing on the discussion of Shiloh. Whereas Wellhausen regarded the Shilonite priesthood as being of Mushite origin, Dillmann considered the Elides to have been descendants of Ithamar, and the Zadokites to have been descendants of Eleazar.[55] Dillmann further dated the promise to an eternal priesthood to Phineas, the son of Eleazar (Num. 25.10-13), to some time during the divided monarchy, since such a prophecy *ex eventu* would presuppose not only the end of the line of Ithamar, represented by Abiathar, the last surviving Elide, but also at least a generation of unbroken dominance of the priesthood by the line of Eleazar.[56]

Dillmann thus departed from the Graf-Wellhausen synthesis in two major points. First, he insisted on the antiquity of the priestly source of the Hexateuch vis-à-vis Deuteronomy and tried to show that deuteronomic law actually was dependent upon the priestly legislation. Second, he took the historical testimony of the books of Chronicles seriously. Both issues had originally been defined by de Wette, and these issues continued to form the basis of debate three quarters of a century later.

2.4.2 *Delitzsch*

Simultaneously with Dillmann's critique, Franz Delitzsch raised his own objections to the synthesis of Graf and Wellhausen. Delitzsch, like Dillmann, argued for the historicity of the tabernacle.[57] According to his analysis, there were two views of the tent shrine: that of J, and that of E (i.e. P), and these two different views shared the same historical basis. In J, the tabernacle was merely the oracular tent, whereas the tabernacle in E (P) was both the oracular tent and the center of the cultic services. But the J tradition presupposed the holy tent of the priestly writings and was itself only a lifeless sketch needing to be fleshed out. The holy tent in J probably also belonged with the ark, although this was never reported.[58] The references to the ark (1 Sam. 3.3; 4.4) and the tent of meeting in Shiloh (Josh. 18.1; 19.51b; 1 Sam. 2.22b) suggested to Delitzsch that the tabernacle and the ark had, in fact, belonged together, as in the priestly stratum of the Pentateuch. Furthermore, while the details of the furnishings of the tent of meeting were largely beyond historical control, the historical books preserved traces of the existence of a wandering sanctuary down to the early monarchical period (2 Sam. 7.6; 1 Chron. 7.5; 1 Kgs 8.4). Furthermore, there was evidence, aside from that of Joshua 18–21, that the tent of meeting had been stationed at Shiloh (Ps. 78.60, 67; 1 Sam. 2.22b).[59] Finally, Delitzsch pointed out that the tent which David had erected for the ark, had had a sacrifical altar (Ps. 27.6; 1 Kgs 2.28). On the basis of such evidence Delitzsch concluded that the priestly depiction of the tent of meeting rested on actual tradition, just as did that of J.

Delitzsch also challenged the Graf-Wellhausen school on the issue

of centralization. The laws pertaining to sacrifice at the tent of
meeting applied only to the wilderness period and had been
abrogated by Deuteronomy 12.[60] Moreover, it was nowhere said that
one might sacrifice wherever one pleased, but only wherever Yahweh
would cause his name to be established. Thus, the issue of
centralization re-emerged in Delitzsch's treatment, and Shiloh, as
the site of the tent shrine, still played a major role in this
discussion.

Lastly, Delitzsch's treatment of the office of the 'high priest' must
be noted.[61] Delitzsch pointed out that the standard designation for
the 'high priest' in the late pre-monarchical and early monarchical
periods was merely the absolute *hakkōhēn* ('the priest'). This
designation occurred in connection with Eli, Ahijah, Ahimelech,
Abiathar, Zadok, Jehoiada, Hilkiah, and Azariah, just as it did with
Aaron in the Pentateuch. Moreover, the Pentateuch knew of no
union of temporal and spiritual authority in the person of the high
priest, as Wellhausen had argued: nowhere in the history of Israel
and Judah had a high priest emerged on the order of Innocent or
Gregory of Rome. Indeed, Wellhausen's entire treatment of the
position of the high priest vis-à-vis the other priests was based upon
the model of the Pope over and against the other bishops, a picture
which had been read into the text by Wellhausen, but for which there
was no historical basis. Indeed, the priesthood of the late pre-
monarchical and early monarchical times had followed a similar
pattern—one which paired the reigning high priest with a reigning
'temporal' ruler. This pattern was to be found in the pairs Joshua-
Eleazar, Saul-Ahijah, David-Abiathar, and Solomon-Zadok.[62] Not
even the post-exilic period exhibited the hierocratic system depicted
by Wellhausen. Rather, this era had been dominated by such non-
priestly figures as Ezra the scribe and Nehemiah the governor.
Against these figures of post-exilic history, the accompanying
priesthood was lifeless and colorless. The priestly order described in
Wellhausen's writings did not in fact come into existence until the
time of the Maccabees, and that order contradicted the priestly order
of the Pentateuch. Moreover, the post-exilic order down to the
Maccabean era could not be accurately depicted as a hierocracy;
rather, it was 'nomistic', and corresponded neither to Wellhausen's
papal order, nor to that of the Priestly stratum of the Pentateuch.
While this argument did not relate directly to Shiloh, it did take

notice of the paradigmatic relationship between the priests and the non-priestly rulers in the pre-monarchical and monarchical period. In this context, Eli appears to have been the only one of the pre-monarchic priests who attained an exalted independent status with temporal functions.[63]

2.4.3 *Kittel*

Rudolf Kittel's work closely followed that of Dillmann in both time and substance,[64] but Kittel advanced his own general critique of the Graf-Wellhausen hypothesis, especially with regard to the extremely late dating of the priestly writings. To begin, Kittel argued that the Graf-Wellhausen hypothesis rested on a massive argument from silence. The lack of evidence in the historical books for the cultic prescriptions of the priestly tradition was paralleled by a similar silence with regard to even those cultic institutions which Graf, Kuenen, Wellhausen, and their followers considered the most ancient. Thus, only one of the festivals considered ancient by the school of Graf and Wellhausen, Succoth, occurred in the historical books.[65] Furthermore, Kittel claimed that the prophets could not be expected to have cited the priestly legislation directly, since these materials were not publicly recognized documents, but comprised, rather, an *innerpriesterliche Privatschrift*—the sacred writings and regulations to which the priests alone were privy, and by which the cultus was administered. Kittel added the contention that P rested on old traditions, that the priestly code contained early traditions which had recieved a final post-exilic redaction. Only when the content of P had stemmed from older traditional materials would it have made any sense to have given it a place alongside those older traditions.[66]

According to Kittel, it was ludicrous to think that there had been no codification of ritual law during the entire period in which the first temple had stood or that the first attempt at technical cultic legislation had occurred with Ezekiel. So late a codification would have been absurd in light of the existence of an established priesthood at the Jerusalem temple during the entire monarchical period. Moreover, writing had been in use throughout this period, so that it was unlikely that cultic ritual had been handed on only through oral tradition. Just as far-fetched was the idea that sacrifices had been carried out solely according to individual whims and incidental urges prior to the exile. Just as one could not dispute the fact that the priests had continually refined their rituals during the period of the first temple, one could not avoid the fact that most of the priestly forms of sacrifice had been on hand then as well. These arguments were in accord with those of Dillmann, who had drawn on Assyrian, Babylonian, Phoenician, and Egyptian parallels to demonstrate that there must have been a cultic order for sacrifice during the monarchy. Even the centralization movement had begun under the monarchy, at least as early as the reign of Hezekiah. Certain priestly materials calling for centralization derived from that period at the latest, thus pre-dating Deuteronomy.[67]

Wellhausen had stated the principle of critical historical dating thus: 'Within the traditions of the ancient period we must preferrably hold ourselves to those points which diverge from the later conceptions and customs'.[68] Kittel accepted this proposition, but in further agreement with Dillmann he argued that many priestly institutions did not fit into post-exilic Judean society. Among these were (a) the tribal allotments; (b) the levitical cities; (c) the laws of warfare and spoils; (d) the laws pertaining to the ark; (e) the laws regarding the Urim and Thummim; (f) the anointing of the high priest, and (g) the agricultural laws presuposing the free use of the land. Thus, Kittel challenged Wellhausen's reconstruction on the basis of the very principles from which Wellhausen claimed to have worked, not by attacking the methodological assumptions on which Wellhausen's synthesis rested. Indeed, Kittel criticized key elements of the historical reconstruction on which Wellhausen had based his analysis of pentateuchal laws and institutions: that a system of sacral prescriptions for the administration of cultic services had emerged only at a very late date in the history of the Israelite people, that the priestly cultus of the Hexateuch had its historical setting in the exilic and post-exilic periods, and that the centralization of the cult had been enacted first under King Josiah.

With regard to Shiloh, Kittel offered a detailed reconstruction in which he depicted Shiloh as the center for and seat of the transmission of the true Yahwistic faith imparted to Israel by Moses.[69] Shiloh had been the most important Yahwistic sanctuary for the Israelites in Canaan: the ark had been stationed there since the conquest of the land, and the Shilonite cult was administered by an hereditary levitical priesthood tracing its descent directly from Moses.[70] According to Kittel, Shiloh had preserved the true Mosaic religion until the fall of the sanctuary there. The site had possessed no temple for most of its history under Israelite rule, but only an ark and the tent in which it had been housed. The ark and tent comprised the ancient *Wanderheiligthum*—the portable tent sanctuary which went back to Israel's birth in the desert.[71] This cultic center, with its levitical priests, its ark, and its holy tent, was the true bearer of the Mosaic tradition of worship without images.[72]

The Shiloh sanctuary, moreover, would have had its own set of ritual prescriptions, but these were no longer extant, though 1 Sam. 2.13-17 hinted at them. Furthermore, women had taken part in the services there (1 Sam. 2.22b), and a lamp was kept burning in the temple. The main festival at Shiloh had been the autumnal feast, which had been celebrated as a pilgrimage.

The turning point in Shiloh's history had been the battle of Ebenezer, which had led to the destruction of the temple, the capture of the ark, and the setting up of a Philistine governor or victory stele at Gibeah.[73] As a result of this calamity, Eli's descendants had transferred their residence to Nob, where they erected another sanctuary, at the center of which stood an *'ēphôd*—as either an image or some other oracular means—rather than the ark. Shewbread and votive offerings were also to be found at Nob.

The loss of the ark and the shift of the Elide priesthood to Nob brought about the resurgence of images in the cult. David's restoration of the ark, however, led to the suppression of these 'foreign things', since image-free worship had originally been linked to the ark.[74] The retrieval of the ark from captivity with the Philistines further led to a resurgence of the levitical priests, because the levitical priesthood had been closely linked to the Mosaic cult of the ark. Thus, from David's time on, pressure had been brought to bear upon the ancient non-levitical lay priests, such as those who ministered at Dan (cf. Judg. 17-18), to secure a legitimate levitical descent. Thus, even the founder of the Danite priesthood was made into a grandson of Moses at a later date, a fact which for Kittel corroborated the close ties between Levi and Moses.[75] The Mosaic tradition which had been transmitted through the Shiloh priests had been carried on first by Samuel, then by Nathan, who had opposed the temple, and finally by Ahijah the Shilonite. All of these prophetic figures had in common their rejection of the degradation of the worship of Yahweh through modernization, which entailed a high degree of syncretism with the Canaanite fertility cults.

2.4.4 *Baudissin*

While Franz Delitzsch had continued many of the lines of argument laid down by the scholars of the mid-century consensus, the works of Kittel and Dillmann were serious critical responses to the substance and method of the synthesis advanced by Graf, Kuenen, and Wellhausen. Wolf Wilhelm Grafen Baudissin, having accepted the validity of many of the basic claims of the Graf-Wellhausen hypothesis, nonetheless charted his own analysis along lines which had affinities with the views of Dillmann and Kittel.[76]

Baudissin began his history of the priesthood by accepting the basic principle that the priestly materials embodied a retrojection of the Jerusalem temple and cult back into the wilderness period of Israel's history—i.e. that the tabernacle was really a figure for the Solomonic temple. He also agreed with Wellhausen that the priestly writings presuposed the centralization of the cult, and thus had to reflect the period following the reform of Josiah. But here their similarities ended. While Baudissin conceded the *general* correctness of certain of the overarching claims of the school of Graf and Wellhausen, his own exegesis led him to markedly different conclusions at key points. Thus, Baudissin held that a *Grundstock* of P pre-dated D, and that both D and Ezekiel had been dependent upon this pre-exilic P material.[77] Baudissin also reiterated Kittel's important notion that P had been on hand as an *innerpriesterliche Privatschrift* long before the priestly legislation had been publicly recognized.[78]

Moreover, Aaron was not the fictional ancestor of the Zadokite priesthood but the historical figure from whom the ancient Ephraimite priesthood had traced its descent.[79] The line of Eli in Shiloh had been directly related to the Aaronite line of Eleazar and Phineas, as was evident in the recurrence of the name of Phineas in Eli's line. Conversely, the Zadokites were a non-Aaronite line, though probably a levitical one.[80] These supplanted the Aaronite line of Eli and served merely as 'Zadokites' in Jerusalem. Only at a later time did the Jerusalem priests adopt as their own the ancient designation of the Ephraimite priesthood, on account of its established antiquity and legitimacy. As late as Ezekiel, however, the Jerusalemite priesthood was designated merely as Zadokite. The Zadokite expropriation of the Aaronite heritage of Ephraim came about in part because of the migration of the ancient Ephraimite priesthood to the Jerusalem cult following Josiah's reform.[81] Thus, the Aaronite priesthood of the post-exilic era did not include the Zadokites alone. Rather, 'the sons of Aaron' was an inclusive term referring to the totality of the priestly families, of which the Zadokites were only one group. Even the Ithamarides had served as Aaronite priests in the post-exilic community, with no evidence of an attempt to exclude them. Thus, the genealogical connection between Aaron and Zadok was artificial. The Zadokites, whose own descent was uncertain, had usurped the legitimate claim of the Elide line of descent from Eleazar, the son of Aaron.[82] Consequently, the connection between Eli and Ithamar (1 Chron. 24.3) was an artificial one meant to place the Elides in a position of secondary status over and against the Zadokites.[83]

Baudissin further disputed the assumption that the priestly legislation was a fictional addition to the Mosaic tradition. The formulation of new laws in the Old Testament had not been effected by the abrupt insertion of new material on its own merits. Rather, new legislation either sanctioned the ancient tradition, or carried the threads of older traditions further. Thus, while each new giving of law superseded and went beyond the old order, it could be seen at the same time as belonging to that old order, even though the connection to that older order might have been merely implied. A mere invention would scarcely have been believed, let alone accepted.[84]

With regard to Shiloh itself, Baudissin staked out a median position between the older consensus and the school of Graf and Wellhausen. Shiloh, while not the *central* sanctuary, had been the *Hauptheiligtum* or *main* sanctuary in the period immediately preceding the monarchy. This sanctuary had been the hereditary possession of the line of Eli, a levitical priesthood tracing its origins to Phineas, the son of Eleazar, the son of Aaron. The Shiloh cult had been characterized by at times peculiar cultic institutions such as the 'ēphôd, a special oracular means. After the destruction of the Shilonite sanctuary at the hands of the Philistines, the surviving priests of the Elide line established a new sanctuary at Nob. Under Saul, Ahijah the son of Ahitub, the son of Phineas, the son of Eli, the priest of Yahweh at Shiloh, was the 'bearer of the ephod' (1 Sam. 14.3). When Saul massacred the priests at Nob, Abiathar, the lone survivor, fled to David with the 'ēphôd—the special oracular means of the Shiloh priests. Abiathar then served as priest to David, in which position he held a status higher than Zadok,[85] until he was himself banished from the Solomonic court and succeeded by Zadok.

With Abiathar's fall from royal favor, the Aaronite influence at the Davidic court in Jerusalem was replaced by that of the Zadokites. The Aaronite priests, in turn, became the priesthood at the high places in the North, notably Bethel, and returned to Jerusalem only as a result of Josiah's reform.

Thus, while Baudissin accepted some of the formal arguments of the school of Graf and Wellhausen, the details of his own reconstruction, e.g. his arguments for the antiquity of the priestly legislation, the authenticity of the Aaronite descent of the Elide priesthood, and of the line of Aaron and Eleazar more generally, deviated significantly from the new synthesis.

2.5 *Other Departures from the Synthesis of Graf and Wellhausen*

While the school of Graf and Wellhausen sought to replace the 'reigning consensus' of the mid-nineteenth century with its own radical reconstruction of the origins and composition of the Pentateuch, those same scholars had been in substantial agreement with many of their opponents concerning the history of Shiloh, at least in its broad outlines. Thus, several aspects of Shiloh's history were almost universally accepted. First, Shiloh had been the site of a temple, if only for a short time. Moreover, this temple had been associated with the ark, and the presence of the ark had afforded Shiloh a special status among the cultic sites of Israel, although it was not generally agreed as to just what that special status had entailed. Shiloh's priesthood had also enjoyed a singular status through its association with the ark. Finally, the peculiar position of Shiloh in Israel had come to an abrupt end with the capture of the ark and the destruction of the sanctuary at Shiloh as a result of the disaster at Ebenezer. Thus, a slightly modified version of Ewald's reconstruction of Shiloh's history, sustained by Wellhausen, came to dominate the critical consensus.

2.5.1 *Buhl*

Nevertheless, opposition to this view continued. In 1896, the Danish Semiticist and lexicographer, Frants Buhl, published his work, *Die Geographie des alten Palästinas*,[86] in which he argued that Shiloh had not been destroyed until late in Israel's history, when the northern kingdom had fallen to the Assyrians. Buhl built his position on the same evidential grounds cited by Graf in his original treatment of Shiloh.[87] According to Buhl, Shiloh had been the permanent site of the ark until that cult object fell into the hands of the Philistines under the tenure of Eli and his sons. The city itself remained inhabited, however, since the prophet Ahijah resided in Shiloh (1 Kgs 11.29). The destruction of Shiloh mentioned in Jer. 7.12 most likely referred to the destruction of Ephraim under the Assyrians. At the same time, Jer. 41.5 demonstrated that Shiloh had been reoccupied after 722 BCE. Buhl's analysis contradicted the most widely established opinions of the day with regard to the history of Shiloh; consequently, it found little audience. Still, Buhl's work had a decisive bearing on the debate in the twentieth century, especially through the work of Marie-Louise Buhl, the former Curator of Ancient Collections at the Danish National Museum in Copenhagen.[88]

2.5.2 Procksch

In addition to Buhl, two other scholars who wrote under the shadow of the Graf-Wellhausen hypothesis offered significantly divergent opinions on the issue of biblical Shiloh. The first of these was Otto Procksch.[89] Procksch's views on Shiloh were contained in a work which was important for its development of a *traditionsgeschichtlich* approach to the study of Israelite history, which was most effectively exploited by Alt and Noth: *Das nordhebräische Sagenbuch: Die Elohimquelle*.[90] In this work, Procksch attributed to Shiloh a far greater role than had heretofore been recognized by any other scholar. While his historical reconstruction followed the lines of the school of Wellhausen—i.e. Shiloh was the seat of the ark and the chief sanctuary of Joseph, and fell into oblivion following the capture of the ark by the Philistines at Ebenezer.[91]—Procksch developed the idea that Shiloh had been the pre-eminent seat of the Holy Law, the place where the Elohistic laws of Exodus 21–23 had been developed and handed on in the spirit of the Mosaic covenant. Here Procksch expanded upon an idea first introduced by Kittel, namely that Shiloh had been the center of the Mosaic cultus, an idea which also squared somewhat with Wellhausen's identification of the Shilonite priesthood as Mushite.[92] Procksch further argued for the reliability of the priestly account of the setting up of the ark in Shiloh in Joshua, thereby linking the Covenant Code to the levitical priesthood in Shiloh. On this basis Procksch asserted that the connection between

Exodus 21–23 and the time of Moses could be established. To be sure, the laws of the Covenant Code reflected the culture of Israel after the settlement, rather than that of pastoral nomadism, but they continued in the ethical spirit of the lawgiver from the desert, and they reflected as well the arrangement of the Decalogue. Moreover, the Shilonite sanctuary had been the place where the national Elohistic saga was cultivated and formed.[93] At the same time that Shiloh actually had been the chief sanctuary of the Joseph tribes, it bacame the guardian of the national treasure—the national memory of the people (*die Volkserinnerungen*). The national saga had grown at Shiloh, the experience of Joseph had become the experience of his brothers, and thus the national consciousness awoke in the soul of Israel. In Procksch's view, this development had been completed by David's day. Procksch further maintained that the Shilonite priesthood had collected and shaped the Covenant Code.[94] The ground for this argument was that there was no king in the Covenant Code, but rather, a priestly court with judicial powers.[95] Thus, the Book of the Covenant had been in the hands of the priests: not the royal priests, but those who had been conscious that they, as the representatives of God, were the highest guardians of the Law and were dependent upon no one.[96] Since Shiloh had been the dominant sanctuary immediately prior to the rise of the monarchy, and its priesthood had guarded the ark, and because this sanctuary had enjoyed considerable public esteem, it was likely that the Covenant Code had been formulated as an Ephraimite law book by the Shilonite priests.

The historical-cultural milieu of Exodus 21–23 confirmed for Procksch such a provenance for the Covenant Code. In these laws, Israel was a settled agrarian society, and apparently had been for a considerable time. The Canaanites might still have been present in the land, but were no longer a threat. The Israelites comprised a society of farmers, and were not city-dwellers. Animal husbandry consisted mainly of sheep and goats, and the ass was the beast of burden. There was no mention of either horses or camels, as one would have expected from a nomadic culture. This picture corresponded exactly to what was known of Israelite life from the son of Deborah and the story of Saul's search for the lost asses.

Procksch's analysis, therefore, led him to the assignment of a far greater role to Shiloh in the early history of Israel than had been the case with his contemporaries. Shiloh, while not serving as the central shrine for the entire nation in the sense of Deuteronomy 12, had served as the center for the transmission and development of the national saga and the concomitant covenant theology. Thus, Shiloh, with its Ephraimite priesthood, had fostered the emergence of a national consciousness, which had led to the creation of the monarchy. Despite the far-reaching implications of Procksch's conclusions, his work had little immediate impact on the overall discussion of biblical Shiloh. Only much later would his development of the role of Shiloh in the pre-monarchic national life be picked up by later scholars such as Eissfeldt and Lindblom.[97]

2.5.3 *Karge*

Another scholar of note for this study was Paul Karge, a Roman Catholic priest from Breslau. Karge's history of the covenantal idea in the Old Testament[99] is one of the 'lost works' of Old Testament scholarship: a groundbreaking study which received little contemporary and even less later attention. Nonetheless, Karge's peculiar approach to the history of the theology of covenant was developed as a significant position by scholars such as G.E. Mendenhall in the fifties and sixties.[99] Of special note in this regard was Karge's appeal to ancient Near Eastern treaty forms to explain the phenomenon of covenant in the Old Testament.[100]

While Karge's treatment of Shiloh followed the fairly standard outlines of his day, there were some important exceptions. For example, he argued in agreement with Graf and Wellhausen that a temple building had stood at Shiloh, but at the same time he considered this temple to have been the national sanctuary. Furthermore, Karge argued that cultic ritual and liturgy had played an important role in the life of the sanctuary at Shiloh.[101] Thus he advocated the early origins of Israel's cultic life in general, as well as the antiquity of many of Israel's cultic prescriptions, a view reminiscent of Dillmann, Kittel, and Baudissin.[102] Otherwise, Karge's treatment of Shiloh was in accord with the critical consensus of his day. The Josephide sanctuary at Shiloh had served as the site of an autumnal pilgrimage and had been administered by a Mushite priesthood. The Philistine victory at Ebenezer in the mid-eleventh century had brought about the destruction of Shiloh and the abandonment of its sanctuary. The Elide priesthood had resettled at Nob and continued its ministry under Saul, but came to an end when Abiathar was expelled from the court of Solomon.[103]

2.5.4 *Smend*: *'Mosiden und Aharoniden'*

The last major work published by a scholar from the Wellhausian era was Rudolf Smend's *Die Erzählung des Hexateuch*.[104] This work followed the same lines developed earlier by Smend, but included a detailed treatment of the relationship between the Mushite and Aaronite priesthoods.[105] While Smend appeared to maintain his old view that Aaron had been the legitimate ancestor of the northern priesthood, he argued that the Zadokites had sought from the earliest days to pass themselves off as Aaronites. Exodus 32, in fact, was the Elohistic reproach of the priests of Jerusalem, not because the Zadokites had been guilty of perpetuating the bull-iconography, but because they sought to trace themselves from Aaron. From this point on, Smend followed Wellhausen's reconstruction: the Shilonite priesthood had been Mushite, since Eleazar, the son of Aaron, had originally been Eliezer, the son of Moses. Abiathar had continued the Mushite line of Shiloh at Anathoth, of which Jeremiah was also a descendant.

The publication of Smend's work brought the period of discussion which had been sparked by the revolutionary writings of Graf, Kuenen and Wellhausen to an end. The last voice of opposition had been Karge's; thereafter a practical orthodoxy reigned with regard to the literary-critical and historical-critical reconstructions. No really new elements would be introduced into the discussion of Shiloh until the emergence of biblical archaeology as a full-blown discipline in its own right, with its concomitant importance for the discussion of biblical history and literature.

Chapter 3

THE DISCUSSION OF SHILOH
IN THE TWENTIETH CENTURY

3.1 *The Heritage of the Nineteenth Century*

The debate regarding Shiloh in the nineteenth century turned on two issues: the centralization of the cult as defined by de Wette at the beginning of the century, and the antiquity and validity of the priestly source of the Pentateuch as advocated at mid-century by Ewald, and opposed by Vatke, Graf, Kuenen, Wellhausen, Reuss *et al*. It was Wellhausen more than any other scholar who set the terms for the ensuing discussion regarding Shiloh. While he himself stood in the critical line of de Wette, Vatke, and Graf, Wellhausen was the pupil of Ewald, and it was a modified form of Ewald's reconstruction of Shiloh's history which Wellhausen furthered. That Shiloh had been the resting-place for the ark, that this sanctuary had attained special status shortly before the emergence of the monarchy, only to be destroyed in the wake of the disaster at Ebenezer, were the basic elements of the view which had come to dominate biblical scholarship by the close of the nineteenth century. Indeed, Ewald's reconstruction of Shiloh's later history had actually become, through Wellhausen, a 'firm conclusion' of Old Testament scholarship.

Yet two factors emerged during the early years of the twentieth century which expanded the dimensions of the debate over Shiloh. The first of these factors was the introduction of comparative Semitic evidence pertaining to the rituals of priestly sacrifice in the Old Testament. This material, especially that from the Syro-Phoenician sources, was first published in a 1914 monograph by Rene Dussaud.[1] Dussaud followed this work with the publication of his famous *Les origines cananéenes du sacrifice israélite* seven years later.[2] His third work on this subject, *Les découvertes de Ras Shamra et l'Ancien Testament*, appeared subsequent to the discovery of the library at Ras Shamra-Ugarit.[3] The data assembled by Dussaud indicated that the priestly sacrificial ordinances, so far from being an invention of post-exilic Judaism, were actually related to the ancient Canaanite tradition of cultic ritual. Thus Dussaud's work at least partially vindicated the appeal made by Dillmann and Kittel to the culture of the ancient Near East as a means of confirming the antiquity of the priestly traditions. Dussaud's studies had a significant influence upon French scholars such as Adolphe Lods and Roland de Vaux and provided the basis for the position later taken by scholars of the Albrightian school, that the priestly stratum of the Pentateuch, while only extant in a late literary form, in fact reflected an ancient tradition in Israel. Such a position had significant ramifications for the history of biblical Shiloh, since those texts in the historical books which seemed to make Shiloh the central sanctuary in the period following the Conquest are found only in the priestly layers of the book of Joshua (Josh. 18–22).[4]

The second factor to emerge in a crucial role in the debate over the course of Shiloh's history was the consideration of archaeological evidence in the reconstruction of Israelite history. Excavations and archaeological research in Palestine had been gaining impetus since the last decade of the nineteenth century, and the application of this form of investigation to the site of ancient Shiloh came under consideration for the first time in 1913. In that year, a committee of Danish scholars was formed to fund and carry out excavations at Tell Seilun, the accepted site of biblical Shiloh since the publication of Robinson and Smith's *Biblical Researches*.[5] The outbreak of World War I prevented the Danes from digging as planned in 1915, and soundings by the team under Dr Aage Schmidt were not made at the site until 1922. Excavations only began in earnest in 1926, under the direction of Hans Kjaer, Deputy Keeper of the National Museum in Copenhagen. Subsequent expeditions under Kjaer returned to Tell Seilun in 1929 and 1932, with the final Danish excavations being carried out by Svend Holm-Nielsen and Marie-Louise Buhl in 1963. The Danish excavations of Shiloh not only provided material to be discussed in connection with the prevalent view of Shiloh's history, but owing to the ambivalence of the artifactual evidence uncovered there, they also served as an important catalyst in the overall debate.

3.2 *The Beginnings of the Archaeological Debate*

From the very beginning, the debate over the interpretation of the artifactual evidence from Seilun was overshadowed by the long-standing historical assumption that Shiloh had been destroyed by the Philistines, and that it had not been reoccupied thereafter. Already in 1913 Aage Schmidt had expressed the view that Shiloh 'no doubt was suddenly destroyed at the time of Eli's death'.[6] Similarly, W.F. Albright, in his article on the first Danish soundings at Seilun, generally followed the standard reconstruction of the history of Shiloh and noted that the artifactual remains of Seilun agreed 'remarkably well with biblical indications'.[7] Albright thus noted an abundance of Iron I pottery and an absence of Iron II pottery and took this evidence as confirmation that the Shiloh sanctuary had been destroyed by the Philistines after the Israelite defeat at Ebenezer. As a result of this calamity, the place had been largely abandoned, aside from a few inhabitants, who were still present at the accession of Jeroboam to the throne of the northern kingdom (1 Kgs 11.29). Yet Jeroboam's selection of Dan and Bethel as his chief cultic sites spelled the end of any hope that Shiloh might have been restored to its original prestige. By Jeremiah's time, 'Shiloh lay in ruins, and had apparently been destroyed so long before that it was proverbial'. Thus, the compiler of the book of Judges had been constrained to give specific directions as to the location of the site, since by his day the place had been largely forgotten.

Ironically, the first controversy to break out as a result of the Danish decision to excavate at Tell Seilun had to do with the actual location of biblical Shiloh. The assumption that Tell Seilun was the site of ancient Shiloh was challenged by A.T. Richardson in 1925.[8] Richardson argued that the Palestinian site of Beit Sila, near Gibeon in the Wadi Imyash, offered a more likely spot for the famous shrine than did Tell Seilun. According to him, the description of Shiloh in Judg. 21.19, 'on the north of Bethel, on the east side of the highway that goes up from Bethel to Shechem, and on the south of Lebonah', most likely referred to a lesser-known site which later became confused with the original Shiloh after the destruction of that sanctuary by the Philistines. Richardson followed this line of argument with an article two years later in which he expanded his case.[9] There Richardson argued that two sites originally had existed—Sila and Silo(n)—and this distinction was reflected in the variant Masoretic spellings of *šlh* and *šlw*. Sila, 'in the land of Canaan' (Judg. 21.12), referred to the site of the great holy place. This site, in the neighborhood of Gibeon, was identified as being 'in the land of Canaan' because Gibeon and its environs had remained in the hands of the Hivites down to the period of the early monarchy. The proximity of the central sanctuary to Gibeon explained the fact that the Hivites had been put to work as hewers of wood and drawers of water (Josh. 9.21, 23, 27) for the tent sanctuary. On the other hand, Silo (or Silon) designated the site of Tell Seilun, a little-known village which had been raided by the Benjaminites for wives, and the location of which required explicit directions. Richardson supported his contention with other literary evidence and cited interesting corelations between his theory and the alternating spelling *šlh* and *šlw* in the account of Judges 21.

Richardson's arguments, however, were never taken up in the ensuing discussion. In the same issue in which Richardson published his final arguments on the site of Shiloh, Albright, then head of the American Schools of Oriental Research in Jerusalem, challenged Richardson's views.[10] Although Albright did not deal with the substance of Richardson's claims, he did suggest that 'Mr. Richardson' raise around ten punds to pay for several test holes to be dug on the site of Beit Sila, so that he might see for himself that there were no traces of ancient occupation there. No record of any such soundings at Beit Sila exists; Albright's note apparently put the matter to rest.

3.3 *The Danish Excavations*

After Aage Schmidt's soundings in the fall of 1922, the Danish excavations at Seilun were resumed in 1926, and the results were published in preliminary fashion in 1927.[11] In his preliminary report on the site and its history, Hans Kjaer expressed the view of Frants Buhl, that Shiloh had suffered no real catastrophe until much later than the disaster in which the ark had been lost, although from that time, certainly, the town's prestige had waned. Still, the place was apparently never destroyed *in toto*. Kjaer offered this opinion as an introduction to the results of that year's excavations, which uncovered only the later strata of the tell down to the Hellenistic period.

No evidence pertaining to the fate of the biblical sanctuary city was unearthed until the second Danish expedition in 1929.[12] The team concentrated primarily on an exposed wall line on the western edge of the tell, approximately 60 meters from the summit. On the outside of this wall, which was subsequently determined to date from the Roman period, a room containing a layer of ash was uncovered. This room was designated 'House A'. There the excavators unearthed seven large 'collared-rim' jars, some of which contained deposits of ash. Albright, who was on site to interpret technical matters relating to pottery dating, among other things, immediately connected the 'destruction layer' of 'House A' and the 'collared-rim' jars which had been found *in situ* with the theoretical destruction of Shiloh by the Philistines in the mid-eleventh century BCE. On the basis of this interpretation, Kjaer reversed his earlier view and concurred with Albright's suggestion.

Nevertheless, not all the archaeological community accepted Albright's interpretation. C.C. McCown, who succeeded Albright as director of the American school in Jerusalem, wrote in 1930:

> Was the place unoccupied during the Middle and Late Iron Ages, that is, after the loss of the ark? And was it destroyed by the Philistines, or did it gradually fall into ruins after the loss of the ark?[13]

Indeed, the discovery of certain sherds similar to Iron II types in the same destruction layer containing the large *pithoi* lent strength to McCown's skepticism.[14] Nevertheless, the Iron II sherds did not enter the discussion until much later. Most of these sherds were never publicised or even returned to Denmark until twenty years later. Instead, Schmidt kept them with him in Jerusalem until his death in 1953.[15] Thus were McCown's remarks forgotten, and Kjaer's subsequent reconstructions and dating tailored to Albright's historical assumptions.

The excavations of 1929 and 1932 brought to light new evidence which compelled Kjaer to modify certain aspects of the reconstruction of Shiloh's history. Chief among these data was the discovery of numerous sherds from the MB II and LB I-II periods, which lent weight to earlier assertions that Shiloh originally had been a Canaanite site which later was taken over by the Israelites.[16] The results of the 1932 excavations were not published, however, until Marie-Louise Buhl and Svend Holm-Nielsen compiled and edited the notes from all these various expeditions after the completion of the final Danish season in 1963.[17] The Danish excavations of the twenties and thirties, then, strengthened the prevailing consensus concerning the course of Shiloh's history.

The work of Buhl and Holm-Nielsen, however, raised a serious challenge to this dominant view. While the original Danish excavations had been carried on during the 'pioneer days' of Palestinian archaeology, those of 1963 had the advantage of nearly two generations of excavations as well as the concomitant pottery and stratigraphy studies. Thus, the better part of Buhl and Holm-Nielsen's work on Shiloh was concerned with the *reinterpretation* of the earlier Danish evidence. The earlier Danish excavations had identified extensive occupation of Seilun in the Iron I period, with little evidence of habitation during Iron II, and renewal of occupation during the Iron III, or Hellenistic period. When Buhl and Holm-Nielsen re-evaluated this evidence in light of more recent excavations and stratigraphic data, they concluded that Seilun had first been settled during MB II, and that this habitation had continued through LB I and II, and on into Iron I and II, finally coming to an end around the close of the seventh century BCE.[18]

A critical aspect of the work of Buhl and Holm-Nielsen was their identification of numerous sherds from Iron II, both in key sectors of the excavations and among the surface sherds taken from the tell at the outset of the excavations.[19] The most controversial aspect of their treatment, however, was the redating of the large storage jars found in House A in 1929 from Iron I to Iron II. They made this distinction on the basis of parallels from Hazor strata VI and V, excavated under the direction of Yigael Yadin in four seasons from 1955 to 1958. The vessels in question were those designated 176I-176VI in the original Danish reports, but cataloged under the numbers 187-192 by Buhl and Holm-Nielsen.[20] During the earlier Danish excavations under Hans Kjaer, Albright had been the principal authority on the pottery of the Holy Land, and the real author of the pottery sequence in Palestinian archaeology. Pottery dating during the twenties and thirties, however, was still in its formative stages. Whereas Albright saw the 'collared-rim' jar as a specifically *early Israelite* artifact, subsequent excavations demonstrated that this form continued in widespread use down into the latter part of Iron II. Buhl and Holm-Nielsen based their revisions of the previous interpretation of the evidence by Albright and Kjaer on this more recent development in the study of Iron Age Palestinian pottery, especially with regard to what they saw as the stronger parallels between the storage vessels of 'House A' and the artifacts of Strata VI and V at Hazor.

In addition to their archaeological work, Buhl and Holm-Nielsen concluded their study with a survey of the biblical traditions regarding Shiloh.[21] Holm-Nielsen denied the historical authenticity of the references to Shiloh in the book of Joshua. According to him, these derived from later traditions which had built upon the importance of Shiloh as a cultic center in late pre-monarchic times. In this respect, Holm-Nielsen displayed an affinity with the school of Wellhausen. He further suggested that Shiloh in these passages had replaced original references to Gilgal or Shechem. Conversely, Holm-Nielsen held the traditions about Shiloh in the book of Judges to be reliable, especially that of the annual 'Feast of Yahweh' in Judg. 21.19, which he compared with the similar tradition in 1 Sam. 1.3. Holm-Nielsen also stressed the apparently special connection between Benjamin and Shiloh, and suggested that this relationship might go back to Shiloh's status as the object of a cultic pilgrimage

> for an earlier immigrated Benjamin tribe before Ephraim settled in central Palestine. If so, it would mean that when Ephraim later immigrated into the country, Benjamin was forced to withdraw to the south. This would explain why Benjamin's special connection with Shiloh was still preserved in the later pan-Israelite traditions.[22]

Holm-Nielsen also argued that there had been a 'strong Cana'anite weft in the Shiloh cult'.[23] The dancing girls in Judges 21 might refer to Canaanite fertility rites, while 1 Sam. 2.22b might hint at sacral prostitution. Indeed, recurrent reference to 'Shiloh, in the land of Canaan' and the need for explicit directions to the site in Judg. 21.19 might have originated at a time when Shiloh was a Canaanite settlement not yet under Israelite control, although it may have had cultural and religious ties to the tribes of Israel, especially Benjamin. Accordingly, the formerly Canaanite city of Shiloh may have had special connections to the tribe of Benjamin, but it had fallen under Ephraimite suzerainty sometime during the twelfth century BCE. There was, however, no tradition of an Israelite conquest of the place.

More importantly, Holm-Nielsen denied any justification for the conclusion that Shiloh as a cultic center had been destroyed as a result of the battle at Ebenezer. In support of this position, he pointed to the archaeological evidence amassed by himself and Buhl which indicated that Shiloh had continued in existence as an inhabited town down to the end of Iron II. He appealed, moreover, to the biblical references which earlier had been cited by Graf and Frants Buhl, but which had been overlooked or ignored by the rest of the academic community. Moreover, the traditions which had been used to identify a destruction of Shiloh during the mid-eleventh century did not afford an unequivocal picture on that score. The story of the ark's Philistine captivity might have been no more than an 'unhistorical cult legend'. If, on the other hand, the capture of the ark actually had taken place, the setting-up of the ark in Kiriath-jearim would have occurred because that town was in Philistine territory, not because Shiloh had been destroyed. That Shiloh was not mentioned again after 1 Samuel 3 derived from the fact that after 2 Samuel 7, the narrative was no longer concerned with the ark. Therefore, Buhl and Holm-Nielsen concluded their work with an attempted refutation of the widely accepted reconstruction, suggested by Hengstenberg and worked out by Ewald, that Shiloh had been destroyed following the battle at Ebenezer during the mid-eleventh century.

3.4 *The Reaction to the Work of Buhl and Holm-Nielsen*

The publication and reinterpretation of the data from the Danish excavations at Shiloh by Buhl and Holm-Nielsen sparked a broad but mixed reaction within the community of biblical scholars and archaeologists. On the one hand, the work won new support for the views originally propounded by Graf and Frants Buhl. Thus, a number of articles appeared in the ensuing years contradicting the prevailing consensus,[24] and Holm-Nielsen wrote the article on Shiloh in *IDBS*, 1976.[25] Thus, the widespread agreement on the course of Shiloh's history, which had dominated Old Testament studies since the days of Wellhausen, met for the first time with serious, broad-based opposition.

Nonetheless, the work of Buhl and Holm-Nielsen did not go unopposed. Yigael Shiloh, the noted Israeli archaeologist, wrote a critical dissenting review of the Danish treatment, in which he attacked the pottery analysis of Buhl concerning the key storage jars found during the 1929 expedition in House A.[26] As Shiloh correctly noted, the fundamental problem with regard to the dating of the Danish pottery was that no overall stratigraphy of the site had ever been established. Thus, Buhl had been thrown back on the straight comparative data of the sherds themselves. It was at that facet of Buhl's work that Shiloh leveled his critique. According to Shiloh, Buhl did 'not differentiate between the typical Iron Age I "collared rim", in whith the "collar" is at the base of the neck, or the top of the shoulder' and the later type, which, while it was ' a development of the early type', had 'the "collar" further up', creating 'a ridge at the middle of the neck'. Shiloh argued, moreover, that the Iron II examples of this form of jar were all considerably smaller than their Iron I prototypes. Shiloh raised the additional claim, made since Albright's pioneering work at Tell Beit Mirsim and Tell el-Ful, that the so-called 'collared-rim jar' was to be associated with the initial settlement of the Israelites in Palestine. Finally, Shiloh denied that Plate 14 of Buhl's treatment of the pottery remains contained a single example of an Iron II sherd, thus challenging her judgment in more than half of the over twenty-five sherds displayed there. The intent of Shiloh's critique was to discredit the contention of Buhl and Holm-Nielsen that the Iron Age settlement at Tell Seilun had not been destroyed until the late seventh century, and to reinforce the earlier consensus that biblical Shiloh had been destroyed by the Philistines in the eleventh century. At the same time, the rest of Buhl and Holm-Nielsen's data, which indicated that Tell Seilun had continued as an inhabited site during the period of the Divided Monarchy, was accepted by Shiloh in lieu of earlier arguments that the town had been abandoned after its destruction and never resettled. Similarly, John Day, in seeking to refute the arguments of Holm-Nielsen, Pearce, and van Rossum concerning the destruction of the Shilonite sanctuary sometime in the late seventh, or perhaps the eighth, century BCE, was compelled to admit that Shiloh had continued as a viable settlement even after the destruction of its sanctuary.[27]

The reversal of the interpretation of the archaeological evidence from Shiloh provided by Buhl and Holm-Nielsen went a long way toward breaking the long-standing consensus concerning the fate of Shiloh's settlement and sanctuary. Even the adherents of the older view have had to modify their claims regarding Shiloh's destruction after Ebenezer. Thus, Shiloh admitted to the continuation of the town at Tell Seilum down into the Iron II period, while Day argued for the destruction of the sanctuary alone, not the settlement as a whole.[28] Nevertheless, the Danish scholars did not succeed in establishing a new consensus.

At present, an Israeli team under the direction of Israel Finkelstein of the Bar-Ilan University has renewed excavations at Tell Seilun with the hope of clearing up the major technical points at issue. The results of this work have been published as noted, and in Prof. Finkelstein's newly published work on the Israelite settlement.[29] The preliminary reports assert on architectural grounds that the stratum in which House A and House B of the Danish excavations were found belong to the Iron I period.[30] Moreover, it is claimed that this entire level perished 'in a fierce fire, the signs of which are to be seen everywhere—ash on the floors and collapse of stone and baked mud-brick'.[31] Final assessment of the archaeological evidence, however, must await publication of the complete site reports before any definitive judgment can be reached regarding the accuracy of these new claims.

Finkelstein's work has nonetheless provided a good overview of the settlement history of the site, and this evidence has important bearing on the interpretation of the biblical traditions. The first occupation of Tell Seilun occurred in MB IIB (1750-1650 BCE), in the form of an unwalled settlement. During MB IICC (1650-1550 BCE) Seilun became the site of a walled city, complete with a massive, beaten-earth glacis supporting the main wall, which reached a height of twenty-five feet in some sectors and varied in thickness from ten to seventeen feet. Even at that time Seilun apparently had been the site of a Canaanite shrine, as small votive bowls and cultic stands taken from the storerooms along the city wall indicate. Since no houses of this period have been found in the tell to date, Finkelstein has suggested that during MB IIC the inhabitants of the small villages of Ephraim may have built fortress-cities such as Shiloh as places of refuge during times of attack. This MB IIC city was destroyed sometime in the sixteenth century BCE, as evidenced by fire in the rooms adjacent to the city. While activity resumed at Shiloh during the Late Bronze Age, very little construction and no real settlement took place. The largest concentration of LB remains, in fact, seems to have been a 'dump' or 'intentional deposit'. This evidence led Finkelstein to interpret the LB site as an isolated cultic place to which offerings were brought by people from various places in the region. The fact that there were very few permanent Late Bronze sites anywhere in the vicinity of Shiloh may indicate that these people lived in pastoral groups, in temporary dwellings. It is probable that these offerings, many of them Late Bronze I (15th century B.C.) in date, were brought to the site of the destroyed Middle Bronze Age sanctuary, which may even have been reconstructed. The steadily declining amount of pottery indicates a decrease in activity at the site, and then a complete cessation, apparently before the end of the Late Bronze Age.[32]

Seilun was reoccupied at the beginning of the Early Iron period, and the Israeli team found the buildings from this period built into the MB IIC glacis. According to Finkelstein, these were 'public' structures, and may have been 'annexes to the cultic complex that stood farther uphill'.[33] Finkelstein then argued that these buildings had been erected 'no earlier that the second half or end of the twelfth century B.C.', since this dating would be in agreement with the evidence for the creation of the 'first supratribal center', and 'especially the date of the beginning of the process of Israelite settlement'.[34]

In conjunction with the ongoing excavations at Tell Seilun, the Israeli team has also been conducting a survey of the Ephraimite hill country, which has yielded some important data for the evaluation of Shiloh's importance in the early period of Israelite settlement. The results of this survey are as follows. (a) During the Middle Bronze Age, small settlements dotted the Ephraimite hill country but were abandoned before the end of that period. (b) During the Late Bronze Age, an even more precipitous decline in population occurred, with the number of sites decreasing from fifty to five, and with the size of those settlements falling off as well. (c) Occupation increased again at the beginning of Iron I, and the area around Seilun was the focus of much of this settlement. In fact, out of one hundred sites surveyed from this period, twenty-two were found within a three-to-four mile radius around Seilun, and over half of these emerged later in Iron I. By comparison, Bethel further south had only twelve Iron I settlements in close proximity to it.

Finkelstein draws several important conclusions from this evidence. Starting from the premise that the large, 'collared-rim' pithoi found at Seilun are characteristic of an ethnically *Israelite* group, he asserts

that the Israelite settlement at Shiloh can be traced to no earlier than
the twelfth century BCE.[35] Accordingly, Shiloh became an important
cult center 'no earlier than the second half or end of the 12th century
B.C.', a view which, for Finkelstein, agrees with the rest of the
chronological indicators. The centers of Israelite worship changed,
however, as the population moved southward. With Shiloh's
destruction around 1050 BCE, Benjamin became the center of
Israelite settlement, and Bethel became an important shrine.[36]

Finally, Finkelstein offers a new interpretation of the settlement at
Shiloh. The Iron I occupation covered no more than three acres, and
Finkelstein argued that this area probably contained the 'complex of
the tabernacle and its auxiliary buildings'. Furthermore, since the
LB remains are an indication of the nature and function of the Iron I
site, he suggests that Iron Age Seilun was most likely a 'sacred
temenos'—a specially marked off area devoted to cultic purposes.
Finkelstein further ventures to identify the summit of the tell as the
site of the tabernacle, and adduces various arguments for this
conclusion, at the same time admitting that the question is
unanswerable.[37]

The current Israeli excavations, then, are being interpreted as
supporting the traditional theory that Shiloh was destroyed in the
mid-eveventh century. Moreover, this reconstruction is associated by
the excavators with a twelfth-century entrance of the Israelite tribes
into Canaan. The latter assumption carries with it other mainstays of
the Albrightian synthesis, most notably the identification of the
'collared-rim' jar with an ethnically Israelite culture. Thus, much of
Finkelstein's interpretation is open to question, at least, on the basis
of the archaeological and historical assumptions from which he has
obviously worked.

3.5 *Interpreting Shiloh's Archaeological Remains*

The interpretation of the results of the original Danish excavations
at Tell Seilun as supporting the prevalent consensus regarding
Shiloh's destruction in the mid-eleventh century BCE has been one of
the fundamental dynamics in the ensuing debate. Consequently, the
reinterpretation of those data by Marie-Louise Buhl and Svend
Holm-Nielsen called that view into question and opened the way for
a different treatment of Shiloh's history. The work of Buhl and

Holm-Nielsen has itself come under fire, however, so that the archaeological evidence must itself be considered problematic. Yigael Shiloh touched upon this problem when he noted that the Danish excavations had failed to yield a general stratigraphy for the site. Indeed, the disputed 'destruction layer' was known to be located only in Houses A and B, until the present Israeli excavations got under way. This basic lack of stratigraphic evidence has made the interpretation of the pottery remains difficult, to say the least. Moreover, the dabate over the dating of this destruction level has centered on seven storage jars of a similar type. Ideally, an archaeologist would have preferred a number of dissimilar types of vessels and sherds from which to date such a crucial stratum. Since only one basic pottery form has emerged to cast light on this problem, and since that form has a long history, from the beginning of Iron I to the close of Iron II, it should come as no surprise that there is considerable disagreement among those most familiar with this evidence over its significance for the dating of the stratum in question.

Additional disagreement has been spawned by the employment of previously accepted, but now questionable hypotheses. Thus, both Shiloh and Finkelstein have reasserted Albright's claim that the 'collared-rim' jar represents an ethnically Israelite pottery type. Yet evidence from elsewhere in Palestine, Hazor, for example, indicates widespread precursors of this form from the Late Bronze Age onwards.[38] Forerunners of this type may even occur as early as MB II.[39] Excavations in the Transjordan have revealed a wider distribution of the 'collared-rim' jar than was previously thought to be the case. This fact has led one archaeologist to argue that this form is to be connected with a socio-economic milieu, rather than a specific ethnic group.[40] Thus, the 'collared-rim' jar, which has figured so prominently in attempts to identify the first 'Israelite' strata in Palestinian sites, appears to be simply a development on the native Canaanite storage jar which originated in the Middle Bronze Age. The identification of the first levels of 'Israelite' occupation by the presence of these peculiar, but culturally widespread pithoi is therefore fallacious. These 'collared-rim' jars comprise just one aspect of a common Palestine-Transjordan culture during Iron I, which had origins in earlier periods.

Another problem raised in this connection by Shiloh is the relative dating of the evolving forms of these pithoi by the position of the 'collar' in relationship to the neck and shoulder of the jar. While it is now clear that this basic form persisted until the end of Iron II, Shiloh has maintained that Iron I 'collars' were set at the base of the neck, or the top of the shoulder of the jar, whereas Iron II 'collars' had moved up to the middle of the neck, and were somewhat smaller than their Iron I counterparts: 0.4–0.6m, as against 1.1–1.2m. Still, there is evidence of the 'earlier' type of 'collared-rim' jar, as identified by Shiloh, in Stratum VA from Hazor, although the jar in question is somewhat smaller than its couterparts at Tell Seilun.[41] Another jar from the same stratum at Hazor,[42] however, exhibits the 'collar' just below the rim, a form which Shiloh considers typical of the later period.[43] The occurrence of these two allegedly different forms of vessel in the same Iron II stratum at Hazor suggests that the problem of Tell Seilun's pottery is more ambiguous than has heretofore been realized. Some forms may have actually continued to enjoy limited popularity, even after they had fallen into wide disuse. This seems to be the logical conclusion of the evidence of Hazor VA.

Nonetheless, Shiloh's observation that the large size of the Iron I 'collared-rim' jars is a distinctive feature of the storage jars of that period, in contrast to the smaller vessels of that style found in Iron II, bears consideration. In fact, Finkelstein's team has unearthed an impressive collection of jars of similar size and form to those found by the Danes nearly sixty years ago, and these in conjunction with other Iron I pottery.[44] Although these massive pithoi do not seem to have survived past the end of Iron I (despite the continuation of the general form of the 'collared-rim' jar down to the end of Iron II), it is also possible that such large jars remained in use in some places long after they had fallen out of general use. The polemical nature of the debate over this issue, especially from the side of those who operate out of the assumption that Shiloh was destroyed by the Philistines, allows little ground for a resolution.

Further objections to the interpretation offered by Finkelstein may be raised as well. It is doubtful, for instance, whether the first 'Israelites' in Palestine can be identified by the material remains of their sedentary culture. Indeed, the tradition of the Israelites as tent-dwellers in the land seems to have persisted until quite late, and is reflected in the cries 'Each to his tents, O Israel!' (2 Sam. 20.1), and 'To your tents, O Israel!' (1 Kgs 12.16). Judg. 7.8; 1 Sam. 4.10; 13.2

also assume that the Israelites still dwelt in tents. One could therefore argue that the dating of the earliest Israelite elements in Palestine is beyond the reach of archaeology, since nomads leave precious little in the way of artifactual remains. One might take this argument one step father and identify the LB I remains at Seilun, interpreted by Finkelstein as 'an isolated cultic place to which offerings were brought by people from various places in the region',[45] with the Israelites of this period, who at that time may well have been no more than 'people who lived in pastoral groups, in temporary dwellings'.[46] If the Canaanite shrine in the old tradition behind Judg. 21.16-24 had been the MB IIC cultic center at Seilun, this connection might place the Israelite tribes in Palestine as early as the fifteenth century BCE.[47] The archaeological problem is this: if one cannot distinguish a typical Israelite artifact from other types of artifacts, one cannot demonstrate by archaeolgical means when the Israelites were on the scene. Certainly the Alt–Noth hypothesis that the Israelite tribes penetrated Palestine over a long period of time is preferable to that of one sudden conquest, at least in light of the disparate nature of the conquest traditions.[48] The tribe of Asher, which settled in western Galilee adjacent to the Canaanite cities along the Mediterranean coast, may be mentioned in an Egyptian inscription from the end of the fourteenth century BCE.[49] And contrary to Finkelstein's assertion that 'there is no unequivocal *archaeological* evidence that the Israelite settlement began as early as the 13th century B.C.',[50] the Merneptah stele definitely identifies a non-settled group in Palestine as 'Israel' during the last decades of the thirteenth century.[51] Consequently, Finkelstein's attempt to associate the first Israelite settlers in Canaan on the basis of their artifactual and architectural remains is mistaken. How long the various tribes inhabited the land before they settled into agrarian communities and adapted to the local Canaanite culture is unknown. However, the presence of Asher in the fourteenth century BCE, and of Israel in the thirteenth, suggests that at least a century passed during which the tribes that eventually became Israel lived in Palestine as pastoralists—the very culture which Finkelstein associates with the Late Bronze Age in the central hill country. Since the biblical account of the Israelite *Landnahme* is not of one piece, and since the broad conquest of the land ascribed to Joshua is an idealization (as Josh. 13.1-6; 15.63; 17.12-13, 14-18 demonstrate), it is difficult to see how the Israelite occupation of the land can, today, be viewed as a simple, archaeologically objectifiable process tied to a single, culturally distinctive group.

Another difficulty with Finkelstein's reconstruction is the apparent confusion between the temple at Shiloh and the tabernacle. Thus, one is perplexed at his expectation that archaeological evidence might be uncovered which would pinpoint the location of the tabernacle. Moreover, the relationship between the 'cultic complex', which stood uphill from the 'public pillared buildings' on the western slope of the tell,[52] and the tabernacle, is not made clear. It is as if the excavators cannot decide whether they are looking for a tent shrine, a temple, or both. The biblical tradition locates both a temple (1 Sam. 1–3) *and* a tent shrine (Josh. 18–22; 1 Sam. 2.22b) at Shiloh, which in fact merely points up the difficulty of 'confirming' the biblical account of Shiloh through archaeology.

In conclusion, the archaeological evidence from Tell Seilun, just as the biblical narratives of Shiloh, does not afford an unambiguous picture of the history of the Israelite settlement there. While the current Israeli team worked out the periodization of the site, serious interpretative problems remain. Noth's caution against 'the improper search for direct biblical connections'[53] is no less valid today than it was thirty years ago. The biblical traditions present neither a clear picture of Shiloh's history nor a straighforward account of the sanctuary there; and similar problems are posed by the reconstruction of the Israelite *Landnahme*. It is therefore difficult to know just how and where the Shiloh traditions of the Hebrew Bible should relate to the archaeological data from Tell Seilun. For instance, the LB I site could have been the locus of the tabernacle, while the Iron I settlement might have centered on a temple (and other equally plausible reconstructions are possible). At any rate, the complexity of the biblical traditions themselves as to the nature and history of the Shilonite sanctuary defy the positing of 'objective' historical reconstructions based on direct correlations between the biblical traditions and the archaeological data.

3.6 *The Literary-Historical Discussion of Shiloh in the First Third of the Twentieth Century*

At the same time that 'biblical archaeology' was coming of age as a discipline, the historical-critical debate over biblical Shiloh was witnessing the opening of avenues of discussion which were basically antithetical to those laid down in the consensus of the late nineteenth century. Not that any major changes were suggested with regard to the reconstruction of Shiloh's history propounded by Wellhausen, other than those already mentioned above. The twentieth century witnessed a resurrection of the notion of the antiquity and reliability of the priestly source of the Pentateuch, which resulted in a reopening of the older debate concerning the importance of the cult at Shiloh. As early as 1923, Albright had treated the erection of the tabernacle at Shiloh as a foregone conclusion requiring no particular defense, in sharp contrast to the international consensus.[54] Noth's famous study, *Das System der zwölf Stämme Israels*, first published in 1930, argued that important elements of the priestly source preserved older, historical traditions.[55] On the basis of this assertion, Noth theorized that the Israelite tribes originally had been organized in an amphictyony similar to those found in ancient Greece and Etrusca.[56] Noth thus sought to redeem as historical what had been regarded by the previous generation as merely idealistic, historicizing fiction. In so doing, he had gone back to the work of Ewald, the mainstay of the mid-nineteenth century consensus.[57] The amphictyonic members, Noth argued, had been bound together by the obligation to protect and maintain the cultic service at the *central sanctuary*[58]— the communal cult there forming the binding element between the various tribes.[59] A six-member amphictyony of the Leah tribes had at one time occupied the central hill country of Palestine and had served the sanctuary at Shechen, which tradition is still preserved in Joshua 24.[60] It was this six-tribe amphictyony which had formed the basis for the later twelve-tribe amphictyony. But when the amphictyony expanded to include the tribes of Joseph and Benjamin, the ark, the old nomadic shrine of the tribe of Joseph, became the actual central shrine of the tribal amphictyony.[61] The original permanent locus of the ark had been Shechem, but the ark was transferred at least once in the pre-monarchical period to Shiloh.[62] The occasion of this transfer, according to Noth, may have been the destruction of Shechem by Abimelech.[63]

Noth's groundbreaking work opened the way for a thoroughgoing reevaluation of the historicity of the pre-monarchic traditions of the unity of the Israelite tribes. Even more significantly, the amphictyonic theory established a basis for the credibility of the pre-monarchic existence of Israel as a *cultic community*, a phenomenon which Wellhausen had associated with Second-Temple Judaism. With its emphasis on the concrete pre-monarchic cultic unity of the Israelite tribes, Noth's thesis paralleled the contemporary work of S. Mowinckel, whose *Psalmenstudien* emphasized the role and importance of the cult during the period of the monarchy.[64]

The first third of the twentieth century, then, saw significant breaks with the historical-critical presuppositions established at the end of the nineteenth century, primarily with regard to the antiquity of the cultic institutions of Israel. This new climate sparked changes in the discussion of biblical Shiloh and produced conclusions sometimes resembling those reached by the dissenting historians of the late nineteenth century: Dillmann, Kittel, and Baudissin.

3.7 *The Work of Kaufmann, de Vaux, and Haran*

In addition to Noth's work on the amphictyony, several other scholars made significant contributions to understanding Israel's cultic traditions preserved in the priestly strata of the Hexateuch in the context of Israel's early history. The scholars who deserve credit for this work came from two different schools: the French school, which began with the work of Dussaud on the connection between Canaanite and Israelite sacrifice, and the Israeli school, which began with Yehezkel Kaufmann. The principal figure among the French scholars was Roland de Vaux. Among the Israeli scholars, Kaufmann's work has been taken up by a whole generation of scholars, among whom Menahem Haran is of special concern to this study.

3.7.1 *Yehezkel Kaufmann*

The most distinctive work on the history of the religion of Israel written in the twentieth century was that of the Israeli scholar, Yehezkel Kaufmann.[65] Kaufmann formulated his work as an alternative to the Wellhausian synthesis. In so doing, he revived arguments which had been first raised by Saalschütz, Riehm, Bleek, Dillmann and other nineteenth-century German scholars. The central claim of Kaufmann was that the priestly source of the Pentateuch was older than and independent of the deuteronomic code, and consequently, that P presented a true picture of Israel's life and worship in the wilderness period. Kaufmann made this point in several ways. He argued that the cultic unity of the priestly source was presupposed by JE, which also reported for the desert period only one camp, one ark, and one tent.[66] Moreover, the priestly source did not betray a hint of the kind of cultic centralization demanded in Deuteronomy.[67] The only instance where such an interpretation might have been possible was Leviticus 17. Yet this text, which prohibited the slaughtering of animals away from the 'entrance' to the Tent of Meeting, would have effectively banned the eating of meat outside of Jerusalem, if it had been written under the influence of the deuteronomic code. Hence, the only possibility for Kaufmann was that Lev. 17.3 actually presupposed a multiplicity of legitimate local Yahwistic sanctuaries.[68] To be sure, the priestly source identified only a single, legitinate sanctuary: the tent of meeting. But after the entry into Palestine, the tent sanctuary had been regarded as a thing of the past, and many sanctuaries were recognized and 'identified' with the tent of meeting. That is why the priestly source was silent regarding sacrifice on the high places: it recognized no such sin. Indeed, Lev. 26.31 showed that P recognized the multiple holy places when it threatened destruction of the Israelite *temples* for failure to comply with the strictures of the Holiness Code. The pronounced emphasis on a single, central place of worship with a specific geographic locus, according to Kaufmann, was a peculiarity of the deuteronomic code. Kaufmann further stressed the oracular, prophetic, and military aspects of the priestly cult, none of which found a place in the Second Temple.[69] Those few points of contact between the priestly code and the institutions of the post-exilic community derived from the attempt by redactors of that later period to put the old priestly legislation into effect, no matter to what limited extent such an exercise might have been possible.

Kaufmann's work thus comprised an attempted rebuttal of the reigning consensus on pentateuchal criticism, as far as the authenticity of the priestly source was concerned. However, he did not argue in the manner of the scholars of the mid-nineteenth century, that is, by trying to show the antiquity of the centralization tradition. Rather, Kaufmann acknowledged the lateness of the deuteronomic demand for centralization of the cult and argued that P, so far from presupposing centralization, as Wellhausen had maintained, actually assumed multiple places of worship.

With regard to Shiloh, Kaufmann departed from the tendency among conservative scholars to regard as historical the tradition that Shiloh had been the first place where Yahweh had made his name to dwell. He maintained instead that Jeremiah's appeal to Shiloh's fate recast 'the past in accord with the Deuteronomistic requirement', especially when Jeremiah designated Shiloh as 'the place where I caused my name to dwell at first' (Jer. 7.12). To Kaufmann, Jeremiah was himself responsible for this connection between the centralization tradition and Shiloh, and it was Jeremiah's view which had laid the basis for the later Mishmaic tradition (*m. Zebah.* 14.4-10).[70]

3.7.2 Roland de Vaux

Another scholar to argue for the authenticity of the priestly material of the Old Testament, although to a lesser extent than Kaufmann, was Roland de Vaux. De Vaux's views were published in his monumental work on *The Early History of Israel*,[71] and in his smaller, but equally valuable *Ancient Israel*.[72] De Vaux continued the tradition begun by Rene Dussaud's studies of sacrifice, in that he relied heavily upon the extra-biblical evidence to clarify and explain the biblical traditions. Thus, he appealed to the ancient Arab institution of the portable tent-shrine to substantiate the biblical tradition of the tabernacle. According to de Vaux, the pre-Islamic Arabs had maintained a tent-shrine called a *qubba*: a red leather tent housing the tribe's stone idols, and cared for by women. In this connection, de Vaux noted that the priestly *miškān* was covered with ram skins dyed red, and was served by women. Furthermore, the priestly tabernacle had housed the stone tablets of the Covenant.[73] Just as the Israelites had carried the ark, with its stone tablets, into battle, the Arabs and even the Carthaginians had carried their respective tent-shrines into war. Finally, the term *qubba* actually occurs in Num. 25.8, possibly in connection with the tent. From this evidence, de Vaux argued that the tabernacle had been the actual Israelite tent-sanctuary, which had been set up last on the plains of Moab, prior to the entry into the land.[74]

With regard to the ark, de Vaux maintained that this item had been an integral part of the desert worship, but at the same time was older than the tabernacle. The ark had had two functions. In the first place it had served as the throne, or footstool, of Yahweh. Its further function had been as a repository for the tablets of the Covenant. De

Vaux cited Egyptian and Hittite parallels in which religious documents, treaties, oaths, and other forms of attestation were deposited 'at the feet of the god'.[75] While the oldest traditions, i.e. those of JE, did not connect the ark with the tabernacle, de Vaux argued that these two institutions probably had been linked, and that the omission of this linkage in JE was the result of the fragmentary form in which those traditions had been preserved. With respect to this latter argument, de Vaux suggested that the $l\hat{o}$ of Exod. 33.7 could possibly have referred to the ark, as opposed to Moses or Yahweh, if Exod. 33.7-11 had been separated from its original context. De Vaux raised additional considerations in support of the validity of the priestly tradition which connected the ark with the tabernacle: (a) the ark must have been housed in *something* in the desert, probably a tent; (b) the tent of meeting likewise must have housed something, just as the Arabic *quabba* had housed divine symbols. Thus, de Vaux concluded that the ark and the tabernacle should not be separated. The priestly depiction of the desert sanctuary, however colored by the Solomonic Temple, represented an authentic, historical tradition of the early Israelite cult.[76]

Although de Vaux maintained the validity of the priestly tradition of the desert shrine, he was skeptical of the other priestly tradition of the erection of the tabernacle at Shiloh at the end of the conquest. He pointed out that it was Gilgal, not Shiloh, where the memory of the entry into the land had been preserved. Shiloh, however, had eclipsed the sanctuary at Gilgal during the period of the Judges, and had become the *central sanctuary* of the tribal confederacy. At Shiloh, a temple, rather than a tent, had housed the ark. Moreover, the Shilonite cult designated Yahweh for the first time as 'Sebaoth, who sits above the Cherubim'. Otherwise, de Vaux doubted that much more could be known of the Shiloh sanctuary, other than that it had been sacked in the aftermath of the disaster at Aphek. The last valid reference to the history of the tabernacle concerned its erection on the plains of Moab, and no further reliable mention of this shrine was preserved. David's tent for the ark merely emulated the tabernacle of the wilderness period, and it was this latter tent which the glossator in 1 Kgs 8.4 had identified as the tent of meeting. The Chronicler's presentation of the tent of meeting was, on the other hand, entirely pretended.

De Vaux thus continued certain of the arguments from Wellhausen's synthesis, while at the same time following lines of argument laid down by scholars such as Dussaud and Noth, which undercut the force of Wellhausen's critique of the priestly source. Nevertheless, de Vaux did not carry his vindication of the antiquity of the priestly traditions over to his treatment of those traditions as they appeared in the latter chapters of the book of Joshua. Therefore, his discussion of the Shilonite cult was nearly identical to that of Wellhausen, with the sole exception of his identification of Shiloh's heyday with its status as the central sanctuary of the tribal confederacy, an idea which was derived from Noth's important work.

3.7.3 *Menahem Haran*

The final major work of the twentieth century to deal with Shiloh in an important way has been that of Menahem Haran.[77] Haran's study, like that of Kaufmann, attempted to demonstrate the antiquity of 'all the material embodied in the pentateuchal priestly source' and to show that 'the literary crystallization of P must have taken place in pre-exilic times'. At the same time, however, Haran contended that the priestly law had not been *canonized* until the period of Ezra, when it became 'a cornerstone of Jewish communal life'. In this latter connection, Haran advanced the idea, first developed by Dillmann, and promulgated by Kittel and Baudissin, that the priestly document had originated as the rules and regulations of the ritual cult which had been maintained and handed on in the closed company of the priesthood.[78]

With regard to Shiloh, Haran both continued and broke with the Wellhausian tradition. First of all, Haran treated Shiloh as one among many pre-monarchic temples, but argued that Shiloh had been the most prestigious of these pre-monarchic holy places.[79] Shiloh's prestige had declined following the loss of the ark to the Philistines, though there was no literary evidence that Shiloh or its sanctuary were at this time destroyed. The destruction of the town and shrine did not occur, in fact, until the general destruction which befell the entire northern kingdom in the last quarter of the eighth century, and even after that a small settlement may have continued on the site.[80]

Moreover, the Shilonite priesthood had been Aaronite, even though the Aaronites had their origins in Judah and Benjamin.[81] This was demonstrated by the fact that all of the Levitical cities which were assigned to the Aaronites were located within the territory of these two tribes. The fact that the Elide Abiathar, banished from the court of Solomon, went to his inheritance in Anathoth, and that Jeremiah, the only prophet to mention Shiloh, was also from Anathoth, confirmed for Haran the Aaronite pedigree of the priests of Shiloh.[82]

Haran's most important contention, however, was his argument that the tent of meeting was not a figure for the Jerusalem temple, but for the temple at Shiloh.[83] The priestly traditions had thus had their origin in Shiloh, as had the priestly legislation. Haran noted, moreover, that the tabernacle in P was not provisional, to be replaced by a temple, but was itself an object of veneration, meant to stand in the land for many generations after the settlement. Furthermore, the priestly tradition never linked the temple in Jerusalem to the tent of meeting, despite the traces of a priestly hand in 1 Kgs 8.4.[84] Instead, the priestly tradition saw the tent of meeting in Shiloh as a figure for the Shilonite sanctuary. Haran, however, denied that a temple originally had stood at Shiloh. The texts which treated Shiloh as the site of a temple derived from the period of the monarchy, and had been written from the standpoint of those later conditions. In fact, the sanctuary at Shiloh had been the tabernacle, which had continued in use from the nomadic period down to the time of the settlement in Canaan simply out of a strict adherence to a venerable old institution.[85] Nevertheless, the priestly legislation regarding the tabernacle—i.e. the priestly 'temple legend'—was not the old Shilonite legend, per se, but the Jerusalemite version of it, in which the tabernacle, having long since passed out of existence, was unconsciously portrayed in the garb of the extant temple of Jerusalem.[86]

To recover the historical reality of the priestly tabernacle, Haran compared the traditions of the tent shrine in JE with those of P. He concluded that all of these traditions agreed with one another in identifying the divine revelation with a fixed institution.[87] However, the priestly tradition had linked divine revelation to the inner sanctum, the *miškān*, located at the center of the camp. The *miškān* paralleled the later institution of the temple, since both served as a 'dwelling-place' for the deity. Conversely, the traditions of JE focused upon the *'ōhel-mô'ēd*, located *outside* the camp (Exod. 33.7-11), where the focal point of revelation had been the *entrance* to the tent. This tent shrine of JE was a unique prophetic institution, but it had been superseded by the belief that prophetic revelation could occur anywhere, and had been absorbed into the hierocentric priestly tradition. Thus, the *'ōhel-mô'ēd* and the *miškān* became interchangeable terms in the priestly materials in the Hexateuch. In point of fact, the JE tradition of the *'ōhel-mô'ēd* was the older, but in P this was made indistinguishable from the *miškān*.[88]

In working from the views of Kaufmann, Haran likewise broke with the legacy of Wellhausen and the late nineteenth century and advocated the antiquity of the priestly traditions. Haran's argumentation on this point is based upon a careful reading of the Hebrew text, and cannot be dismissed as apologetic or uncritical. With specific regard to Shiloh, Haran has maintained the authenticity of the tradition of the tent shrine there, contending that the tent shrine is not a figure for the Jerusalem temple. Finally, Haran has appealed to the same exegetical evidence cited by Graf, Buhl, and Holm-Nielsen to argue that no biblical evidence exists for a destruction of Shiloh in the mid-eveventh century BCE.

3.8 *The Work of Eissfeldt, Cody, and Cross*

While significant inroads were made against Wellhausen's synthesis during the twentieth century, his ideas also continued to recieve creative support and were further developed with regard to biblical Shiloh. The treatments of Eissfeldt, Cody, and Cross all represent expansions on the sythesis of Wellhausen with regard to Shiloh, its history, and its priesthood.

3.8.1 *Otto Eissfeldt*
Otto Eissfeldt presented an essay before the International Congress for the Study of the Old Testament in Strasbourg, France, in 1956, in which he expanded upon the *religionsgeschichtlich* aspects of the relationship between Jerusalem and Shiloh.[89] In the introduction to this paper, Eissfeldt concurred with Albright and Kjaer, that the archaeological excavations at Shiloh had proven the accuracy of the view that Shiloh had been destroyed violently in the eleventh century BCEE, and that this destruction was, at least with high probability, alluded to in Jer. 7.12, 14; 26.6, 9; and Ps. 78.60, where the destruction of the temple at Shiloh was either explicitly narrated,

or unmistakably implied.[90] In terms of the historical scenario which was presupposed, then, Eissfeldt's essay followed the reconstruction of Shiloh's history which had dominated biblical studies since the time of Wellhausen.

Nevertheless, the basic thesis of Eissfeldt's paper was at odds with the spirit of the Wellhausian synthesis, insofar as Eissfeldt contended that during the pre-monarchic period

> Shiloh had for the history of Israel, and with it the history of humanity, the same significance as Jerusalem, inasmuch as Jerusalem, without Shiloh, would never have become what it [actually] became.[91]

According to Eissfeldt, Shiloh had embodied the national and religious unity and consciousness prior to the Davidic monarchy. After David had seized power and made the Jebusite fortress city his capital, he had to solve the problem of maintaining the Jebusite cult of El Elyon in the city, represented by the priesthood of Zadok, while at the same time preserving the heritage of the Israelite faith in Yahweh. David did not accomplish this task by 'going to Shiloh', as is perhaps implied in Gen. 49.10.[92] Rather, David 'brought Shiloh to Jerusalem'—that is, he brought the ark, the cult object which symbolized the values of Israel's pre-Canaanite past—up into the city. Yet this act by David entailed far more than the mere introduction of an Israelite cult object and priesthood into the Jebusite stronghold. By this action, David had transferred to the Yahweh of Jerusalem the divine epithet of the Shilonite diety: 'Seba'oth, who is enthroned above the cherubim'. Thus, Yahweh had become 'Yahweh Seba'oth, who is enthroned above the cherubim'.[93] According to Eissfeldt, this fundamental change in the divine name was of as great a magnitude as the revelation of the divine name Yahweh to Moses in Exod. 6.2-3, in that it brought about a dramatic expansion in the concept of God, especially with regard to the power and majesty of Yahweh, Moreover, Shiloh's stone temple had inspired David to erect a temple to Yahweh in Jerusalem, and Shiloh's cult had inspired Solomon's two gold-covered cherubim which stood over the ark in the holy of holies in Jerusalem.

The central contribution of Eissfeldt's essay was his development of the significance of the role of Shiloh in the emergence of the Yahwistic religion during the early monarchy. These ideas were not altogether new: Martin Noth had argued already in 1950 that in bringing the ark to Jerusalem, David had tied Canaanite Jerusalem to the Israelite tradition.[94] Furthermore, the religious significance of Jerusalem had increased independently of the status of the Davidic house during the period of the later monarchy due to the presence of the ark—the focus of Israel's *vorpalästinische* tradition. Thus, Eissfeldt's treatment of Shiloh and Jerusalem, while it presumed Wellhausen's reconstruction of the history of the Shiloh sanctuary, actually furthered the *religionsgeschichtlich* views of Martin Noth. These views, as has been shown above, stood in basic contradiction to those of Wellhausen, in that Noth insisted on the pre-monarchic cultic unity of the Israelite tribes.

3.8.2 *Aelred Cody*

The contribution of Aelred Cody to the discussion of Shiloh has come mainly in regard to his treatment of the Shilonite priesthood.[95] Cody displayed the tendency of the majority of scholars in the middle third of the twentieth century to accept the credibility of the traditions regarding the pre-Canaanite origins of Israel's cult. For instance, Cody argued that the biblical traditions regarding Moses' appointment of the Levites *prior to the entry into Canaan* as attendants to the ark may actually have had an historical nucleus. In connection with the priesthood of Eli, Cody contended that Eli's family had been an hereditary order of levitical descent, attached to the shrine at Shiloh because of the presence of the ark there.[96] This levitical ancestry of the Elides Cody found confirmed in the recurring names of Hophni and Phileas, which were both Egyptian in origin.[97] Furthermore, Cody accepted the tradition of the judgeship of Eli on the basis of Exod. 18.13-26; Deut. 17.8-13; 21.5. Thus, he interpreted the Shilonite priesthood as one of sanctuary attendants

> whose oracular consultation was perhaps developed into judicial *tora*, or beginning to develop into that kind of *tora*. The Elides had no monopoly on sacrifice, however, for . . . Samuel's father Elkanah sacrificed as a pilgrim to the sanctuary they frequented (1 Sam. 1:3).[98]

Samuel, on the other hand, had been neither priest nor Levite. According to 1 Sam. 2.13, Samuel was a *na'ar-hakkōhēn*. Since *na'ar* was a technical Phoenician designation for a lower temple servant.

Samuel had shared this status.[99] This position corresponded best to Hannah's humble vow to Yahweh (1 Sam. 1.28). The material placing Samuel in the Shilonite cult had been preserved not to demonstrate Samuel's own priesthood, but to 'root' him 'in the place which was the center of the pre-monarchical Yahwistic spirit, leading up to his climax showing Samuel as a prophet in that spirit's tradition'. Samuel as an adult was both judge and prophet, as Deborah had been (Judg. 4). His cultic role had been limited to these functions as well, and had not extended to those of the priesthood.[100]

Shiloh had been destroyed as a cultic center following the battle of Ebenezer, and Nob had succeeded it as the center of the covenantal traditions, and was administered by the descendants of Eli, while the ark remained in Kiriath-Jearim. In all of his reconstruction, Cody maintained a tenuous balance between the views of Wellhausen, which held the priestly literature to be late, and the consensus of the mid-twentieth century, which held that that literature was based upon authentic traditions. Cody also relied heavily upon the comparative methodology first established by Dussaud. Thus, he arrived at a view of Shiloh's history and priesthood which was a melding of elements from various competing perspectives.

3.8.3 *F.M. Cross*

Another important treatment of the Shilonite priesthood written under the influence of both the Wellhausian tradition and the consensus of the middle third of the twentieth century was that of Cross.[101] Cross began his treatment by accepting Wellhausen's reconstruction of the history of the priesthood: the earliest age, characterized by independent, hereditary priesthoods; the age of the monarchy, when the Levites formed a rising priestly class; and the post-exilic age, when the Aaronites became the dominant priestly class, and the Levites had been demoted to the status of hierodules.[102] Furthermore, Cross maintained Wellhausen's view that the Elide priesthood, along with that of Jonathan ben Gershom in Dan, had been Mushite, and not Aaronite.[103] The Mushite priests at Shiloh, in fact, not the priesthood in Jerusalem, was responsible for the Elohistic polemic against Aaron (Exod. 32). The bull iconography must have been centered at Bethel,[104] and the Bethel priests must originally have traced their heritage directly to Aaron. Cross further appealed to the lone reference to the ministry of Phineas, the son of

Eleazar, the son of Aaron, at Bethel (Judg. 20.27-28) as confirmation
of the Aaronite origins of the Bethel priests.[105] Thus Cross reasoned
that Jeroboam I appointed two competing priesthoods: the Mushite
line at Dan, and the Aaronite line at Bethel. This move was not an
innovation, but an attempt to ground the national cult on the
people's ancient traditions. Therefore, the cult at Bethel had eclipsed
that at Shiloh, even though Shiloh had been the center of the
formulation of the Elohistic tradition.[106]

Cross found further evidence for this Mushite versus Aaronite
competition in the connection between Moses and the Midianite
priesthood of Jethro. The Mushite priesthood had been of mixed
origin and had served at the sanctuaries of Dan, Arad, Kadesh-
Naphtali, and Shiloh. The mixed heritage of the Mushite line was
reflected in the story of Moses' Cushite (i.e. from the Midianite clan
of Kusan, or from Ethiopia) wife, as well (Num. 12). Moreover,
Mirian and Aaron had opposed Moses in this matter, for which
Miriam was smitten with leprosy, in a demonstration of (a) the
legitimacy of the Mushite priesthood despite its mixed blood and (b)
the superiority of Moses to Aaron as a divine mediator.[107] Conversely,
the priestly tradition of Num. 25.6-15 portrayed the Midianites as
arch-enemies of Israel. The same incident was implied by the gloss in
1 Sam. 2.22b, which was designed to impugn the Mushite priesthood
of Shiloh by tying it to that incident. That is, the reference to the
sons of Eli lying with the 'women who served at the door of the tent
of meeting' (1 Sam. 2.22b) was meant to recall the Israelite who
brought his Midianite wife into his tent while the congregation was
weeping at the door to the tent of meeting (Num. 25.6). Such tales,
Cross theorized, reflected the much wider conflict between competing
priestly families which once existed, but have not survived in the
present sources.[108]

Having located the Aaronite priesthood at Bethel and the Mushite
at Shiloh, Dan, Arad, and Kadesh-Naphtali (in line with Wellhausen's
thesis that the northern priesthoods had generally traced their
heritage from Moses), Cross went on tha argue that the Aaronites
actually had been the ancient Judahite priesthood.[109] Thus, Zadok
had not founded an entirely new line,[110] but was a true representative
of the Aaronite priesthood of Judah.[111] In support of this point, Cross
pointed to the Aaronites in service to David, among them, Jehoiada
and Zadok (1 Chron. 12.27-29). Thus, Cross both supported

Wellhausen's reconstruction, and at the same time argued for the antiquity of the Aaronite, and for him, Zadokite priesthood, which he considered Judahite.[112]

There are, however, serious difficulties with Cross's theory. To begin, it was precisely the priests of Bethel whom Josiah is said to have sacrificed upon the altar there (1 Kgs 13.1-3; 2 Kgs 23.15-20), and there is no disagreement but that these were Aaronites. What connection existed, however, between the Aaronites at Bethel and the supposedly Aaronite priests of the line of Zadok? It is in fact more logical to assume that the polemic against the Aaronites in Bethel (as preserved in Exod. 32, 1 Kgs 13 and 2 Kgs 23) came from Jerusalem and not Shiloh, since the priests in Jerusalem had waged a two hundred-year struggle against Bethel and its priestly house. Moreover, that Phineas the son of Eleazar was an Aaronite is taken for granted by Cross, but he makes no mention of the connection between this Phineas and the son of Eli, both of whom are primarily associated with Shiloh, and not Bethel. Thus Cross's reconstruction contradicts the most intractable evidence regarding the identity of the Aaronite priesthood.

3.9 *Synopsis: Shiloh's Place in the Twentieth-Century Debate*

In conclusion, the discussion of the Israelite cult in the twentieth century has witnessed the weakening of the older consensus on the relative dating of the pentateuchal sources, especially as regards the reliability of the materials of the priestly source. While the Graf-Wellhausen hypothesis is not dead, a succession of critical scholars and a wealth of comparative data from elsewhere in the ancient world have brought continued pressure upon the older reconstruction, so that that synthesis can no longer be considered to be above debate. The single strand which has unified the critics of the Graf-Wellhausen hypothesis has been the insistence on the antiquity of the priestly code.

The twentieth-century discussion of Shiloh, however, has witnessed only the continuation of the discussion, begun in the nineteenth, with no major variations in the opposing positions first taken by Graf and Ewald. The theory of the destruction of Shiloh as a result of the disaster at Ebenezer remains the crux of the historical debate. Some, such as Day, have reiterated Ewald's thesis point for point and have sought to strengthen it as well.[113] Others, such as Buhl, Holm-Nielsen, and Haran, have continued to point up the lack of direct biblical evidence that the Philistines destroyed Shiloh. With regard to more peripheral issues, such as the ancestry of Shiloh's priests, one is stilll confronted by Wellhausen's reconstruction and variations on it, or by the opposing views of those who still accept the Aaronite origin of the Elide line.[114] The same can be said of the Shiloh sanctuary: there has been no clear resolution of whether the old wilderness tent shrine, or the Elide temple, or *both*, or *neither*, stood there. Thus, after nearly a century and a half of debate, there has been no substantial progress toward the resolution of the issues involved in the reconstruction of Shiloh's history.

3.10 *Conclusion: Summary of the Critical Issues Pertaining to the Discussion of Biblical Shiloh*

3.10.1 *The Broader Issues Relating to Shiloh*

In the debate over biblical Shiloh during the last 180 years, the city's role in the history of Israel has generally been discussed in the context of larger issues. The chief of these issues has been the question of the historicity of the pentateuchal cultus and the relationship of this cultus to Israelite life in Palestine in general and to Shiloh in particular. The conviction that there had been an historical period of wilderness wanderings, in which the Israelites had possessed a distinctive cultus, the outlines at least of which are presented in the priestly stratum of the Pentateuch, led to an emphasis on Shiloh as the center of this cultus in Palestine. This position was taken by scholars of the mid-nineteenth-century consensus, such as Hengstenberg, Ewald, Saalschütz, Riehm, and others. Conversely, those scholars—such as de Wette, Graf, and Wellhausen—who advocated a later provenance for the pentateuchal cultus and consequently, the priestly stratum, denied that authentic traces of this cultus could be found in the historical books of the Old Testament and were inclined to see a number of independent sanctuaries as characteristic of pre-monarchic Israelite life, among which Shiloh had risen to prominence through the influence of the priestly family of Eli.

Directly related to the issue of the historicity of the pentateuchal cultus and its attestation during the settlement period was a second major issue, namely, the problem of the centralization of the cult. As a rule, two positions have prevailed in this discussion. On the one hand, de Wette, Vatke, Graf and Wellhausen argued that cultic centralization had constituted a late stage in Israel's religious development. The deuteronomic demand for a single central place of worship first emerged during Josiah's reform (2 Kgs 22–23) at the end of the seventh century. According to Wellhausen, the priestly stratum, although it never mentioned centralization, actually *presupposed* a single central place of worship, which was fictionally represented in the wilderness period by the tabernacle, but which post-dated Deuteronomy.

In response to the position advocated by scholars such as de Wette, various approaches were employed to argue that cultic centralization was not a late development, but actually a pre-monarchic phenomenon. The most consistent counterpoint to Wellhausen's formulation of the issue of cultic centralization in P has been that P knew of centralization in terms of the tent shrine. Delitzsch and Kleinert argued that the deuteronomic 'place where Yahweh will cause his name to dwell' actually referred to any place where the tent shrine was erected. Kaufmann, on the other hand, contended that in P, the tent shrine was representative of any local shrine. Along different lines, Noth argued in favor of early centralization, and concluded that the central amphictyonic shrine had been the ark, the seat of which had been transferred at least once during the pre-monarchic period, from Shechem to Shiloh.

Rooted in the first two problems of the historicity of the pentateuchal cultus and the centralization of the cult was a third, already alluded to: the date of the priestly stratum of the Pentateuch. For scholars who accepted Wellhausen's reconstruction of pentateuchal sources and his general methodology, P was invariably late in both content and outlook. Many scholars, however, raised objections to the late dating of P. The most important of these arguments, namely, that the antiquity of the pentateuchal cultus was attested by extra-biblical evidence from the ancient Near East, first introduced by Dillmann, was taken up by Kittel and reached its fullest development during the twentieth century. In a similar vein, scholars such as S.I. Curtiss looked to contemporary Bedouin custom and practice to understand the early Israelite cultus. Although Wellhausen also argued that the culture of the late pre-Islamic Arabs was the best source for understanding ancient Israelite life, he did not believe that this material corroborated the antiquity of the pentateuchal cultus. The appeal to ancient Near Eastern evidence and modern Arab custom to establish the antiquity of the pentateuchal cultus, or at least key elements of it, was followed by French scholars of the twentieth century, notably Dussaud and de Vaux. De Vaux accepted the lateness of P's literary form, but argued for the antiquity of certain elements of the priestly cultus, such as the ark and the tent shrine. W.F. Albright and his students adopted a similar postion.

A second major development which was used by those scholars who maintained the antiquity of P was the traditio-historical methodology developed by Gunkel. While Gunkel and his students accepted the Wellhausian source-hypothesis, they sought to recover the pre-literary history of the traditions embodied in the text. This methodology was put to use in connection with Shiloh most notably by Procksch and, later, Noth. Taken together, these two new approaches, the one employing extra-biblical evidence, the other Gunkel's traditio-historical method, led many to conclude that while the final literary form of P may have been late, the priestly stratum itself contained much early material. Many scholars thus sought to transcend the polarized debate over the relative age of the literary sources of the Pentateuch, while maintaining a certain confidence in the authenticity of the pentateuchal cultus during the early period of Israel's history.

At the same time, some scholars have continued to adduce evidence in support of the older theory of the literary antiquity of the priestly source. The most notable work of this persuasion has been supplied by Yehezkel Kaufmann and his students. Among these, Haran has argued that the priestly cultus in fact traced itself to the sanctuary at Shiloh, and not Jerusalem.

Thus, a broad spectrum of views, on hand already in the late nineteenth century, persists between those scholars who maintain the antiquity and authenticity of the priestly source of the Pentateuch, and those who have accepted Wellhausen's reconstruction.

In addition to the issues of the composition, dating, and historicity of the various sources of the Pentateuch, the question of the narrative shape and extent of these materials has been a topic of debate. This problem can be summarized in terms of three theses: (a) the pentateuchal sources extended into the book of Joshua, and formed the conclusion to the Hexateuch [Graf, Wellhausen, Mowinckel, von Rad]; (b) the sources of the Pentateuch, especially J and E, could be traced into the books of Samuel [esp. Budde]; (c) the pentateuchal sources had at one time been hexateuchal in form, but the original ending to this 'Hexateuch' had been broken off and replaced by the Deuteronomistic History (Deuteronomy-2 Kings), leaving the Tetrateuch and Deuteronomistic History as the basic literary entities between Genesis and 2 Kings (Noth). The importance of this issue to the discussion of biblical Shiloh was that one's treatment of Shiloh could vary significantly, depending on which of these theses one held to be correct. Thus, Wellhausen, accepted the literary theory of a Hexateuch, considered the Shiloh references in Joshua to be priestly, and hence, late, over and against the central content of the historical books, which he held to be early, and thus more reliable. Since Budde held that the earlier strands of the pentateuchal narratives were continued in the books of Judges and Samuel, his position was not substantially different from that of Wellhausen. He accepted the late, priestly origin of the Shiloh references in Joshua and sought the more reliable historical testimony with regard to Shiloh in the continuation of JE into Judges and Samuel. Noth's theory of the Deuteronomistic history, which denied the continuation of the pentateuchal sources beyond Numbers, explains much of the material in Joshua previously considered priestly as deuteronomistic, while at the same time discounting the Shiloh references in Joshua as miscellaneous and late additions.

Finally, if one accepts the priestly origin of the Shiloh materials in Joshua, the question arises of why P, an ostensibly Jerusalemite document, would have concluded the account of the *Landnahme* with the hallowing of Shiloh, and not Jerusalem, as the site of the legitimate cultus of Israel. If the references to Shiloh in Joshua do inhere in the priestly corpus, there are solid grounds for doubting that P represents a pro-Jerusalem viewpoint. As will be demonstrated below, the attitude of the Jerusalem cultus towards Shiloh was far from the positive depiction exhibited in the materials of priestly affinity in Joshua.

3.10.2 *Particular Issues Relating to Shiloh's History*

In addition to the wider questions which have an important bearing on the reconstruction of Shiloh's role in Israelite history, past

attempts to trace the history of biblical Shiloh have involved a series
of more specific issues. The first of these might be defined as the
nature of the Shilonite cultus. This issue subsumes six basic
problems: (a) the nature of the sanctuary at Shiloh (i.e., was it a tent
[Hengstenberg, *et al.*, Haran], a temple [Graf, Wellhausen, Dibelius,
de Vaux], or both [cf. von Haneberg]?); (b) the relationship of the ark
to the Shilonite cultus; (c) the ancestral origins of the Shilonite
priesthood (i.e., was Shiloh's priesthood Mushite [Reuss, Wellhausen,
Cross] or Aaronite [Graf, Baudissin, Haran]?), and in the same
connection, the origin of the priesthood of Aaron (i.e., was Aaron a
fictional figure for the Zadokite priesthood in Jerusalem [Wellhausen,
Reuss, Cross], or was Aaron the traditional ancestor of the northern
priests [Smend, Baudissin, Haran]?); (d) the role and status of the
Shiloh sanctuary in Israelite life during the pre-monarchical period;
and (e) the role and status of Shiloh during the late monarchy.

A second major focus of debate has been the relationship of
Samuel to Shiloh, and the relationship of Samuel and Shiloh to Saul
and the rise of the monarchy. The issues here have to do with
Samuel's role in the establishment of the first king of Israel, and the
connection between Samuel and the Elide priesthood at Shiloh. A
related issue is whether there was any historical connection between
Samuel and Shiloh at all.

A third major problem, which only emerged during the twentieth
century, has to do with the nature and interpretation of the
archaeological evidence from Tell Seilun (the Palestinian site
traditionally identified with biblical Shiloh). That is, does the
archaeological evidence support the theory, first proposed by
Hengstenberg, and later developed by Ewald, that Shiloh was
destroyed after the battle at Ebenezer, where the ark was lost and the
Elide priests slaughtered (1 Sam. 4)? This theory, and the assumption
of its veracity, have dominated treatments of the history of biblical
Shiloh since the time of Wellhausen. Objections to this position,
initially raised by Graf (though later abandoned by him), have since
been reiterated, first by Frants Buhl, and later by Marie-Louise Buhl
and Svend Holm-Nielsen, among others. Even advocates of the
dominant viewpoint have had to admit as a result of the archaeological
evidence brought to light by the Danish excavations at Tell Seilun
that Shiloh continued in existence into the later period of the
monarchy.

A fourth and final issue, dealt with by Eissfeldt, Haran, and Mettinger, has to do with the relationship of the Jerusalem cultus to that at Shiloh. This issue subsumes three basic questions: (a) provided that Shiloh had once enjoyed a peculiar status among the Israelite shrines, did Jerusalem succeed to that status? (b) in what ways, if any, did the Jerusalem cultus continue elements of the Shilonite cultus? and (c) finally, how did the Jerusalem cultus perceive its relationship to the cult at Shiloh? These questions are *religionsgeschichtlich* in nature, and arise in connection with texts such as Ps. 78.60-72; Jer. 7.12-15; 26.6-9.

Chapter 4

SHILOH IN THE BOOK OF JOSHUA

4.1 *Introduction: The Priestly Documents of Joshua 13–22*

Aside from the Shiloh oracle in Gen. 49.10-12 (see below, 6.7.1), the biblical references to Shiloh begin in the book of Joshua, where Shiloh occurs eight times in the MT, and ten in the LXX. In the MT, all of these references occur in Joshua 18–22. Two additional references are found in the LXX of Josh. 24.1, 25, where the MT reads 'Shechem'.[1]

All of the MT references, moreover, occur in the broad literary context describing the occupation of the land by the Israelites and the distribution of the tribal inheritances. Josh. 18.1 records the erection of the tent of meeting at Shiloh immediately following the Joseph tribes' taking of the central hill country. (Josh. 17.14-18). In Josh. 18.1-10 and 19.51, Shiloh is the site where Joshua the son of Nun and Eleazar the priest cast lots *lipnê-Yhwh* to determine the inheritances of the seven northern tribes. The war-camp is also found at Shiloh (Josh. 18.9), and Josh 21.1-2 gives 'Shiloh in the land of Canaan' as the site of the appointment of the levitical cities. Finally, Josh. 22.9-34 records the erection of an altar in the region of the Jordan by the Transjordanian tribes, an act which is considered heretical by the tribes dwelling in Palestine. The apparent point of this account is that the sole legitimate place of sacrifice for the Israelite tribes is the altar which stands before the *miškan-Yhwh* at 'Shiloh, which is the land of Canaan'.

Shiloh is mentioned in the MT of Joshua primarily in four lists. These lists recount, in order, the inheritances of the Transjordanian tribes (Josh. 13), the inheritances of the tribes who settled in Palestine (Josh. 14–19), the appointment of the cities of refuge (Josh. 20), and the apportionment of the levitical cities (Josh. 21). Only Joshua 22 is not a list.

The scholars of the nineteenth century considered most of the passages in Joshua referring to Shiloh to have been priestly. While this view has not been consistently supported by more recent scholars, important considerations have been raised in favor of it. First, Joshua 14–21 contains information arranged in lists, a favorite device of the priestly source of the Pentateuch. Second, the formulaic language characteristic of P is preserved in these lists, especially in the superscriptions and subscriptions (cf. e.g. Josh. 14.1-5; 19.51; 21.1-2). Of particular note in this regard is the consistent use of the term *maṭṭēh* for tribe in the lists of tribal inheritances, and the emphasis on the apportionment of the land by lot (*gôrāl*). Third, each list fulfills a specific injunction given in the priestly stratum of the book of Numbers. Thus, Joshua 13, which gives the inheritances of the tribes in the Transjordan, fulfills the commandment of Moses in Num. 32.28-32. The list in Joshua 14–19 fulfills Moses' charge in Numbers 34 to Joshua the son of Nun and Eleazar the priest to divide the land in Palestine by lot. Joshua 20 precisely follows the injunction in Num. 35.9-34 to appoint cities of refuge. Finally, Joshua 21 satisfies the command to set aside cities for the Levites in Num. 35.1-8. Each of these texts in Numbers is distinguished by language characteristic of the priestly source. Furthermore, the employment of lists as a basic mode of conveying information is a primary feature of P. Accordingly, many nineteenth-century scholars recognized the lists in Joshua 13–21 as belonging to P. Although Josh. 22.9-34 does not form a list, the language and motifs employed in it are distinctly priestly. In addition, Josh. 18.1, which introduces Shiloh in the account of the allotment of the tribal inheritances, contains two crucial priestly motifs: the erection of the tent sanctuary in the Promised Land (Josh. 18.1a), and the subjugation of the land (Josh. 18.1b).[2]

Thus, although other strata besides P were acknowledged to be present in Joshua 13–22, notably JE, the passages in which Shiloh inhered were generally attributed to P. Wellhausen, for instance, gave the following breakdown of the pentateuchal sources in Joshua 13–22:

P: 13.15-14.5; 15 (except vv. 13-19); 16.1-8; 17.1-10; 18.1, 11-25; 19.1-48, 51; 20; 21 (except vv. 43-45); 22.9-34;

JE: 16.9-10; 17.11-18; 18.2-10; 19.49-50; 21.43-45; 22.8; 24;

D: 22.1-6; 23.

Since the work of Alt and Noth in this century, however, the provenance of these chapters has been a matter of dispute.[3] According to Noth, Deuteronomy-2 Kings originally constituted a single, unified historical work, the 'Deuteronomistic History'. Noth further argued that an original hexateuchal narrative, as recognized by the scholars of the nineteenth century, had at one time existed, but that the conclusion to this material had been suppressed in favor of the Deuteronomistic History. In its present form, the Genesis-2 Kings continuum comprised two distinct works: the Tetrateuch (Genesis-Numbers) and the Deuteronomistic History. Noth also denied the existence of a systematic deuteronomistic redaction of the Genesis-Numbers traditions. Finally, Noth argued that the lists in Joshua 13-19, which made reference to Shiloh and which earlier had been identified as priestly, and hence late, were actually quite ancient, and preserved the boundaries of the pre-monarchic Israelite tribes.[4] While Alt sought to tie some of the same lists to the reign of Josiah, the thrust of both scholars' work was the same: to deny the priestly provenance of these lists, and to date them to an earlier period than heretofore would have been admitted.

The views of Alt and Noth met with critical opposition in the work of Sigmund Mowinckel.[5] Mowinckel reiterated the position of the nineteenth-century critics that there had been an original Hexateuch extending from Genesis to Joshua. Accordingly, he assigned Joshua 13-19 to the priestly stratum of the Pentateuch, as Wellhausen had done before him. At the same time, Mowinckel entered the most important critique to date of Noth's treatment of the pentateuchal sources in the book of Joshua.

Mowinckel began his critique of Noth's position with regard to Joshua 13-19 by pointing out that Noth had based his denial of a priestly provenance for this material on the supposition that P had hs no *Landnahme* tradition. To this point, however, Mowinckel countered by pointing out that several priestly fragments in Numbers anticipate an account of the conquest. He listed these as Num. 13.2; 20.12b; 22.1; 27.12-23, and took them as proof that P had contained a conquest-settlement report. Morover, Numbers 32 betrayed important stylistic and linguistic characteristics of P, while Num. 33.50-34.29 also stemmed from P on the basis of both style and content. Mowinckel therefore concluded that the boundary descriptions in Joshua 13-19 which depended upon the priestly stratum in Numbers must also have originated with P.[6]

Mowinckel's critique of Noth thus concluded by reiterating the
strong literary connections between the priestly stratum of Numbers
and the description of the tribal inheritances in Joshua 13-19. In
addition, Mowinckel noted the connections between Joshua 20 and
21 and the priestly account of Numbers. However, after establishing
the dependence of Joshua 20 on Num. 35.9-15, Mowinckel later
rejected ch. 20 as an intergral part of the priestly account of the
settlement, and with Noth, treated it as a later insertion based on
Deuteronomy 19.[7] Thus, Mowinckel reckoned only Joshua 14–
19+21 to P. Mowinckel raised other considerations as well, but those
given here are sufficient to point out what had been obvious before
the publication of Noth's theory: namely, that the narratives which
ran from Genesis to Numbers found their proper conclusion in the
book of Joshua. Since Genesis–Numbers was not in itself a complete
work, no 'Tetrateuch' had in fact ever existed.[8]

4.1.1 *The Critical Perspective of the Present Investigation*
In the subsequent treatment it is accepted, on the basis of language
and style as well as the deliberate literary connectives between the
final priestly chapters of Numbers and the material in Joshua 14–22,
that the priestly conclusion to the Hexateuch is found in Joshua.
Thus far, this investigation is in basic accord with the literary-critical
observations of the late nineteenth century. At the same time, the
matter of the dating of the priestly strata of Joshua is left open here.
The dating of Old Testament traditions and literary strata is a fragile
undertaking at best, and neither the late dating of P advocated by
Wellhausen and those who followed him, nor the early dating of the
lists of tribal inheritances in Joshua advanced by Noth can be
adequately substantiated. A further departure from Wellhausen's
source analysis is the argument in the present work for a deuteronomistic redaction of the priestly stratum of Joshua 13–22. This evidence
has critical implications for the relative dating of the pentateuchal
sources, and consequently, for the problem of the antiquity of the
priestly materials which refer to Shiloh.

Nonetheless, the primary concern here is not the dating of the
pentateuchal sources, nor specifically the dating of P, though this
matter is of considerable ancillary significance. Rather, the foremost
interest of this treatment is to understand the place of Shiloh in P's
traditions and theology, and thus the possible historical connection
between the priestly tradition and Shiloh.

The methodology employed in this study may be characterized generally as literary-critical, as the term was understood by Wellhausen and those who followed him, though this work is not predicated upon Wellhausen's conclusions. Rather, by working from the language and style of P in Genesis–Numbers, conclusions similar to those of Graf and Wellhausen have been reached here. In a similar manner, what is 'deuteronomic' (dtn) has been determined on the basis of what is typically and exclusively characteristic of the language, style, and theology of Deuteronomy. What is 'deuteronomistic' (dtr) has been established on the basis of what has been generally accepted, even before Noth's epochal work, as that historical and redactional framework of the former prophets based upon, but not necessarily identical with, the rhetorical language and style of Deuteronomy.[9] It is here accepted, moreover, that at least traces of this redaction can be found in the Pentateuch.[10] In sum, while this work does not represent a strict adherence to any of the particular theories of pentateuchal sources which have been offered to date, it stands in general accord with the identification of the priestly source in Joshua offered by Wellhausen and reiterated by Mowinckel. At the same time, this investigation departs from each of those treatments at important points. This seeming incongruity arises from the conviction that it is not so much the conclusions of previous generations of scholars which should provide the basis of subsequent debate, but the literary evidence with which those scholars were wrestling. Thus, one may find oneself in general agreement with the specific observations of one's predecessors, without simultaneously advocating the same conclusions.

4.2 The Nature and Function of Joshua 14–22 in the Priestly History

4.2.1 The Nature of the Priestly Stratum in Joshua 14–19

Before proceeding to an evaluation of Shiloh's place in the overall priestly narrative, it is necessary first to examine in detail the texts in Joshua in which Shiloh receives mention, in both their general and more particular contexts. Although the first references to Shiloh in Joshua occur in 18.1-10, this passage is found in the context of the list of tribal inheritances in Joshua 14–19. The tribal allotments are introduced in Josh. 14.1 by a superscription in the priestly style known elsewhere in the Pentateuch: *'ēlleh 'ăšer-nāḥălû běnê-Yiśrā'ēl be'ereṣ kěna'an 'ăšer nāḥălû 'ōtām 'el'āzār hakkōhēn wîhôšua' binnûn wěro'šê 'ăbôt hammaṭṭôt libnê Yiśrā'ēl* (These are that which the Israelites inherited in the land of Canaan, which Eleazar the priest and Joshua the son of Nun and the heads of the fathers of the tribes of the Israelites apportioned to them'). Equally important is the subscription in Josh. 19.51 which concludes the list begun in Josh. 14.1: *'ēlleh hanněḥālôt 'ăšer niḥălû 'el'āzār hakkōhēn wîhôšua' binnûn wěro'šê hā'ăbôt lěmaṭṭôt běnê-Yiśrā'ēl* ('These are the inheritances which Eleazar the priest and Joshua the son of Nun and the heads of the fathers of the tribes of the Israelites apportioned . . . '). These formulae in Josh. 14.1 and 19.51 mark the beginning and end of a long list of tribal inheritances which provides the basis for these six chapters. The formal arrangement of the list, according to its superscriptions and subscriptions, has been outlined below in Tables 1 and 2 (see Appendix).

The greater list which forms the basis of Joshua 14–19 is characterized by the inclusion of smaller sublists regarding the inheritance of each tribe. These sublists delineate either the 'boundary' (*gěbûl*) of a given tribe, or the 'cities' (*'ārîm*) of that tribe, or both. As with the greater list, these smaller lists contain introductory and concluding formulae, or superscriptions and subscriptions, which distinguish them from one another (see Tables 1 and 2). It can be seen from the arrangement of superscriptions and subscriptions that the sublists were generally ordered according to a superscription regarding the allotment (*gôrāl*) of the tribe, and subscription regarding the inheritance (*naḥălāh*) of the tribe. Exceptions to this pattern occur in connection with Judah, Ephraim, Manasseh, and Benjamin. (1) In the case of the tribes of Judah and Benjamin, the initial descriptions of the allotments are given in the form of the delineation of boundaries. These boundary descriptions are then concluded with their own subscriptions:

> *zeh gěbûl běnê-yěhûudāh sābîb lěmišpěḥōtām* ('This is the boundary of the Judahites round about, according to their families')

> *zō't naḥălat běnê binyāmin ligbûlōtêhā sābîb lěmišpěḥōtām* ('This is the inheritance of the Benjaminites according to its boundaries round about, according to their families').

(2) In addition, Judah and Benjamin also include lists which have their own superscriptions:

zō't naḥălat bĕnê-yĕhûdāh lĕmišpĕḥōtām ('This is the inheritance of the Judahites according to their families')

wĕhāyû he'ārîm lĕmaṭṭēh bĕnê binyāmin lĕmišĕḥōtêhem ('And the cities of the tribe of the Benjaminites were according to their families')

as well as subscriptions:

wayyihyû he'ārîm (miqṣēh) lĕmaṭṭēh bĕnê yĕhûdāh lĕmišpĕḥōtām ('And the cities from the outer boundary of the tribe of the Judahites were according to their families')

zō't naḥălat bĕnê-binyāmin lĕemišpĕḥōtām ('This is the inheritance of the Benjaminites according to their families')

(3) The pattern of these formulae in the case of Judah is somewhat irregular. In the present text, the formula *zō't naḥălat bĕnê-yĕhûdāh lĕmišĕḥōtām* ('This is the inheritance of the Judahites according to their families'), which in most other cases functions as the regular subscription to the descriptions of the respective tribal allotments, stands as the superscription to the Judahite inheritance. The narrative introduction to the Judahite city-list may at one time have served as the subscription to the same city-list, if the tribe of Benjamin may be taken as a model.[11]

(4) A disorder similar to that in the list for the tribe of Judah exists with regard to the allotments to Ephraim and Manasseh as well. To begin, a general superscription is given for Joseph, which is prefixed to the description of Ephraim's southern boundary. This superscription uses the verb *yāṣā'*, which occurs in the superscriptions for Simeon, Issachar, Asher, Naphtali and Dan. Those of Benjamin and Zebulun use *'ālāh*, while Judah, Ephraim and Manasseh employ *hāyāh*. This fact, along with the otherwise regular formulae, places the superscription for Joseph within the order of the greater list. Nonetheless, no specific inheritance is ascribed to Joseph, so that one might wonder whether Joseph in fact belongs in the list. Moreover, Ephraim is the only tribe which carries a superscription for its boundary (*gĕbûl*), although Judah bears a subscription for its boundary (Josh. 15.12b). Furthermore, Manasseh has no subscription, though it does retain a regular superscription.

It is difficult to determine what has led to these variations in a document which otherwise is so orderly. Mowinckel may have been right is ascribing some of these variations to the freedom of the author's style or to textual corruption.[12] On the other hand, the confusion between Joseph and Ephraim may simply reflect an early ambiguity with regard to the relationship between these two entities.[13]

(5) A further difficulty is posed by the uneven presence of the city-lists. The most extensive of the sublists is that of the cities of Judah (Josh. 15.21-62), which comprises twelve separate listings of Judahite towns and villages. In addition to Judah, each of the descriptions of the inheritances of Benjamin, Zebulun, Issachar, Asher, Naphtali and Dan, i.e. the last seven tribes, includes some sort of city-list. This fact led Alt to argue that the list of tribal boundaries in Joshua 13–19 combined two originally separate lists, a city-list and a boundary list. Alt was followed in this view by Noth, and more recently by Aharoni.[14] That both cities and boundaries have been included in the greater list is obvious. Nonetheless, only Judah and Benjamin possess independent city-lists. That the subscriptions elsewhere for the cities within the tribal boundaries serve merely as addenda to the description of the inheritances belies Alt's claim. In fact, most of the tribal lists contain no independent city-lists at all. The present form of Joshua 14–19, therefore, apart from the variations noted above, is a self-contained entity, whatever the deficiencies in its content may be.[15] This fact is demonstrated by the regularity of the arrangement of the superscriptions and subscriptions.

Moreover, the considerable confusion in the super- and subscriptions pertaining to Judah, Joseph, Ephraim and Manasseh may be the result of the insertion of other material into the framework of the list at these points. The list of tribal inheritances in Joshua 14–19, in fact, has been supplemented with three different kinds of information: (a) various settlement traditions relating to particular tribes, or to clans within a particular tribe (e.g. under Judah's list of inheritances, the inclusion of Caleb and Othniel); (b) historical anecdotes, often explaining why the inheritance of a certain tribe was not occupied or settled in the area allotted in the list (e.g. Josh. 15.63, the continued presence of the Jebusites in Jerusalem); and (c) introductory and concluding statements which serve to incorporate the greater list into the overall priestly history (e.g. Josh. 14.2-5, the explanation of the division of the land by lots). These materials are of uncertain origin. The settlement traditions (see Table 3, p. 204) have traditionally been ascribed to JE.

Many inconsistencies have emerged in the list as a result of these myriad expansions, and the greatest confusion exists with regard to the lists for Judah, Joseph, and Ephraim, where the most significant intrusions in the list are found, mostly in the form of settlement traditions. Nevertheless, the parameters of the list can still be established on the basis of the superscription in 14.1 and the subscription in 19.51a. Within these boundaries, the materials belonging to the original list are readily separated from the later supplementation, which, however, has not shattered the overall structure of the list. While the inclusion of this traditional and historically explanatory material in the framework of the list has led to a great deal of controversy as to the source and/or origin of the list itself, the historical introduction in Josh. 14.1-5 and the conclusion in 19.51, as well as the formulaic super- and subscriptions throughout the list, which are priestly in both language and style, identify the list as priestly, regardless of the material added to it.

Contrary to Mowinckel's arguments, moreover, Joshua 14–19 does not depend upon any earlier hexateuchal source for its arrangement. Instead, it is an independent entity, and its arrangement has served as the basis for the expansion of the narratives of Joshua by the piecemeal addition of isolated settlement traditions at the relevant places in the list, as is illustrated by the confusion wrought in the list by the insertion of the tradition in Josh. 14.6-15. Moreover, the incorporation of this list into the greater hexateuchal context demanded some modifications, especially in the addition of historical introductions to bring the list into line with the overall hexateuchal narrative, and in the inclusion of historical anecdotes by which the list of inheritances was made consistent with the historical realities known to the priestly writer(s).

These modifications and additions to the list of tribal inheritances were necessary because the basic priestly document in Joshua 14–19 reflects an idealized view of the land of Israel. The classic priestly statement of this ideal is given in Numbers 34. This Israel was considered to have inherited the land of Canaan, according to the borders of the former Egyptian province.[16] Thus, the boundaries of the land run down to the sea on the west. In the same manner, the Canaanite cities in the Jezreel and along the coast, which were not incorporated into Israel proper until the time of David and Solomon, and the Philistine cities in the southwest, which remained independent of the Israelite kingdoms, are ignored in the list proper, and are only noted in the anecdotes to the list.

In conclusion, Joshua 14–19 contains several literary strata. The basis of the whole is provided by the priestly list of tribal inheritances. This list, in turn, has been supplemented with several kinds of information: (a) old *Volkstraditionen*, silimar to what one finds, for example, in JE; (b) historical anecdotes, clarifying certain parts of the list in light of comtemporary reality; and (c) introductory and conclusory historical material which incorporate the list into the overall schema of the priestly history.

4.2.2 *Shiloh in Josh. 18.1-10; 19.51*

The most important addendum to the list in Joshua 14–19 is the pericope in Josh. 18.1-10. This passage recounts the setting up of the tent of meeting at Shiloh and the subsequent division of the land among the remaining seven tribes by Joshua the son of Nun and Eleazar the Priest:

> (18.1) And the whole congregation of the Israelites assembled at Shiloh, and they erected there the tent of meeting. And the land lay subdued before them. (2) And there remained among the Israelites seven tribes who had not received their inheritance. (3) And Joshua said to the Israelites, 'How long will you neglect to go and take possession of the land which Yahweh, the god of your fathers, has given to you? (4) Commission three men per tribe, and I will send them, and they will arise, and they will go throughout the land, and they will write it down, according to the edict of the inheritances, and will come unto me. (5) And they will apportion it in seven portions, Judah standing against his border in the south, and the house of Joseph standing against their border to the north. (6) And you will write down the land (in) seven portions, and you will bring it unto me here. And I will cast lots for you here before Yahweh our god. (7) (Because there is no portion for the Levites in your midst, because the priesthood of Yahweh is their inheritance; and Gad and Reuben, and the half-tribe of Manasseh have taken their inheritances beyond the Jordan to the east, which Moses, the servant of Yahweh, gave to them.) (8) And the men arose, and they went. And Joshua commanded those who were going to write down the land, saying, 'Go, and and go throughout the land, and write it down, and return unto me. And I will cast lots for you before Yahweh at Shiloh'. (9) And the men went, and they traversed the land, and they wrote it down according to cities, according to seven

portions, upon a scroll. And they came to Joshua—unto the camp at Shiloh. (10) And Joshua cast lots for them at Shiloh before Yahweh. And Joshua divided the land there for the Israelites according to their allotments.

The origin of this passage and its original place in the list (if indeed it had one!) have long been matters of controversy. Wellhausen argued that because of the statement in 18.1b, 'and the land lay subdued before them', 18.1 actually belonged at the beginning of the list, preceding 14.1.[17] More recently, Mowinckel has advanced the same argument.[18] Furthermore, there was a long-standing tendency on the part of nineteenth century literary critics to ascribe the basic stratum of Josh. 18.1-10 to E or J,[19] while the introduction and conclusion were attributed to P, or to some other secondary redactor.[20] Mowinckel, however, attributed Josh. 18.2-9 to the dtr *Grundlage*, which introduced the concept of the distribution of the land in two stages: the initial allocation of inheritances to Judah, Ephraim, and half-Manasseh, and the subsequent allotment to the seven smaller northern tribes.[21] Noth, on the other hand, regarded 18.1 as an individual addition to the text, as he did Josh. 14.1 and 19.51, without connection to a broader hexateuchal narrative. At the same time he held 18.2-10 to be the second layer of expansion to the original list of tribal inheritances. Noth further regarded this list as the basis for Joshua 13-19.[22]

In the context of this three-way debate, several points must be made. First, Wellhausen's observation that 18.1b ('and the land lay subdued before them') originally must have preceded 14.1 is probably correct, because one would naturally expect to find such a statement immediately following the conquest and prefacing the allotment of the tribal inheritances. This conclusion is supported by 19.51a, which knows of only a single allotment proceedure, and that 'by lot at Shiloh before Yahweh, at the door of the tent of meeting'.[23] The distribution of the inheritances in two stages reflects a secondary revision of the material, probably by a dtr hand, as will be shown below. Third, Noth's treatment of 18.1 as an individual addition to the text is not far off: 18.1 is no different in form from other anecdotes in the list, such as 15.63, 16.10, or 17.12-13. Nevertheless, 18.1 is more than simply a single notation. Its wider connection to P's hexateuchal narrative is confirmed by the dependence of 19.51a; 21.1-3; 22.9-34 upon this singular event. Again it will be demonstrated below that 18.2-10 are dependent upon 18.1, and some portions are even tied directly to the present placement of 18.1. Moreover, 14.1 and 19.51a cannot serve as a model for excising 18.1 from the list as secondary since these two verses comprise the proper super- and subscription, respectively, to the list as a whole. Indeed, so far from standing as a mere individual gloss, 18.1 is part of a specific redactional layer of Joshua 14–19. This redaction entailed the modification of an important aspect of the list in Joshua 14–19, namely, the subscription in 19.51a. Josh. 21.1-3 also conforms to the view laid out in 18.1-10 and 19.51a, that Shiloh, in the land of Canaan, had been the site of the final distribution of the land. Josh. 22.9-34 assumes this same scenario. Inasmuch as certain priestly elements unite all of these materials in Joshua 18–22, it is logical to regard these materials as part of a unitary priestly recension of the book of Joshua.

The chief characteristic of this recension is that basic lists, such as those which form the *Grundlage* for Joshua 14–19, 20 and 21, have been brought into the historical framework of the Hexateuch by the prefacing of those lists with brief historical introductions. Indeed, Josh. 18.1-10 serves in its present position as a kind of introductory passage to the lists of the last seven tribes (Josh. 18.11–19.48). Furthermore, each of these historical introductions reflects the language and conceptual historical framework of the priestly source, and most relate explicitly to priestly passages in the book of Numbers. Thus, Josh. 14.2-5 relates to Num. 34.13-15; Josh. 20.1-6 describes the fulfillment of Num. 35.9-34; and Josh. 21.1-3 refers back to Num. 35.1-8.

That 18.1 did not originally belong to the list is evidenced by its anecdotal character, and Wellhausen and Mowinckel are correct in finding the original locus of Josh. 18.1 prior to 14.1. Conversely, the separation of 18.2-10 from 18.1 has been advocated by nearly every critical scholar who has examined this material, usually on the assumption of a non-priestly *Grundlage* which knew of no particular site of the distribution of the inheritances, or which actually assumed Gilgal to have been the place. These two problems, the placement of 18.1 within the list as a whole, and the relationship of 18.1 to 18.2-10, lie at the heart of the question of the importance of Shiloh in the priestly tradition, as well as the more controversial issue of the historical origin of the connection between Shiloh and P.

The first question of importance in this connection regards the literary placement of Josh. 18.1 (2-10): i.e., why has the erection of the tent of meeting and the casting of lots at Shiloh been postponed until Judah, Ephraim, and Manasseh have received their inheritances? The most logical answer is that this change of scene was influenced by the insertion of the tradition in Josh. 17.14-18.[24] There the Joseph tribes complain that they cannot take possession of the land in the valleys, since the Canaanites there have chariots of iron. Joshua therefore commands the people of Joseph to go up and clear the hill country, to dwell in it. The inclusion of the tradition of Joseph's settlement of the central mountains in which Shiloh lay brought about the transfer of Josh. 18.1-10 to its present place in the list. The reason for this transfer of 18.1 to immediately after 17.14-18 probably derived from the association of Shiloh's cultus specifically with the tribe of Joseph.[25]

The next problem is the specific literary provenance of Josh. 18.1-10. The priestly character of 18.1a is clear from its language. *wayyiqqāhălû kol-'ădat běnê-Yiśrā'ēl* reflects the distinctive language, style and theology of P. The centrality to the priestly ideology of the congregation (*'ēdāh*) which assembles (*qāhal*) is indisputable and requires no further proof. Blenkinsopp has shown that 18.1b is priestly as well, since *wěhā'āreṣ nikběšāh lipnêhem* reflects the priestly concern for the subjugation of the land expressed in nearly identical language in Gen. 1.28.[26]

The rest of the passage, however, is not of a single piece. It is at least broken by the statement in v 8a—*wayyāqumû hā'ănāšîm wayyēlēkû* ('And the men arose, and they went')—which precedes Joshua's command to those sent out to 'write down' the land in v. 8b. Furthermore, v. 9a again reads *wayyēlēkû hā'ănāšîm wayya'abrû bā'āreṣ* ('And the men went, and they passed through the land'). On the other hand, a simple division of sources on the basis of language is not readily apparent in this text.

In fact, this passage seems to have experienced a gradual expansion, until it reached its present form. Support for this contention is found in the following factors. (a) Verse 6 repeats the instruction given in vv. 4-5a. In doing so, v. 6 assumes the division of the land into *seven* portions, and anticipates the casting of lots, as mentioned in v. 8b. (b) Verse 5b gives instructions to Judah and Joseph to stay within their borders, which might fit into the context, but is somewhat cumbersome. (c) Verse 7-8a have no immediately clear antecedent. *Kî 'ên-ḥēleq lalwiyyim bĕqirbĕkem kî-kĕhunnat Yhwh naḥălātô* ('Because there is no portion for the Levites in your midst, because the priesthood of Yahweh is their inheritance') may have at one time directly followed v. 5a, which commands the writing down of only seven tribal inheritances. Nonetheless, vv. 7-8a read like many of the other brief harmonistic comments in these chapters, and therefore do not belong to the traditional *Vorlage* of the present text.

In order to account for these discrepancies in Josh. 18.1-10, the theory is offered here that the basic account of Josh. 18.1-10 is priestly. It includes the obviously priestly introduction in 18.1, and thereafter, vv. 3a, 4, 8b, 9 (with the exception of the phrase, *lĕ'ārîm lĕšib'āh ḥălāqîm 'al-sēper*—'according to cities, according to seven portions, upon a scroll'—which is dtr) and 10. This *Grundlage* would have read as follows:

> (1) And the whole congregation of the children of Israel assembled at Shiloh, and they caused to dwell there the tent of meeting. And the land lay subdued before them. (3a) And Joshua said unto the children of Israel, (4a) 'Choose for yourselves three men per tribe, and I will send them, and they will arise and go throughout the land, and they will write it down according to the decree of their inheritance, and they will come unto to me'. (8b) And Joshua commanded those who were to go to write down the land saying, 'Go, and criss-coss the land, and write it down, and here I will cast for you lots, before Yahweh at Shiloh'. (9) And the ment went, and traversed the land, and wrote it down, and they came unto Joshua, unto the camp at Shiloh. (10) And Joshua cast for them lots, at Shiloh, before Yahweh. And Joshua apportioned there the land for the children of Israel, according to their allotments.

This *Grundlage* reflects the priestly theology that the land was distributed among the various tribes by Joshua, after the erection of the wilderness cultus in the Promised Land. It also uses consistent priestly phraseology, e.g. in the formula *hišlîk gôrāl*, in reference to the casting of lots. Most important, however, is the repeated reference to Shiloh, first as the place where the tent of meeting is set up (v. 1), and thereafter in 8b, 9b, and 10a, where Shiloh is the place where Joshua casts lots for the inheritances. A notable feature of the *Grundlage* as a whole is its innocence of the division of the land in two stages.

This *Grundlage* has been expanded by a dtr hand through the addition of the dtr motif of the seven tribes yet to receive their inheritances in vv. 2, 5a, and 9a. A dtr hand is also recognizable in the distinctly dtr clauses *lābô' lārešet 'et-hā'āreṣ* ('to go to take possession of the land'),[27] and *'ăšer nātan lākem Yhwh 'ĕlōhê 'ăbôtêkem* ('which Yahweh, the god of your fathers, has given to you').[28] A final dtr addition is found in v. 7. An important characteristic of the dtr redaction of the Hexateuch, according to Wellhausen, was the insertion 'everywhere' of the two-and-a-half Transjordanian tribes and the Levites.[29] Indeed, the priestly lists in 13–19 account for the twelve tribes without reference to the Levites.[30] Moreover, while v. 7 employs the otherwise exclusively priestly term *kĕhunnāh* ('priesthood'), the concept of the Levites forming a 'priesthood of Yahweh' comes from the book of Deuteronomy.[31] Verse 7b also shares with v. 5b an interest in explaining what has already transpired, namely the apportionment of the inheritances of Reuben, Gad, and half-Manasseh in Transjordan (7b) and the allotment of the inheritances of Judah and Joseph in the Promised Land (5b).

This dtr expansion of the priestly *Grundlage* of Josh. 18.1-10 also confirms the truth of the possibility raised by Mowinckel, namely, that Dtr was responsible for the view of a division of the land in two stages. The dtr interest in a distribution of the tribal inheritances in two phases further suggests that Dtr may also have been responsible for the shift of Josh. 18.1-10 from its original place at the head of the list in Joshua 14–19 to its present locus. The priestly recension, at any rate, knew of only a single, ritual division of the land, as is demonstrated both by 14.1 and 19.51.

In addition to the dtr redaction of the priestly *Grundlage* of Josh. 18.1-10, traces of a further expansion of the passage are in evidence in vv. 6 and 8a which must be seen as a repetition of vv. 4b, 9a. Verses 6 and 8a, in fact, cause the severest breaks in the text of the *Grundlage*. Their origin probably lies with a later independent expansion.

In conclusion, Josh. 18.1-10 originated with the priestly writer and introduced the final critical sequence in the priestly history: the establishment in the Promised Land of the cultus practiced in the wilderness and the distribution of the land among the tribes by lot. This passage was expanded over time, most conspicuously by the dtr

additions in vv. 2, 3b, 5, 7, 9a, and later by the addenda in vv. 6, 8a.
Mowinckel's argument that 18.2-9 reflects the dtr view of a two-stage
allocation of the inheritances is correct. That these verses originated
with dtr and subsequently received a priestly modification, is
incorrect.[32] One cannot arbitrarily assume that there was a dtr report
of this event and then assign the *only* extant treatment to Dtr. In fact,
the theology of the underlying stratum of 18.1-10 is demonstrably
priestly. The dtr hand is clearest in those verses, such as 5 and 7,
which constitute unmistakable addenda to the *Grundlage*. The dtr
editorial activity in Josh. 18.1-10 is otherwise limited to a few
parenetic notices, e.g. 18.3b, 5 and 7, which give a dtr flavor to a non-
dtr passage.[33] Despite dtr editing, then, there is no evidence of an
actual dtr source for Josh. 18.1-10. Nor can the *Grundlage* of Josh.
18.2-10 be ascribed to JE, since there are no clear indicators of that
stratum to be found here. Verse 5b, which seems to presuppose a
setting at Gilgal, simply reflects the anachronistic dtr view based on
the tradition in Josh. 14.6-15.

A further problem with the interpretation of the Shiloh references
in 18.1-10 has been the assigning of vv. 2-10 to JE, and each
occurrence of Shiloh to a secondary recension of this pericope. Both
Noth[34] and Eissfeldt[35] represent this position. Their view, however,
is not compelling. The idea that Gilgal, and not Shiloh, was the
original setting for the distribution of the tribal inheritances by lot
overlooks two facts. First, there is no connection, traditional or
otherwise, between Gilgal and the allotment of the tribal possessions.
The presence of Gilgal in Josh. 14.6 neither inheres in the priestly list
in Joshua 14–19, nor evinces a connection to the tradition that
Joshua and Eleazar divided the land by lot. Rather, Gilgal in Josh.
14.6 is part of the independent Caleb tradition and has nothing to do
with the account of the distribution of the tribal inheritances.

Nor is there a sound grammatical basis for regarding the Shiloh
references as secondary. Josh. 18.1 would hardly make sense without
mention of a geographic location, and Shiloh is the only reading for
such a site which attested for this verse. Moreover, the *'ōhel-mô'ēd* is
nowhere associated with Gilgal. Nor is the problem of the tent of
meeting at Shiloh solved by reducing 18.1 to a secondary addition to
the passage, since the entire passage hangs on this verse. Shiloh
belongs in v. 9b as well, where its deletion is nothing less than
capricious.[36] Indeed, *'el-hammaḥăneh šilōh* ('unto the camp at

Shiloh'), is a traditional element known also from Judg. 21.12 and parallels *'el yĕhôšua'* ('unto Joshua'). This appositional usage is typical of stylistic parallelism, and there are no grounds for deleting the second member of the parallel. The presence of Shiloh in v. 10a is also necessary from the standpoint of the MT, since *wayḥalleq-šām yĕhôšua' 'et-hā'āreṣ* ('and Joshua apportioned there the land') in v. 10b demands a geographic antecedent. Although the LXX does not contain v. 10b, it does render v. 10a literally, including the specification of Shiloh as the place where Joshua cast lots before Yahweh. Therefore, while it might be argued that v. 10b is a later instrusion into the text, the LXX has retained the presence of Shiloh in v. 10a, anyway, so that the deletion of Shiloh here depends upon doubtful literary-critical considerations.[37]

To sum up, Shiloh inheres indisputably in 18.1-10 in vv. 1, 9b and 10a. The assumption of an Elohistic *Grundlage* is unfounded: there is no trace of the key feature of the Elohist as known from Genesis and the first chapters of Exodus: Elohim as the unqualified proper name of God. Moreover, no connection between JE and the distribution of land by Joshua by lot can be established. Instead, the *Grundlage* of Josh. 18.1-10 is characterized by priestly language and interests, and these center on the erection of the tent of meeting at Shiloh and the apportioning of the tribal inheritances there by lot. Indeed, Shiloh is the unambiguous geographic focus of the priestly narrative of Josh. 18.1-10.

The role of Shiloh at this point of the priestly history has far-reaching consequences for the understanding of the rest of the book of Joshua, as well as for the theology and historical background of P. Josh. 18.1-10 marks a critical development in the history of the settlement for the priestly source. With the establishement of the tent of meeting at Shiloh, the Shiloh sanctuary becomes of central importance in the narrative framework of P. Thus, for example, the subscription to the long list of tribal inheritances in Josh. 19.51 has been modified by the addition of a notation marking the exact cultic-geographic locus of the land division: *bĕšilōh lipnê Yhwh petaḥ 'ōhel mô'ēd* ('in Shiloh before Yahweh, at the door of the tent of meeting'). That this notation is an addition to the subscription to the list of tribal allotments is suggested by the fact that the superscription of the list in Josh. 14.1 makes no mention of the geographic setting of the distribution of the inheritances. Thus, 19.51a is based directly upon 18.1, and brings the subscription into conformity with the priestly historical perspective that the allotment of the tribal inheritances took place before the tent of meeting at Shiloh.

The concluding formula in Josh. 19.51b, *waykallû mēhallēq 'et-hā'āreṣ* ('and they finished apportioning the land'), likewise belongs to P's historical framework, where it serves as a summary conclusion to the historical narrative produced by P's casting of the list of tribal inheritances in narrative form. It is important to note in this context that this phrase is quite similar to the priestly conclusion to the account of Creation in Gen. 2.1: *waykullû haššāmayim wĕhā'āreṣ wĕkol-ṣĕbā'ām* ('And the heavens and the earth and all their host were completed'). Blenkinsopp has shown on the basis of the conjunction of the standard conclusion formulae and the more solemn execution formulae in P that there are three critical moments in P's history: (a) the creation of the world; (b) the construction of the sanctuary; and (c) the establishment of the sanctuary in the land and the associated division of the land between the tribes.[38] This structural evidence not only supports the literary claims made thus far, namely, that Joshua 13–22 forms the conclusion to P's version of Israel's origins, but also demonstrates that the themes of the erection of the wilderness tent shrine in the Promised Land and the allotment of the tribal inheritances were of critical moment to P's overall theology. Furthermore, that Shiloh was the site which P associated with the culmination of the settlement in the Promised Land means that the Shilonite cultus held a special status, one above all other sanctuaries, in the priestly tradition.

4.2.3 *Shiloh in Joshua 20 and 21*

The priestly materials in the Hexateuch which follow the crucial events of Joshua 14–19 are found in Josh. 20; 21; 22.9-34. Joshua 20 is the priestly version of the appointment of cities of refuge for the manslayer, as commanded in the priestly text of Num. 35.6-34.[41] Mention of Shiloh is not found in this chapter, however, but only in the subsequent account of the levitical cities in Josh. 21.1-42, where Shiloh occurs in v. 2 in the historical introduction to this list. Indeed, Josh. 21.1-2 comprises the literary *Fortsetzung* of the theme established in 18.1-10, namely that the Israelites had set up the wilderness tent shrine at Shiloh and had divided the land there by lot. That no trace of this motif is found in Josh. 20.1-9 probably is to be attributed to the fact that Josh. 19.51 and 21.1-2 bracket the account of the appointment of the cities of refuge, making additional mention of Shiloh superfluous in this account.

The priestly list of the levitical cities in Josh. 21.1-42,[42] as with the list of tribal inheritances in Joshua 14–19, initially included no specific mention of the geographical locus of the activity. Both lists, in fact, seem to have been merely that: lists, with brief super- and subscriptions. Like Joshua 14–19, moreover, Josh. 21.1-42 has been brought into the priestly narrative by the appending of a brief introductory statement in the priestly style to the beginning of the list. This introduction gives the historical and geographical setting of the list, and in Josh. 21.1-2 reads:

> *wayyiggĕšû ro'šê 'ăbôt halwiyyim 'el-'el'āzār hakkōhēn wĕ'el-*
> *yĕhôšua' bin-nûn wĕ'el-ro'šê 'ăbôt hammaṭṭôt libnê Yuśrā'ēl;*
> *waydabbĕrû 'ălêhem bĕšilōh bĕ'ereṣ kĕna'an lē'mōr: Yhwh ṣiwwāh*
> *bĕyad-mōšeh lātet-lānû 'ārîm lāšābet ûmigrĕšêhen libhemtēnû*

> And the heads of the fathers of the Levites drew near unto Eleazar the priest and unto Joshua the son of Nun and unto the heads of the fathers of the tribes of the children of Israel; and they spoke to them at Shiloh in the land of Canaan saying, 'Yahweh commanded by the hand of Moses to give to us cities to inhabit, and their pasture lands for our livestock'.

Whether Josh. 21.3 ever served as the superscription to this list, or whether the original superscription has been integrated into P's historical introduction (cf. the language of 14.1 vis-à-vis 21.1) is impossible to say. What is clear is that the formal superscriptions to the various sublists of levitical cities, apportioned according to families, actually begin in v. 4, in a form known also from the list of tribal inheritances: *wayyēṣē' haggôrāl lĕmišpĕhōt haqqĕhātî* ('And the lot went out for the Kohathite families'). Shiloh occurs in v. 2 and therefore belongs to the historical introduction, and stems from the same stratum of P (i.e. the narative historical framework, rather than the *Grundlage*, which included the lists in Josh. 13–21) as does the key passage in Josh. 18.1-10, which once served as P's historical introduction to the list in Joshua 14–19. The reiteration of Shiloh in Josh. 21.2 confirms what has been shown previously, namely, that the erection of the tent shrine at Shiloh, and the distribution of the tribal inheritances before the sanctuary there played a key role in P's historical theology.

4.2.4 *Shiloh in Joshua 22*

Unlike Joshua 13-21, the priestly portion of Joshua 22 contains no
list. Rather it seems to have had as its basis an old tradition of a
conflict between the Transjordanian tribes of Reuben and Gad and
the tribes dwelling west of the Jordan. This chapter, however, is not
wholly priestly, as Josh. 22.1-8 bears the marks of dtr editing. The
characteristic dtr language first emerges in v. 4a, with the motif of
Yahweh's granting of rest to the Israelites—a direct reference to
Deut. 3.20. Verse 5 is almost wholly deuteronomistic:

> *raq šimrû mě'ōd la'ăśôt 'et-hammiṣwāh wě'et-hattôrāh 'ăšer ṣiwwāh*
> *'etkem mōšeh 'ebed-Yhwh lě'ahăbāh 'et-Yhwh*
> *'ělōhêkem wělāleket běkol-děrākāyw wělišmōr miṣôtāyw ûlědobqāh bô*
> *ûlě'obdô běkol-lěbabkem ûběkol-napšěkem*

> Only be on guard exceedingly to do the commandment and the law
> which Moses, the servant of Yahweh commanded you: to love
> Yahweh your god and to walk in all his ways and to keep his
> commandments and to cleave to him and to serve him with all your
> heart and with all of your lives.

This verse deliberately takes up the central injunction in Deut. 6.5.
The expression *ûlědobqāh bô* ('to cleave to him') is found exclusively
in Deuteronomy. 'To walk in all his ways' (*lāleket běkol-děrākāyw*)
and 'to keep his commandments' (*lišmōr miṣôtāyw*) are equally
deuteronomistic. The final dtr expression is found in v. 8a. The
mention of the Transjordanian tribes' return to their inheritances
'with very many possessions' (*ûběmiqneh rab mě'ōd*) is tied to Deut.
3.20 and represents the dtr fulfillment of the role of the Transjordanian
tribes in the conquest and settlement.

In addition to the deuteronomistic characteristics in Josh. 22.1-8,
there are also non-deuteronomistic elements, which betray a pre-dtr
Grundlage. *Wělaḥaṣî maṭṭēh měnaššeh* ('and the half-tribe of Manasseh')
in v. 1 is a distinctively non-dtn/dtr usage, the dtn/dtr writers having
preferred the more usual word for tribe, *šebet*, to the exclusion of
maṭṭēh. *Maṭṭēh* is in fact a priestly term, and its presence here
suggests that the original introduction to Joshua 22 was priestly. The
expression *miṣwat Yhwh 'ělōhêkem* is neither clearly priestly nor
clearly dtn/dtr.[43] The use of the word *'ăḥuzzāh* ('inheritance') in v. 4,
however, is further evidence of the priestly provenance of the
hexateuchal *Vorlage*: the term occurs only once in Deuteronomy, in
32.49, in the Yahwistic account of the death of Moses. Otherwise,

'*ăhuzzāh* is largely a priestly term, and must be here so regarded as well.[44] An additional priestly term is present in v. 3 with *mišmeret*: 'charge' or 'injunction', usually given in connection with some specific cultic directive.[45] Since vv. 2-3a refer to the charge of Moses to the Transjordanian tribes in Numbers 32, these must also be considered part of the hexateuchal *Vorlage* of this passage. Finally, v. 6 is devoid of dtr language, and probably belongs with vv. 1-3a, which together form a proper introduction to vv. 9-34. The final difficulty regarding vv. 1-8 has to do with v. 7. This verse comprises an anecdote on the inheritance of the half-tribe of Manasseh in Transjordan. It has no logical antecedent in the passage, and was probably introduced as part of the dtr recension of the passage.[46]

In conclusion. Josh 22.1-8 contains the priestly introduction to the tradition in 22.9-34, and this introduction knew only the two tribes of Reuben and Gad. These verses have experienced a substantial dtr re-editing in the addition of the peculiar dtr rhetoric to the passage and in the correction of the simple pairing of Reuben and Gad to include Manasseh, to conform with the standard dtr order stressing the two and-a-half tribes of Traansjordan. A similar phenomenon is evident in the dtr re-working of Josh. 18.1-10 (see above).

4.2.5 *The Priestly Character of Josh. 22.9-34*

Josh. 22.9-34 conceives of a single legitimate place of sacrifice for the Israelites in the Promised Land and is to be associated with the priestly traditions, rather than with the work of the deuteronomists. These verses are replete with priestly language, which illustrates the priestly origins of the tradition (see Table 5, Appendix).[47]

Given the priestly provenance of this passage, it is necessary to raise a question regarding its literary character: namely, is this passage a literary construct, or is it an older priestly tradition?[48] This problem can only be resolved by consideration of those elements in the passage which would betray an actual tradition, i.e. the traditional figures, motifs, etc. In this connection, Wellhausen's criterion for the antiquity of tradition, namely, to prefer those features as authentic which most clearly departed from the later standards, must be given credence.[49] Conversely, it is extremely difficult to disprove the claim that a particular tradition or account is a fictional literary construct, drawing on earlier elements. Since this type of argument requires precious little evidence, however, it should be regarded with suspicion. Only clearly anachronistic elements betray the later provenance of a document and can reveal the employment of archaic elements in the service of a later *Tendenz*.

The central question with regard to Josh. 22.9-34, is, in fact, whether there is an actual traditional basis for the events described, or whether archaic features have been employed in the composition of a late text, in order to give the appearance of an early provenance. The first pertinent piece of evidence in this connection is the fact that there appears to have been an underlying stratum in this chapter which dealt not with the two and-a-half tribes, but with the Reubenites and Gadites alone (vv. 25, 31, 32, 33, 34). The association of Reuben and Gad alone with the Transjordan is contrary to the later formulation of both dtr and P, which strata adhered to the division of the people of Israel into the nine-and-a-half tribes in Palestine, and the two and-a-half tribes in Transjordan. This later formulation is present in Josh. 22.9, 10, 11, 12, 13, 15, 21. Indeed, a glance at this breakdown reveals a division between the first and second halves of the passage: the first half uses the standard formula, while the second half, and incidentally, that which contains the aetiology of the altar of 'witness', preserves the anomalous pairing of the Reubenites and Gadites, without reference to Manasseh. This evidence suggest that an older tradition has been preserved within the context of a later narrative text.

Other traditional elements play an important role in Josh. 22.9-34 as well. The most notable of these is the figure of Phineas, the son of Eleazar the priest. The first mention of this Phineas in the Hexateuch comes in an anecdote to the priestly list of the levitical families in Exod. 6.16-25. Exod. 6.25a is, in fact, the birth notice of this Phineas: 'And Eleazar the son of Aaron took for himself from the daughters of Puti'el, for himself for a wife, and she bore to him Phineas'. The death notice of Eleazar, the son of Aaron (Josh. 24.33), also mentions this Phineas: 'And Eleazar the son of Aaron died, and they buried him at the hill of Phineas, his son, which had been given to him in the hill country of Ephraim'.

These notices exemplify an important traditional form in Hebrew literature. Similar notices exist regarding Samuel (1 Sam. 7.15-17; 8.1-3; 25.1a), Abraham (Gen. 25.7-10), Isaac (Gen. 35.29), Jacob (Gen. 49.33), each of whom 'breathed his last' and 'was gathered to his people'; also Joseph (Gen. 50.26; Josh. 24.32), Sarah (Gen. 23.1-

2), Rachel (Gen. 35.19), and Joshua (Josh. 24.29-30). Of all of these death notices, those of Joshua and Samuel are most like that of Eleazar: in each case, only a statement of death, and the location of the grave site are given, with a third bit of information. In the case of Eleazar, the third entry is merely a qualification of the grave site: 'the hill of Phineas his son, *which had been given to him in the hill country of Ephraim*'. Since Eleazar's death notice is formally similar to other such notices in Hebrew tradition, and since its location in Ephraim is inconsistent with the later traditions linking the Zadokites of Jerusalem to this Eleazar, Josh. 24.33 should be taken as preserving authentic traditions regarding the Aaronite origins of these two priestly figures.

Two other instances exist in which one finds Phineas, the son of Eleazar, the son of Aaron the priest, taking a central place in hexateuchal tradition: Num. 25.6-13, and Num. 31.1-12. The priestly provenance of each passage is uncontested. In the first, Phineas slays an Israelite and his Midianite wife during the events surrounding Ba'al-Pe'or, an act which stays Yahweh's wrath and prevents the slaughter of more Israelites by the divinely sent plague. As a reward for his zeal, Phineas is then promised an eternal priesthood (cf. Ps. 106.28-31). Num. 31.1-12 is related to this incident, but has to do with the war of vengeance subsequently carried out by Israel against Midian, allegedly for the Midianites' complicity in the seduction of the Israelites 'in the matter of Pe'or' (Num. 31.16).[50]

These priestly texts regarding Phineas the son of Eleazar suggest two conclusions. First, Phineas, the son of Eleazar, the son of Aaron, was an important figure in the priestly lore. He was associated with the wilderness tent shrine (Num. 25.6), and with the holy war carried out against the Midianites (Num. 31.1-12). Second, this Phineas must at one time have played a far greater role in both priestly and popular tradition, since he is promised an *eternal priesthood*, and since the burial site of Eleazar is identified by reference to this, his son Phineas (Josh. 24.33).

This evidence provided by Num. 25.6-13; 31.1-12; Josh. 24.33 has important implications for understanding the role of Phineas in Josh. 22.9-34. To begin, Phineas appears in this pericope in much the same role as he does in the two passages in Numbers: he is a priest, the son of Eleazar, and as such ministers before the tent shrine (Josh. 22.19, 29) in connection with an incident which at least threatens holy war.

Thus, Phineas the son of Eleazar in Josh. 22.9-34 is the same traditional figure as he is in the book of Numbers. Both Num. 25.6-13 and Josh. 22.9-34, in fact, seem to reflect a cycle of independent traditions focusing upon Phineas, the son of Eleazar, which dealt with his exploits in preserving the purity of the Yahwistic cultus. In fact, this figure of Phineas seems eventually to have served as the unspoken foil for the godless sons of Eli, Hophni and Phineas, on whose account Yahweh destroyed the line of the Shilonite priests in 1 Samuel 2-4.[51] Thus, alongside the anomalous pairing of Reubenites with the Gadites and the aetiology of the altar of 'witness', the tradition of Phineas ministering before Yahweh's tabernacle at Shiloh constitutes the third major piece of evidence that Josh. 22.9-34 contains an archaic tradition, or several archaic traditional fragments, which deal with a confrontation of the tribes west of the Jordan with the Reubenites and Gadites over an heretical altar.

On the other hand, evidence that these earlier traditions have been brought together in a later redaction is provided by several links between Josh. 22.9-34 and the preceding narratives of the Hexateuch. First, Josh 22.17 explicitly ties this passage to Num. 25.1-13 and the matter of Ba'al-Pe'or. Second, Josh, 22.20 recalls Achan's theft of the devoted things, and his subsequent punishment in Joshua 7. Third, the erection of the wilderness tent shrine at Shiloh (Josh. 18.1) and the conclusion to the division of the land (Josh. 19.51; 21) is here assumed. These assumptions, and the fact that these events belong to the narrative historical framework of P, indicate that Josh. 22.9-34 in its present literary form belongs to this stratum of P as well.

Nevertheless, the priestly historical narrative in Josh. 22.9-34 (as well as the priestly *Grundlage* of Josh. 22.1-8) preserves elements of older traditions which have been incorporated into P's overall history. These elements include the priesthood of Phineas at the tent shrine, the *two* tribes in Transjordan, and the aetiology of the altar of 'witness', which assumes *two* rather than two and-a-half Transjordanian tribes. In Josh. 22.9-34, then, the evidence is not for the archaizing of a later *Tendenz*, but rather, for the inclusion of older traditions in a later literary form. That several old traditions have been brought together under the rubric of P's extended historical framework in Joshua 22 argues that the priestly stratum of the Hexateuch, whatever the date of its final literary form, preserves much ancient, and possibly authentic, material.

4.3 *Conclusion:*
The Place of Shiloh in Joshua 22 and the Priestly History

The first question with regard to Joshua 22, however, is not whether or not P's account of these events is authentic, but what role Shiloh plays in the passage, and thence, in the overall priestly narrative. In this regard it is significant that while Shiloh is not the central focus of this passage, Shiloh is directly connected to P's dominant concern for the exclusive sanctity of the *miškan-Yhwh* and the altar standing before it which the Israelites erected in the Promised Land at Shiloh. This concern is consistent with Leviticus 17, where the *'ōhel-mô'ēd* and the altar at its entrance constitute the sole permissible place of sacrifice for the Israelites. Transgression of this exclusivity, moreover, is the source of potential harm to the whole community, as the references to the matter of Pe'or (v. 17) and to the fate of Achan (v. 20) make clear. Joshua 22 does not ascribe this exclusive status to Shiloh per se, however, but this status accrues to Shiloh as a direct result of the establishment of the wilderness cultus there. Thus, Shiloh, for P, becomes the geographic focus for the legitimate worship of Yahweh in the Promised Land, because it is the site of the tent shrine and altar.[52]

In the broader context of the priestly recension of Joshua 13-22, Joshua 22 serves as the final cultic injunction to the Israelites settling Palestine. The erection of the wilderness cultus and the distribution of the tribal inheritances, which comprise the third great moment in the priestly history, do not end the priestly narrative. Instead, the priestly history concludes with the retelling of older traditions for the purpose of levelling sanctions against violations of the wilderness cultus established in the Promised Land. For P, then, the legitimate cultus in the Promised Land centered on the tent and the altar which stood before the tent, both of which were located at Shiloh. Moreover, since no provision is made for the transfer of status *from* the wilderness cultus to another form of cultus (e.g. a temple), and since there is no anticipation of a succession of the legitimate cultus from Shiloh to Jerusalem, there is no legitimate basis for regarding Shiloh in P as a late fictional representation of the Jerusalem cult. In fact, the priestly narrative is concerned with Shiloh as the site of the wilderness cultus, and there is no evidence that anything else is intended.

Thus, P's account of the origins of Israel ends with the establishment of the legitimate institutions of the worship of Yahweh at Shiloh, and with the definition of the sole legitimate place of sacrifice in the Promised Land as the altar before Yahweh's tabernacle at Shiloh. Shiloh is, in fact, the focus of the priestly history's interest in the wilderness cultus in the Promised Land. While at least one other shrine is recognized in the priestly stratum of the Hexateuch, i.e. that at Bethel, the connection between Shiloh and the wilderness cultus in P is unique. This fact suggests that the priestly tradition recognized more than one shrine, but that Shiloh held a special status in that tradition, a status which was deliberately emphasized in the priestly recension of the Hexateuch.

Moreover, that the emphasis of the priestly history centered upon a place, Shiloh, and a shrine, the tent sanctuary, which in the Jerusalem tradition were regarded as having been rejected by Yahweh (see below, Chapter 6), provides strong evidence that the priestly tradition did not derive from Jerusalem. Indeed, P's hallowing of Shiloh, along with the heretical temple at Bethel (Gen. 35.9-15), both northern shrines, and the traditions linking the origins of the Aaronite priesthood, represented by Eleazar and Phineas, to Ephraim, suggest that the priestly traditions of the Hexateuch stem from northern Israel, and not from Judah and Jerusalem.

To sum up, Joshua 22 furnishes the final priestly word on the crucial theme of the legitimate Yahwistic cultus in Palestine. This cultus comprises the tent shrine and its altar established at Shiloh. The exclusive legitimacy of the wilderness cultus at Shiloh carried divine sanction, and any breach threatened the entire community. The priestly history, by this means, set the Shiloh sanctuary above all other sanctuaries in Palestine, and made no provision for change in this order, which it presented as an ideal, permanent institution.

Chapter 5

SHILOH IN THE BOOK OF JUDGES

5.1 *Introduction: Shiloh in Judges 17–21*

Shiloh does not appear in the book of Judges until chs. 17–21, in a section sometimes called the 'appendix' to the book of Judges. These chapters center on the theme of the arachic days before any king ruled in Israel, when 'every man did that which was right in his own eyes' (Judg. 17.5; 18.1; 19.1; 21.25). They depart from the framework established in Judg, 2.6-23, which is based on a succession of judge-deliverer stories. Judges 17–21 can be broken down into separate sections. Chapters 17–18 relate how one Micah erected a household shrine in the Ephraimite hill country, and how the Danites robbed him both of his cultic images and his levitical priest. Chapters 19–21 recount the tale of an intra-tribal war against the Benjaminites, which was occasioned by the murder-rape of the concubine of a Levite by the men of Gibeah.

Shiloh first emerges in these narratives in Judg. 18.31, where it receives incidental mention in connection with the cult at Dan. A second incidental reference to Shiloh is found in Judg. 21.12, where Shiloh appears as the site of the war-camp at the end of the Benjaminite war (Judg. 20.1-21.15). Only in Judg. 21.16-24 does Shiloh become the focus of the narrative, There, the Benjaminites raid Shiloh during the annual 'feast of Yahweh' and carry off the dancing maidens for wives. Thus, the references to Shiloh in Judges form no consistent picture of Shiloh's role in the period before the rise of the Israelite monarchy. Difficult, isolated notes, such as Judg. 18.31 and 21.12, combine with the intriguing tale in Judg. 21.16-24 to pose additional problems for understanding the role of the Shilonite cult in pre-monarchic Israel.

5.2 *Judg. 18.30, 31: the House of God at Shiloh*

The first reference to Shiloh which confronts the reader of the book
of Judges occurs in Judg. 18.30-31:

> (30) And the sons of Dan erected for themselves the graven
>   image,
>   And Jonathan, the son of Gershom, the son of Moses,
>   He and his sons were priests to the tribe of the Danites
>   Until the day of the captivity of the land.
>
> (31) And they set up for themselves the graven image of Micah,
>   Which he had made,
>   All the days that the house of God was in Shiloh.

These verses form the conclusion to the story of Micah's shrine in
Judges 17-18 from which the Danites robbed the cultic objects, and
whose priest, a Levite from Bethlehem, established the priesthood of
Dan (Judg. 18.30). Much debate has centered on these verses in
connection with the discussion of the nature and history of the
sanctuary at Shiloh.

First, whereas Shiloh is the site of the Mosaic tent shrine in Joshua
18-22, the first mention of Shiloh in the book of Judges is as the locus
of a *bêt-hā'ĕlōhîm* ('house of God', Judg. 18.31). Graf argued on the
basis of this verse that an actual temple, and not the Mosaic
tabernacle, had stood at Shiloh. Moreover, the phrase *kol-yĕmê
'ăšer hĕyôt bêt-hā'ĕlōhîm bĕšilōh* ('all the days that the house of God
was in Shiloh') stands in parallel with the preceding *'ad-yôm gĕlōt-
hā'āreṣ* ('until the day of the captivity of the land'). The juxtaposition
of these two expressions of time, 'the day of the captivity of the land',
and 'all the days that the house of God was in Shiloh', was taken by
Graf to mean that the sanctuary at Shiloh had continued in existence
'until the day of the captivity of the land', i.e. until the fall of the
northern kingdom to the Assyrians.[1] Graf's position was the first
major opposition voiced with respect to Ewald's theory that Shiloh
and its sanctuary had been destroyed as a result of the Philistine
victory at Aphek (1 Sam. 4). Nonetheless, the relationship between
v. 30 and v. 31 is a matter of dispute: while Graf had read these two
verses as mutually interpretative,[2] Budde saw them as the separate
conclusions to two independent sources.[3]

The historical referent of the *bêt-hā'ĕlōhîm bĕšilōh* in v. 31 has
been variously regarded as a temple[4] or a tent sanctuary.[5] That the

term *bayit* must always refer to a building is shown to be false by 2 Kgs 23.7, which reads:

wayyittōṣ 'et-battê haqqĕdēšîm
'ăšer bĕbêt Yhwh
'ăšer hannāšîm 'ōrĕgôt šām bāttîm lā'ăšērāh

And he tore down the houses of the male prostitutes
which were in the house of Yahweh,
where the women were weaving houses for Asherah.

This verse mentions woven 'houses' in a particular sacral context, and thus demonstrates the *bayit* could refer to something other than an actual building. This appelative *bêt-hā'ĕlōhîm* may have been applied similarly to all manner of sanctuaries, including the tent of meeting at Shiloh. Thus, one cannot rule out altogether the possibility that the *bêt-hā'ĕlōhîm* in Judg. 18.31 may refer to a tent shrine. On the other hand, if this were a reference to the wilderness tent, one would have expected one of the technical appelations, of this institution, *'ōhel-mô'ēd* or *miškan-Yhwh*, since these were its traditional designations (as is clear from Exod. 33.7-11 and Josh. 22.9-34). Even Ps. 78.60-72 refers to the *miškan-Šilô* and the *'ōhel-Yôsēp*, using at least devivatives of the technical priestly appelations. Thus, in the absence of more compelling evidence, *bêt-hā'ĕlōhîm* in v. 31 should be taken as implying its typical referent, a temple. The narratives in 1 Samuel 1-4, in fact, presuppose an actual temple at Shiloh, and probably this same sanctuary is referred to in Judg. 18.31. Thus, the *bêt-hā'ĕlōhîm* in Judg. 18.31 should be taken as referring not to the tent of meeting at Shiloh, but to a temple building which stood there.

The relationship between v. 30 and v. 31, however, is more problematic. On the one hand, vv. 30a, 31a form the kind of doublet used by nineteenth-century source critics to discern the presence of parallel sources. In this context, v. 30a appears to be the legitimate conclusion to the tradition of the Danite migration, and v. 31 the summation of the tradition of Micah's graven image. At the same time, the feature which most clearly distinguishes these verses is not their respective relationships to the foregoing traditions, but the nature of the time referents which they contain. Thus, vv. 30 and 31 may not represent parallel sources, but may instead introduce parallel, or even correlative, time references. Verse 31a may in fact be treated as a *Wiederaufnahme* of v. 30a, a stylistic device whereby the initial phrase of a parallel is taken up at the beginning of the second member of the parallel to introduce a new, albeit related, motif or, in this case, piece of information. If this is the case, vv. 30 and 31 are not the respective conclusions to separate sources, but parallel historical comments which carry the ramifications of the older traditions incorporated into the present text far beyond the historical scope of those traditions. Indeed, the phrases 'until the day of the captivity of the land' and 'all the days that the house of God was in Shiloh' are astonishingly perspicacious historical referents, betraying a broad, schematic perspective which demarcates Israelite history using two key referents: a definitive national event—'the day of the captivity of the land', i.e. the fall of the northern kingdom on 722/721 BCE—and an extended period of national significance—'all the days that the house of God was in Shiloh'. This expansive frame of reference is unusual, and suggests that Judg. 18.30 and 31 do not coincidentally derive from two separate sources or traditions which have been woven together in Judges 17–18. A better explanation for this parallelism would be that these notices are the work of a single redactor/historian whose concern was to provide, at a much later date, a broad historical scheme by which the events of Judges 17–18 might be correlated. It is therefore legitimate to conclude, as Graf did, that v. 31 is intrinsically dependent upon v. 30.[6] These two historical notices probably come from the same hand, and may not have been introduced until long after the traditions in Judges 17–18 had been combined into a single narrative. If this analysis is correct, the correlation of 'the day of the captivity of the land' (v. 30) with 'all the days that the house of God was in Shiloh' (v. 31) would imply that Shiloh had continued as an important sanctuary until the fall of Samaria.[7]

In conclusion, two important pieces of information regarding Shiloh can be gleaned from Judg. 18.30-31. First, whatever Shiloh's relationship to the wilderness tent shrine had been, the place was remembered at a much later period, after the fall of the northern kingdom, as the site of a temple. This information is confirmed in 1 Samuel 1–4. Second, this particular sanctuary—the Shilonite temple—remained in existence until the fall of the northern kingdom. Nothing in Judg. 18.30-31, in fact, supports the theory that Shiloh was destroyed and abandoned in the mid-eleventh century. Rather, a close analysis of these verses confirms Graf's original view that the Shilonite sanctuary continued in existence down to the fall of Samaria, at least according to the associations of the historian/redactor responsible for the insertion of vv. 30 and 31 into this text.

5.3 *Judges 20–21: Shiloh in the Account of the Benjaminite War*

After Judg. 18.30-31, Shiloh is not mentioned again until Judg. 21.12 and 16-24. The first of these references is to 'the camp at Shiloh, which is in the land of Canaan' (Judg. 21.12). This verse forms the conclusion to the account of the Benjaminite war and is notable because it is the only reference to Shiloh in this account; the sanctuaries upon which Judg. 20.1-21.15 otherwise focuses are Mizpah (20.1; 21.1, 8) and Bethel (20.18, 26; 21.2). In fact, the multitude of sanctuaries which emerges, quite unapologetically, in Judges. stands in contrast to the importance of Shiloh as the exclusive legitimate sanctuary of Yahweh following the conquest and settlement of the land in Joshua. In Judg. 18.30-31, the sanctuary at Shiloh is placed without apology alongside that at Dan, and in the story of the Benjaminite War (Judg. 20.1-21.15) Shiloh appears alongside the sanctuaries of Mizpah and Bethel, without any clear distinction in status. Moreover, Judg. 21.16-24 contains a tradition according to which the Benjaminites, on the advice of the 'the elders of the congregation' took the dancing maidens from the vineyards around Shiloh during 'the feast of Yahweh' and carried them off for wives.

The juxtaposition of Shiloh with Mizpah and Bethel in Judges 20–21 was especially important to de Wette's position that the period before the monarchy knew no central sanctuary, only a multitude of local shrines. Thus, 'the congregation assembled . . . to Yahweh at Mizpah' (Judg. 20.1), and the people 'had sworn at Mizpah' (Judg. 21.1a). Similarly, 'the people arose and went up to Bethel, and inquired of God' (Judg. 20.18). Again Judg. 20.26-28a reads:

> Then all the people of Israel, the whole army, went up and came to Bethel and wept; they sat there before Yahweh, and fasted that day until evening, and offered burnt offerings and peace offerings before Yahweh. And the people of Israel inquired of Yahweh, for the ark of the covenant of God was there in those days, and

> Phineas, the son of Eleazar, the son of Aaron, ministered before it
> in those days . . . .

In Judg. 21.2, the Israelites again 'came to Bethel, and sat there until evening before God'. The expression *lipnê Yhwh*, and its Elohistic counterpart, *lipnê hā'ĕlōhîm*, usually indicate the presence of a temple or cultic site.[8]

Despite the contrasting portrayals of Shiloh in Joshua and Judges, certain elements of the depiction of Shiloh in Judges 21 correspond to elements in the priestly stratum of Joshua. Thus, for example, *hammaḥăneh šilōh* ('the camp at Shiloh', Judg. 21.12) occurs only one other time in the Hebrew Bible, in Josh. 18.9. Similarly, *šilōh 'ăšer bĕ'ereṣ kĕna'an* ('Shiloh, which is in the land of Canaan', Judg. 21.12) is found only in Josh. 22.9, and in the related phrase *šilōh bĕ'ereṣ kĕna'an* ('Shiloh in the land of Canaan') in Josh. 21.2. Other elements of the narratives of Judg. 20.1–21.24 can only be described as priestly as well. *Wattiqqāhēl hē'ēdāh* . . . *'el-Yhwh hammiṣpah* ('and the congregation assembled . . . unto Yahweh at Mizpah', Judg. 20.1) recalls Josh. 18.1. Similarly, *ziqnê hā'ēdāh* ('the elders of the congregation', Judg. 21.16) are found otherwise only in Lev. 4.15, while the term *'ēdāh* ('congregation') is itself nearly always priestly. Surprisingly, the most clearly priestly expressions ('and the congregation assembled', 'the elders of the congregation') occur in passages in Judges which presuppose the existence of rightful sanctuaries other than that at Shiloh. It must be remembered in this connection that the priestly tradition of Genesis also hallowed Bethel (Gen. 35.9-15), the sanctuary present in Judg. 20.18, 26, 28; 21.2.[9] These common traditional elements could suggest that the priestly passages in Josh. 18.1-10; 19.51; 21.2; 22.9-34; Judg. 20.1–21.15 derive from a complex of traditions cast in language otherwise known from the priestly stratum of the Hexateuch. Indeed, phrases such as 'the camp at Shiloh' and 'Shiloh which is in the land of Canaan' could imply a common traditional background for all of these stories. The appearance of the same stereotypical phraseology in narratives of such diverse theological cast as the books of Joshua and Judges is best explained by assuming that the priestly materials of the Hexateuch represent a development on an older body of tradition which is in part preserved in Joshua 18–22 and Judg. 20.1–21.15. And while Shiloh played a key role in these traditions (cf. Josh. 18.1-10; 22.9-34), sanctuaries such as Bethel and Mizpah were hallowed as well.

This evidence supports observations already made in connection with the material in Joshua, namely, that P included a number of independent cultic traditions which presupposed a common socio-historical background. This common background included such ideas as the centralization of power in the hands of the 'elders of the congregation', Shiloh as the locus of the war-camp and the wilderness cultus, and the site of Shiloh as being in 'the land of Canaan'. Moreover, within this priestly tradition-complex, cultic centralization was sometimes attested, as in Josh. 22.9-34, and sometimes not, as in Judg. 20.1-21.15. Thus, in addition to the tradition of the exclusive legitimacy of the wilderness cultus, there was a further priestly tradition which hallowed not one but several Yahwistic sanctuaries: Shiloh, Bethel, and Mizpah. That Shiloh was hallowed above any other sanctuary in the final Priestly recension of the Hexateuch, however, attests the antiquity and persistence of the tradition of Shiloh's cultic pre-eminence in early Israel and may explain the bitter Jerusalemite invective against Shiloh in Ps. 78.60-72.[10]

Besides the differences in the views of cultic centralization within the priestly tradition, those traditions in the Hexateuch and their counterparts in Judges have been incorporated into two distinctive narrative frameworks. The ideological concern of P in the Hexateuch centers on the maintenance of the legitimate cultus, centered on the tent shrine and its altar. The final statement of this ideology is found in the prohibition of sacrifice at any altar save for the one before the tabernacle of Yahweh at Shiloh in Josh. 22.9-34. The priestly traditions of Judges 20–21, on the other hand, have been edited to conform to a different set of redactional goals: namely, the depiction of life before the monarchy as characterized by anarchy and senseless violence.

In point of fact, the traditional materials which belong to P in the Hexateuch, such as the traditions of Phineas, are not intrinsically different from those in Judges: they have only been edited to different ends. Many of the hexateuchal traditions of P represent independent cultic stories (cf. Gen. 35.9-15; Num. 25.6-15; Josh. 18.1-10; 22.9-34), just as do Judg. 20.1-21.15 and 21.16-24, at the same time holding much in comon. The stories relating specifically to Shiloh and its priesthood either associate Shiloh with the holy war traditions of the pre-monarchic period (Num. 25.6-15; Josh. 22.9-34; Judg. 21.12) or place it in a unique position vis-à-vis the wilderness cultus and the other sanctuaries of the land (Josh. 18.1-10; 22.9-34). The only exception to these categories is found in Judg. 21.16-24, which seems to preserve the tradition of Shiloh as a pre-Israelite shrine of Yahweh.

5.3.1 *Synopsis*

What these traditions have to say about the role of the Shiloh sanctuary in the early pre-monarchic period is, however, uncertain. It seems that Shiloh was remembered, at least in Judg. 21.16-24, as the site of a non-Israelite shrine. The radical nature of this claim in the face of orthodox tradition makes it likely that Judg. 21.16-24 actually preserves an historical memory of Shiloh before it had been incorporated into the territory of the Israelite tribes. At the same time, the emphasis on Shiloh's singular exclusivity in the hexateuchal framework of P does not impeach the historicity of that tradition. Inasmuch as the Jerusalem cultus assumed that Shiloh was, in a negative sense, heir to the wilderness cultus which Yahweh had rejected,[11] the priestly traditions in Josh. 18.1-10 and 22.9-34 would seem to pre-date the Jerusalem tradition, and may therefore preserve an authentic memory of Shiloh's origins as an Israelite sanctuary. This conclusion is supported by the traditional association of Shiloh with the wilderness tent shrine, the association of both with the Aaronite priesthood of Phineas, and of all three with the traditions of early tribal wars.

To sum up, the traditions in Judg. 20.1–21.15 make three principal contributions to our understanding the role of Shiloh in the early life of the Israelite tribes. First, they attest the existence of pre-monarchic, socio-historical order in which Shiloh was regarded as the locus of the war-camp in early tribal wars. Second, these traditions assume the existence of sacred shrines other than the one at Shiloh, namely, Bethel and Mizpah. Judg. 20.27-28 goes so far as to identify the Aaronite priesthood of Phineas with Bethel, a notable Aaronite shrine in any case. Third, the primacy in pre-monarchic Israel of the tribal council, where power centered on the elders of the congregation, as known from the Priestly stratum of the Hexateuch, is confirmed by the assumption of this order in Judges 20–21. Each of these contributions, in its own way, confirms the antiquity of the priestly traditions of the Hexateuch, especially the recognition of the shrines at Bethel, Mizpah, and Shiloh, all of which were anathema to the cultic community in Jerusalem in later Judean history.

5.4 *The Shilonite Cult in Judg. 21.16-24*

Perhaps the most intriguing of the traditions dealing with Shiloh in the book of Judges is that in Judg. 21.16-24. This pericope recounts how the Benjaminites, on the advice of the elders of the congregation, kidnapped for wives the dancing maidens from the vineyards of Shiloh at the yearly feast of Yahweh. According to Svend Holm-Nielsen,

> It is generally recognized that Judg. 21, as well as I Sam. 1-3, indirectly witness to a strong Cana'anite weft in the Shiloh cult. The young women dancing in the vineyards and the abduction of brides are well-known motives in the Cana'anite fertility cult ... One could also draw attention to Judg. 21.12 where the geographical setting '... Shiloh which is in the land of Cana'an' is peculiar. If a geographical definition was felt necessary one would have expected 'in the land of Ephraim' as opposite to Gilead. Judg. 21.19 gives an even stranger extremely accurate definition: '... Shiloh ... in a place which is on the north side of Bethel, on the east side of the highway that goes up from Bethel to Shechem, and on the south of Lebonah'. Both cases may be accidental and of no importance; but they may also originate from a time when Shiloh was still a Cana'anite town outside the proper Israelite boundaries, though culturally as well as religiously connected with Israelite tribes, especially Benjamin.[12]

Holm-Nielsen further suggests in a footnote that 'Shiloh could even have been the property of a Benjamin tribe which was highly influenced by Cana'anite culture and religion'.[13]

There may be some truth to the observation that the Shilonite cult had been influenced by non-Israelite ritual and practice. The Israelite cultus in general was highly influenced by the practices known elsewhere from Syria-Palestine, as has been demonstrated in the work of Dussaud.[14] The designation of Shiloh as being 'in the land of Canaan' might recall a time when Shiloh lay outside the direct control of the Israelite tribes. The use of the same terminology in Josh. 21.2 and 22.9 might imply a similar setting for these priestly traditions, as would the precise geographical description of Shiloh's location in Judg. 21.19. Of further importance in this respect is the fact that Shiloh is nowhere mentioned as having been destroyed or conquered. Thus, the traditions of the establishment Israelite sanctuary at Shiloh may reflect a relationship between the Israelite tribes in the central hill country, and a non-Israelite sanctuary at Shiloh.

The Israeli excavations at Tell Seilun indicate that Shiloh had been the site of a sanctuary from the Middle Bronze Age on.[15] The LBA site does not appear to have contained anything more than

> an isolated cultic place to which offerings were brought by people from various places in the region. The fact that there were very few permanent Late Bronze sites anywhere in the vicinity of Shiloh may indicate that many of these people lived in pastoral groups, in temporary dwellings.[16]

One can thus infer from both archaeological and written evidence that Seilun during the Middle and Late Bronze Age had been the sanctuary of non-Israelite origin which is depicted in Judg. 21.16-24, from which the Benjaminites had kidnapped non-Israelite maidens for wives. That the kidnapped women were non-Israelite is indicated by the fact that they were considered fair game for the Benjaminites, even though all Israel had sworn not to give their daughters in marriage to Benjamin.

The present text assumes, however, that the maidens actually had been Israelite. The plea, 'Grant them graciously to us, for we did not take each man his wife in battle, for you did not give them to us, *because then you would be guilty*' implies that the Shilonites had participated in the covenant against Benjamin. Nevertheless, this text may have been edited to fit its own context, according to which Shiloh was an *Israelite* shrine. That an older tradition depicting Shiloh as a non-Israelite entity lies behind the present story, however, is suggested by the strong parallel between this story and the Roman tale of the 'Rape of the Sabine Women'.[17] If one accepts that these two stories share a common motif, namely, one group's taking of wives by force from an ethnically different group at a public festival, one can postulate that the tradition in Judg. 21.16-24 originally dealt with a Benjaminite *Weibenraub* carried out at a non-Israelite festival of Yahweh at Shiloh.

If it is impossible to judge the historicity of this particular tradition, it is nonetheless significant that behind the present text of

Judg. 21.16-24 lies the now muted tradition of Shiloh as a Yahwistic shrine beyond the control of the Israelite tribes. The profound difference between this tradition and that of the special cultic status ascribed elsewhere to Shiloh (cf. Josh. 18.1-10; 19.51; 21.1-2; 22.9-34; Judg. 21.12) offers strong evidence that Judg. 21.16-24 preserves the actual memory of a time when Shiloh stood as a Yahwistic holy place outside the territory occupied by the Israelites.

This tradition subsequently was recast to conform to the controlling motif of Judges 17–21, which is expressed via the repeated notation, 'In those days, there was no king in Israel; every man did what was right in his own eyes' (Judg. 17.6; 18.1; 19.1; 21.25). The kidnapping of the dancing girls at the behest of the 'elders of the congregation' in this context serves to pillory the old pre-monarchic order with its tribal and cultic, rather than royal leadership. In this present account, the elders' advice to the Benjaminites is the supreme act of moral cynicism, since the raid is directed against maidens at the chief Israelite sanctuary. The juxtaposition of the rape of the Shilonite and Gileadite maidens with the rape of the concubine at Gibeah (on which account the tribes had made war on the Benjaminites in the first place!), climaxes the perversity of the tribal conduct under the pre-monarchic order. The *Weibenraub* at Shiloh thus serves as a prime example, and the final atrocity, in the depiction of the anarchy among the tribes 'before any king ruled in Israel'.

5.5 Conclusion

The adaptation of the traditions in Judges 17–21 to the overriding motif of pre-monarchic anarchy has been carried out in an extremely subtle fashion, so that tradition and redaction are not always easily separated. Nevertheless, a picture of pre-monarchic institutions can be gleaned from these chapters. The Israelite institutions of this era include the various sacral points of assembly (Bethel, Mizpah, Shiloh), the location of the war-camp at Shiloh and of Shiloh 'in the land of Canaan', and the central role played by the tribal council and the elders of the congregation. The society thus depicted is so different from that which existed during the monarchy, and so contrary to the later (and especially deuteronomistic) view of the ideal order, that its basic features should be taken as historical. At the very least, the redactor and his audience associated certain institutional realities, known also from the Priestly stratum of the Hexateuch, with the pre-monarchic order, and regarded these as having been rightly supplanted by the monarchy.

The connections between Judges 19–21 and the priestly strata of the Hexateuch, especially in the form of traditional elements such as 'the camp at Shiloh', 'Shiloh in the land of Canaan', and the 'elders of the congregation' to name a few, further confirm the importance of Shiloh and its sanctuary in the priestly tradition. Similarly, the traditional figures associated with Shiloh in Joshua 18–22, i.e. Eleazar, Phineas and Joshua, are imbedded in the traditions of the early tribal wars (especially Phineas and Joshua), while Josh. 22.9-34 and Judges 19–21 deal with concerted actions by the *'ēdāh* against an offense by a member tribe. The insertion of Phineas into the account of the Benjaminite war in Judg. 20.27-28 attests to the persistence of the figure of Phineas in Israelite lore. Many of the traditional elements of this narrative further link Shiloh to the period of the tribal confederacy, and to the holy wars waged against both those outside Israel as well as those Israelite tribes which had committed some cultic offense. It is crucial that the argument for the superiority of the monarchical order in the present narrative framework actually presupposes that cultic warfare as depicted in Judges 20–21— governed by elders and sanctioned by priest—was part of a failed archaic order which had been happily superseded by the institution of kingship. That someone in the monarchical period could thus argue precludes the conclusion that the tribal warfare in Judges 20–21 (which is not unlike that in Josh. 22.9-34, nor even Num. 25.6-13; 31.1-12) was the invention of a later age.

Consequently, the priestly traditions pertaining to Shiloh in the book of Judges, whatever their ultimate date of compostion, preserve the memory of a pre-monarchic order. In this order, Shiloh was the site of the war-camp and played a role in the cultic wars waged by the Israelite tribes. At the same time, Judg. 21.16-24 preserves the still older memory of Shiloh as a Yahwistic shrine outside the tribal territory of Israel.

Chapter 6

SHILOH IN THE BOOKS OF SAMUEL

6.1 *Introduction*

The materials in 1 Samuel which directly relate to Shiloh are limited to the narratives of 1 Samuel 1–4 and to brief references in 1 Samuel 14. 1 Samuel 1–4 narrates the birth of Samuel, his dedication to Yahweh before Eli, the head of the priestly family at Shiloh, his growth to full stature as a prophet of Yahweh at Shiloh (in contrast to the corrupt Elide priests), and, finally, the extermination of the Shilonite priests and the loss of the ark to the Philistines in battle. In 1 Samuel 14, the priest with Saul, Ahijah, is tied to the family of Eli, 'the priest of Yahweh at Shiloh'. In addition to these direct references to Shiloh, however, a wide range of material in both 1 and 2 Samuel as well as 1 Kings must be considered, generally in connection with the priesthood of Shiloh and its descendants.

Within the greater compass of the Shiloh traditions in the Old Testament, those in the books of Samuel have been considered the most reliable source of information. The narratives of 1 and 2 Samuel appear at first glance to offer a straightforward historical account of the last days of the house of Eli at Shiloh, the loss and exile of the ark until the time of David, the continuation of the house of Eli through the line of Ahimelech the son of Ahitub at Nob, and the final demise of the Elide line when Solomon expels Abiathar the priest from the court in Jerusalem.

Nevertheless, closer study of this material reveals several disturbing contradictions. To begin, the story of the exile of the ark between the beginning of Samuel's tenure and the elevation of David to the throne in Jerusalem is belied by the plain statement in 1 Sam. 14.18 that the ark was in the camp of Saul during that monarch's Philistine campaigns. Moreover, the apparent re-emergence of descendants of Eli in the priestly house of Nob after the debacle at Aphek goes

wholly without explanation, although one is given the impression
that the priestly office of the Elides was terminated in 1 Samuel 4.
Finally, the story of Samuel's birth and his dedication to cultic
service under the priests of Shiloh is built around the verbal root
šā'al, which would seem to refer to the name of Saul, rather than
Samuel. These problems with the depiction of Shiloh and its
priesthood in the Samuel narratives are not easily resolved and call
into question the historicity of the story of Samuel at Shiloh.

In addition to these difficulties, several other issues regarding
Shiloh's place in Israelite life are raised by the Samuel narratives.
The first of these has to do with the nature of the cultus at Shiloh:
i.e., was there a tent shrine, a temple, or possibly both located at the
site? 1 Samuel 1–4 assumes the presence of a Yahwistic temple at
Shiloh (1 Sam. 1.9, 25, 3.3, 15), while 1 Sam. 2.22 mentions the tent
of meeting. Another difficulty which has already been touched upon
has to do with the origin of the Shilonite priesthood, and the
relationship of this priesthood to other priestly families, such as that
of Ahimelech, the son of Ahitub, at Nob, and that of the Davidic
priest, Zadok. To sum up, many of the most pressing questions
regarding the place of Shiloh in Israelite history come to a head in
the narratives of 1 and 2 Samuel.

6.2 *The Sanctuary at Shiloh*

The first issue to be examined with regard to Shiloh in 1 Samuel has
to do with the nature of the Shilonite sanctuary. 1 Samuel 1–3 clearly
presupposes that a *hêkāl*, or temple, was the central structure of the
cultus at Shiloh (1 Sam. 1.9; 3.3). The use of *bêt-Yhwh* (1 Sam. 1.24;
3.15) in the same context as *hêkal-Yhwh* indicates that this second
term likewise refers to an actual building. Consequently, these
references to Shiloh as the site of a Yahwistic temple (1 Sam. 1.9, 25;
3.3, 15) have been taken as proof that the tent shrine at Shiloh was
merely a fictional construction meant to lend credibility to the
(fictitious) claim that the sacral tent of the wilderness period had
actually existed.[1] Scholars of this persuasion have similarly dismissed
the mention of the tent of meeting (2.22b) as a late, post-exilic
addition, linking the crimes of Eli's sons to that in Num. 25.6-15.[2] If
any item associated with the wilderness cultus had been at Shiloh,
that item had been the ark (3.3; 4.3-5), from which alone Shiloh had

drawn its prestige.[3] Conversely, it has been argued, most recently by Haran,[4] that the references to the tent of meeting reflect the historical sanctuary at Shiloh, and that the assumption of a temple in 1 Samuel 1-3 derives from the influence of the Jerusalem temple upon the writer of these chapters.

The existence of a Shilonite temple, however, does not preclude the erection of the tent shrine at the same place, so that the tradition of the tent of meeting at Shiloh does not confute the presence of a temple there. In fact, there are two well-attested traditions regarding the sacral cult at Shiloh: one of the tent of meeting, the other of a temple. Thus, Ps. 78.60-72, which can be related to the events of 1 Samuel 4, identifies the shrine at Shiloh as a *miškān* and an *'ōhel*. 2 Sam. 7.6, using similar language, claims that Yahweh had never before dwelt in a house (*bayit*), but that he had always gone about *bě'ōhel ûběmiškān* ('in a tent and in a tabernacle/dwelling'). Consequently, the incidental assumption that a temple stood at Shiloh (1 Sam. 1-3) is balanced by the assumption elsewhere that a tent shrine stood there. The Mishnaic tradition that the structure at Shiloh consisted of stone walls with a tent roof is an apparent attempt to harmonize these two separate traditions,[5] just as were the nineteenth century interpretations of *bêt-hā'ĕlōhîm* and *hêkal-Yhwh* as referring to the tent of meeting.[6]

That Shiloh was a pre-Israelite cultic site has been shown both by the archaeological evidence and by the old tradition in Judg. 21.16-24. In addition, it is known that the building of temples was a feature of the settled, pre-Israelite culture of Palestine. Thus, it is possible, at least, that a temple building had stood at Shiloh since before the Israelites' settlement of central hill country. This possibility must be considered alongside the evidence in 1 Samuel 1-3 that Shiloh was remembered as the site of a temple. On the other hand, Shiloh was remembered as the site of a tent shrine not only in the priestly traditions of northern origin, but in the competing Jerusalemite tradition preserved in Ps. 78.60-72.[7] Tradition further claimed that the tent had been moved to Gibeon with the demise of the Elide priesthood, and its final resting place was supposedly the temple in Jerusalem (1 Kgs 8.4).[8] The traditional locus of the tent in all acounts, however, was Shiloh.

In conclusion, the incidental nature of the assumptions regarding the existence of both tent and temple at Shiloh make it likely that both of these traditions reflect historical realities.[9] The tent sanctuary is most clearly linked to the ancient era of holy wars and to the figures of Phineas and Joshua; the temple at Shiloh is associated with the house of Eli. Nevertheless, that the Elides were associated with the tent shrine, and that a temple was known also in the period of Israel's rise, cannot be ruled out entirely.[10]

6.3 *The Elide Priesthood at Shiloh*

According to the priestly traditions of Joshua, the priesthood of Shiloh was Aaronite from Shiloh's earliest days as an Israelite cultic center. Eleazar, the son of Aaron, cast lots with Joshua at Shiloh for the tribal inheritances after the erection of the tent of meeting there (Josh. 19.51; 21.1-2). Eleazar's son Phineas is found ministering before the altar of Yahweh, which stood before the tabernacle at Shiloh during the conflict with the tribes of Reuben and Gad over the erection of a second altar in the region of the Jordan (Josh. 22.2-34).

In the biblical sequence, the death notice of Eleazar in Josh. 24.33 is the last mention of the priesthood at Shiloh until 1 Samuel 1-4. There 1 Sam. 1.3 introduces the priesthood of Eli and his sons as follows, giving no genealogical background:

> Now this man [Elkanah] used to go up year by year from his city to worship and sacrifice to Yahweh *Ṣĕbā'ôth* at Shiloh, where the two sons of Eli, Hophni and Phineas, were priests of Yahweh.

The next piece of information on the Elides comes from the story of the naming of the son of Phineas, Ichabod, upon Phineas' death in 1 Sam. 4.19-22. Through this Ichabod, 1 Sam. 14.3 ties the line of Eli to the priestly house of Nob, whose head, Ahimelech, the son of Ahitub, does not appear in the narrative until 1 Samuel 21-22. The link between the house of Eli and the priestly house of Nob is made in 1 Kgs 2.27, which attributes the expulsion of Abiathar from Solomon's court to the prophecy against Eli and his sons in 1 Sam. 2.27-36. Subsequent references confuse this genealogical picture. Thus, 2 Sam. 8.17 makes Ahimelech the son of Abiathar, in contradiction to 1 Samuel 22, where Abiathar is clearly the son of Ahimelech. Indeed, the priest Zadok in the same verse is made out to be the son of Ahitub, originally the father of Ahimelech and the grandfather of Abiathar. The Chronicles carry on the genealogical tradition of 2 Sam. 8.17, making Ahimelech the son of Abiathar (1 Chron. 18.16; 24.6). It is important to note also that the Chronicles struck the Elides from the priestly tradition altogether, making Ahimelech, the son of Abiathar, the direct descendant of Ithamar, the son of Aaron, and Zadok the descendant of Eleazar (1 Chron. 24.2-3).

The excision of the Elides from the Aaronite genealogies in Chronicles probably was the result of the tradition in 1 Sam. 2.12-17, 22-25, which depicts the sons of Eli as abusing their priestly prerogatives and lying with the women who served at the entrance to the tent of meeting. Indeed, 1 Sam. 2.27-36 prophesies the obliteration of Eli's priestly house and the election of a new 'faithful priest' instead. 1 Sam. 3.11-14 expands upon this prophecy and puts it in the mouth of the boy Samuel. In apparent fulfillment of these oracles, the Philistines capture the ark in battle and slay the two sons of Eli (1 Sam. 4). At the same time, the priestly line of Nob has been related to that of Eli (1 Sam. 14.3) and the curse upon Eli and his sons carried down to Abiathar (1 Kgs 2.27). In sum, both the genealogical and traditional material present a confused picture of the origins and end of the priestly line of Shiloh.

The standard solution was proposed by Wellhausen and Reuss and has been followed more recently by Cross. Despite the connection between the house of Eli and the Aaronite line of Eleazar and Phineas, which is suggested by the recurrence of the name Phineas in both families,[11] these scholars have argued that the Elide priesthood at Shiloh was Mosaic.[12] Key elements of this formulation are the claim that Eliezer, the son of Moses, in Exod. 18.4, is the same person as Eleazar, the son of Aaron, and indeed, that Eleazar only secondarily has been tied to Aaron a double for Moses, the true founder of the cult. This Aaron actually was the fictional ancestor of the Zadokite priests in Jerusalem, who thereby sought to displace the older levitical priesthood, which had traced its descent from Moses.

Nonetheless, important objections to this position have been raised. First, as Baudissin noted, it is absurd to think that the Zadokites, whose pedigree was doubtful, would have been able to overcome this deficiency by the invention of a heretofore unknown brother of Moses, i.e. Aaron, from whom they could then trace the (theoretically) Mosaic line of Eleazar, which had held a recognized public status for centuries.[13] Although Cross does not treat Aaron as a late, fictional creation, his identification of the Zadokites with Aaron is difficult to reconcile with the deep-seated animosity between the priests of Jerusalem and those of Bethel, who were certainly Aaronite. The identification of Aaron with the Zadokites is also a problem for Wellhausen as well, for how is one to believe that the Zadokites would have created a fictional founder of their house, only to identify him with the heretical shrine at Bethel and allow him to bear the blame for the odious calf-worship?

Conversely, Baudissin made a strong case for the Aaronite origins of Shiloh's Eldie priesthood, as well as for the secondary connection between the upstart Zadokites and Aaron.[14] Moreover, even though Reuss correctly recognized that there is no genealogy tying Eli to Aaron,[15] this fact most probably derives from the deliberate purging of Eli's name from the later genealogies, as is clear from the Chronicler's omission of Eli even from the genealogy of Abiathar (1 Chron. 24.3, 6), whom 1 Kgs 2.27 links to the priesthood of Shiloh.

In point of fact, the line of Eli was linked to that of Aaron through the occurrence of the name Phineas for the illustrious son of Eleazar, the son of Aaron, as well as for Phineas, the corrupt son of Eli. The depiction of Eli's corrupt sons in 1 Samuel 2–4 appears to have been written against the backdrop of the earlier traditions of Phineas, the son of Eleazar, a zealous and militant priest in the early traditions of Israel's holy wars (Num. 25.6-13; Josh. 22.9-34; cf. Judg. 20.27-28). Indeed, the tale of the corruption of the sons of Eli, one of whom is named Phineas, seems to be a deliberate reversal of the older tradition of the son of Eleazar by the same name, whose zeal for Yahweh turned back the divine wrath from Israel at Ba'al-Pe'or (Num. 25.6-13). The controversial note in 1 Sam. 2.22b, that the sons of Eli 'lay with the women who served at the door of the tent meeting', whether original to the narrative or not, merely makes explicit the already implicit relationship of Eli's sons to the traditions of Phineas, the son of Eleazar. Therefore, the tradition of Eli's corrupt sons, Hophni and Phineas, presupposes the Aaronite descent of Eli as a rejected line of descent, to be replaced by a wholly new line, that of the sons of Zadok.

At one time the Elide traditions in 1 Samuel 1–4 may even have formed part of a greater cycle of Aaronite traditions which could have included those in Numbers 25; 31; Josh. 22.9-34; 24.33; Judg. 20.1-21.15, as well as many stories which are no longer extant. Such a postulate would explain the notable lack of any formal introduction to Eli and his sons in 1 Samuel 1 as well as the interesting identification of Eleazar's burial site by reference to his son Phineas.[16]

The traditional connnections between the Elide traditions in 1 Samuel and the Aaronite traditions in the Hexateuch form a crucial link between the house of Eli and the priestly line of Aaron. In fact, since a genealogy is never given for Eli, any attempt to reconstruct it must rely on the various incidental notations in the Hexateuch concerning the origins of the priesthood of Phineas, the son of Eleazar. This Phineas, because of the recurrence of his unusual name in the house of Eli, is the one probable ancestor of the priesthood of Shiloh. That the original Phineas was the son of Eleazar, the son of Aaron, and not the grandson of Moses, is indicated by his repeated designation as the son of Eleazar, the son of Aaron (Num. 25.7, 11; Judg. 20.28). Exod. 6.25 actually records the birth of Phineas to Eleazar, the son of Aaron the priest, by one of the daughters of Putiel, and the burial notice of Eleazar (Josh. 24.33) identifies this Phineas as the son of Eleazar, the son of Aaron.[17] This last reference is an important piece of evidence because it indicates that whether Eleazar was the son of Aaron or not he *was* remembered as such at his traditional burial site in the hill country of Ephraim. Conversely, Wellhausen's argument that Moses' son Eliezer was identical with Eleazar, the son of Aaron, is based upon the dubious assumption that where similar names occur the same person must be on hand. There is no evidence in support of this assumption, in the first place, and it condenses biblical traditions along rather arbitrary lines.[18]

Nor is Wellhausen's claim sound that Moses was the traditional *Urpriester* and founder of the Israelite priesthood. In fact, Moses is never depicted as priest, but as prophet and lawgiver; as such he is a transhistorical figure whose primary purpose is to commission Israel's fundamental institutions, including the priesthood. The basic task of the priesthood is to oversee and administer the technical order of the cult—the proper offering of sacrifice, and the correct observance of the prescribed rituals. Moses, however never performs these functions, which are instead relegated to Aaron and his sons. 1

Sam. 2.27-28, which Wellhausen took as referring to Moses, refers to
the election of the *Urpriester* during the Israelite captivity in Egypt,
'to go up to my altar, to burn incense, to wear an ephod before me'.
This text does not recall the traditional functions exercised by
Moses, but describes, rather, the archetypal activities of Aaron and
his sons (cf. Lev. 9.8-10.3). It is Aaron, in fact, who serves as the
traditional *Urpriester*: he understands the technical cultic matters of
the fashioning of images (Exod. 32.1-6) and the employment of
correct language. This traditional background probably lies behind
the designation, 'Aaron, the Levite' in Exod. 4.14, as well as of
Aaron's traditional place as Moses' speaker before the Egyptian court
in J (Exod. 4.10-17).[19]

On the other hand, Wellhausen is correct in arguing that Moses'
grandson, Jonathan ben Gershom, was the founder of the priestly
line at Dan: this tradition (Judg. 18.30) is so disturbing within the
tradition of the primacy of the Aaronite priesthood that it must be
taken as authentic. The Mosaic descent of the Danite priests,
however, lends credibility only to Wellhausen's portrayal of the
disparate priestly houses which at one time ministered at Israel's
various shrines; it shows nothing regarding the Mosaic heritage of
the priests of Shiloh.

Wellhausen's explanation of Aaron as the fictional ancestor of the
Zadokites is the final linchpin in his attempt to break the connection
between the Elides and the priestly line of Aaron. Nevertheless,
1 Samuel 2-4, which implicitly identifies the Elides with the priestly
line of Aaron, shows no evidence linking these Shilonite priests to the
Zadokites, nor anything which would link the Zadokites to the
Aaronites in contrast to the Elides. On the contrary, a demonstrable
connection between the cult in Jerusalem, administered by the
Zadokites, and the Aaronites, who were indisputably linked with
northern shrines, such as the heretical altar at Bethel, is non-
existent. That the founder of the priesthood identified with the
heretical shrine at Bethel should become a figure for the Zadokites of
Jerusalem, who were possibly even Jebusite in origin,[20] is unimaginable.
The dtr polemic against the sanctuary at Bethel with it priesthood
(1 Kgs 12.25-33; 13.1-10; 2 Kgs 23.15-20), which is also Jerusalemite,
furnishes proof enough that the Zadokites and Aaronites were two
different, even opposing groups. Especially striking in this regard is
the ascription to Aaron of the same sin and words for which
Jeroboam the son of Nebat is condemned:

1 Kgs 12.28b:	hinnēh 'ĕlōhêkā Yiśrā'ēl
Exod. 32.4b:	'ēlleh 'ĕlōhêkā Yiśrā'ēl
1 Kgs 12.28b:	'ăšer he'ĕlûkā mē'ereṣ miṣrayim
Exod. 32.4b:	'ăšer he'ĕlûkā mēēreṣ miṣrayim

This crucial passage in Kings could date from the period following Josiah's reform, but may be based on older sources as well. It is at any rate Jerusalemite in origin, and hence Zadokite in its sympathies, and its *Tendenz* is to condemn the Aaronite priesthood and their shrine. This anti-Aaronite polemic of Jerusalemite origin contrasts with the *priestly* tradition in Gen. 35.9-15, which actually hallows Bethel. This fact demonstrates that there was no serious historical link between the Zadokites in Jerusalem and Aaronites as late as the writing of the Deuteronomistic history. In the traditions of Jerusalem, the Aaronite priests were associated with the heretical cult at Bethel and were abhorred by the Zadokite priesthood. Even an exilic writer such as Ezekiel distinguished the Zadokites as a separate priestly group.[21] The connection between Zadok and Aaron was not drawn until the post-exilic period, when the Chronicler for the first time presented the Zadokites as Aaronites.[22]

The anti-Aaronite attitude of the priests the sons of Zadok, can be seen in the earliest traditions, in which the Zadokites seem to have sought to displace the Aaronites altogether. Thus, 1 Sam. 2.35-36, where the priestly line chosen in Egypt is to be replaced by 'a faithful priest'—*kōhēn ne'ĕmān*, probably refers to Zadok.[23] In this connection, Yahweh's choice of a priest who will 'do according to what is in my heart, and what is in my soul'—*ka'ăšer bilbābî ûbĕnapšî ya'ăšeh*— recalls 1 Sam. 13.14, where Yahweh rejects Saul in favor of 'a man according to his [Yahweh's] heart'—*'îš kilbābô*. The striking parallel between Yahweh's unnamed 'faithful priest' in 1 Sam. 2.35-36 and the characterization of David in 1 Sam. 13.14 suggests that the referent of 1 Sam. 2.35-36 was the Davidic and Solomonic priest, Zadok, whose line in Jerusalem displaced that of Abiathar of the priestly house of Ahimelech, the son of Ahitub, at Nob. The anti-Elide prophecy in 1 Sam. 2.27-36, however, probably originated as a judgment oracle against the Elides alone, and stopped at v. 34, as is suggested by the giving of the sign by which Eli would know that this judgment was about to be fulfilled. Verses 35-36 were then added by a later redactor/author so as make the prophecy point to a new priesthood, without pedigree, which would replace the corrupt

Elides. The Zadokite priesthood's claim to authority, then, like that of David rested on divine election rather than pedigree. Therefore, 1 Sam. 2.35-36 can only refer to the line of Zadok. This is the clear meaning of 1 Kgs 2.27, where the prophecy against Eli is made to fall upon Abiathar, the last descendant of the priests of Nob, in favor of Zadok.

The link between Eli and Abiathar, however, is another dubious aspect of the priestly genealogies in Samuel and Kings, although it has scarcely been questioned by previous scholars. The first indication that the Elides and the priests of Nob represented two independent priestly families is provided by the traditional treatment of the respective groups. Thus, Eli's sons, by despising the proper cultic order, bring disaster upon their whole line. It is even said that Eli did not restrain his sons, an accusation which makes him party to their sin. On the other hand, Ahimelech, the son of Ahitub, and his son Abiathar are portrayed only in a positive light, as supporters of David in his struggle against Saul. Indeed one would not know from the narratives which introduce Ahimelech and Abiathar that they were connected to the fallen Elides at all. Only the genealogy of Ahijah (1 Sam. 14.3) and the note in 1 Kgs 2.27 make this connection. Otherwise, one finds two separate priesthoods: that of Eli at Shiloh, which had an illustrious ancestor in Phineas, the son of Eleazar, the son of Aaron, the priest, but whose later representatives had taken on currupt ways; and that of Ahimelech, the son of Ahitub, at Nob, who had been loyal to David, and whose son spent a lifetime in service to the first Judean king.

The next piece of evidence to cast doubt upon the Elide descent of the priests of Nob is provided by the traditional designation of Ahimelech of Nob as 'the son of Ahitub', without further clarification of his pedigree (1 Sam. 22.9, 11, 12, 20). A connection with Shiloh is nowhere drawn. This is a crucial fact. As has been argued in the cases of Phineas and Eleazar above, the traditional designations of popular figures probably offer better evidence for reconstructing these priestly lines than do the artificial genealogies of Samuel and Chronicles.

Moreover, the genealogical material which has been preserved on Abiathar and Zadok is not reliable. Although 1 Sam. 2.35-36 assumes that Zadok was a man without pedigree,[24] Zadok appears in subsequent genealogies as the son of Ahitub, Abiathar's grandfather(!)

(2 Sam. 8.17; 1 Chron. 6.8, 12; 18.16). If this information were true, Zadok would theoretically have been a descendant of the priests of Shiloh as well. The connection of Zadok to Ahitub (if Ahitub really had been the line of Shiloh) would then have meant that the general curse on the descendants of Eli would have fallen upon Zadok's line, too. Moreover, such a connection, had it been known, would have undermined the Zadokite claim to represent a new, divinely chosen priestly house. Despite the traditional conflict between the Zadokite and Aaronite priests, however, the Chronicles make Zadok a descendant of the Aaronite forebear, Eleazar (1 Chron. 24.3) who was the father of Phineas, the probable *Urpriester* of the Elide line at Shiloh. The genealogical materials on Zadok in both Samuel and Chronicles thus contradict the very strong tradition that Zadok was the progenitor of a priestly line, elected by Yahweh to replace the traditional Aaronite priesthood of Shiloh (1 Sam. 2.27-36). The artificiality of the genealogies in Chronicles at this point is illustrated by the fact that the descendants of Ahimelech are made the offspring of the shadowy Ithamar the other surviving son of Aaron (1 Chron. 24.3: 'Ahimelech of the sons of Ithamar'), while Zadok is made a descendant of Aaron through Eleazar. This bifurcation of the Aaronic line to include Zadok is nonsensical, since Zadok, who is treated as the son of Ahitub, Ahimelech's father, is made a descendant of Eleazar, while Ahimelech, also a son of Ahitub, is traced to Ithamar.

The logical explanation for this confusion is that Zadok's connection to Aaron and Eleazar through Ahitub is an artificial device, fashioned at a late date to create a priestly descent where there was none. The descent of Ahimelech from Ithamar is a similar attempt to harmonize the rejection of Abiathar and the Elides with the succession of Eleazar to the priesthood over his brother Ithamar. The wholesale rewriting of the priestly genealogies in Chronicles, in deliberate contradiction to the older traditions and narratives in 1 Samuel, suggests that the Zadokite connection to Eleazar was the result of post-exilic editing. The link between Zadok and Ahitub, which overlooks the anti-Abiathar Tendenz of 1 Kgs 2.27 and plays upon the tradition of loyalty between the priests of Nob and David, resulted from later editing, when the Zadokites were given a traditional lineage.

In fact, there were probably two stages in the development of the

Zadokite pedigree. During the first stage, Zadok and his descendants sought to maintain their station by appeal to divine election, similar to the appeal made for David by his advocates. This was the position taken by the Zadokite priests throughout the monarchy and the exile. The second stage occurred during the post-exilic period: Ahitub was selected as Zadok's father, and made a descendant of the ancient Aaronite priest, Eleazar, probably on the strength of the tradition of the loyalty of Ahimelech, the son of Ahitub, to the cause of David (1 Sam. 22). The name of Zadok's father may indeed have been Ahitub, but this Ahitub has subsequently been identified with the Ahitub of Nob, if only implicitly.

In addition to altering their own genealogical heritage, the Zadokites made corresponding alterations in the relationship between the priests of Shiloh and the house of Ahitub at Nob. At first, the house at Zadok, on friendly terms with Abiathar of Nob, aspired merely to discredit and replace the priesthood of Eli and his sons at Shiloh. After the expulsion of Abiathar from the Solomonic court, however, it was convenient to tie Abiathar to the Elides (1 Sam. 14.3), and to let the curse upon Eli and his sons fall upon Abiathar. In view of this reasoning, the genealogy of Ahijah (1 Sam. 14.3) probably read, in its original form: 'Ahijah, the son of Phineas, the son of Eli, the priest of Yahweh at Shiloh'. This move was meant to strengthen the claims of the Zadokites to an exclusive election and to justify the exile of Abiathar.[25] Finally, during the post-exilic period, the Elides were excised from the Aaronite line altogether, and the genealogy known from Chronicles was formulated, making Zadok the descendant of Eleazar, and Abiathar the representative of the line of Ithamar.

6.3.1 *Summary*

To sum up, the genealogies of Zadok and Abiathar are suspect, and with them, the blood descent of Abiathar from Eli. In fact, in its present state, the biblical text cannot be relied upon for an accurate record of the priestly lines of Shiloh, Nob, and Jerusalem. These must be reconstructed rather, from the literary and traditional evidence otherwise available. Particularly with regard to the house of Eli and the house of Ahimelech the son of Ahitub, the considerably different treatments which these two priestly families receive in the narratives of 1 Samuel belie their genealogical relationship. The

Aaronite lineage of Zadok given in Samuel, Kings, and Chronicles likewise confounds the earlier traditions of Zadok, which depicted him as a new man, holding office, like David, by divine election alone. In place of the express genealogical relationships, the traditions of the Elides, the priests of Nob, and the Zadokites indicate that these families comprised three independent priestly houses. The Elides could trace their heritage to Israel's earliest days (cf. 1 Sam. 2.27-28) and were Aaronite in origin. Their most illustrious ancestor was Phineas, an important priest in the early tribal wars. Less can be gleaned from the traditions of the priests of Nob. Located in the vicinity of Jerusalem, the shrine of Nob was adminstered by Ahimelech, the son of Ahitub. Ahimelech and the rest of the priests were allegedly slain at Saul's behest, and only Abiathar escaped to minister under David. Zadok, who became priest under David, and who succeeded Abiathar under Solomon, laid claim to no traditional priestly line of Israel. Nor did he or his heirs seek such a pedigree, if the traditions are correct. This Zadok probably had been the priest of El-Elyon in Jerusalem, prior to David's rise, and his descendants maintained their independent status down into the post-exilic period. The pro-Zadokite recensions of the traditions of the Shilonite priesthood sought first to descredit the house of Eli, and later, through the artificial connection between Shiloh and Nob (1 Sam. 14.3), to discredit the house of Abiather as well. The pro-Zadokite *Tendenz* was originally coupled with an affirmation of the independent, non-Aaronite, indeed, *non-levitical* origins of the line of Zadok (1 Sam. 2.37-36; 1 Kgs 2.27). This situation persisted down to the time of the exile, and even later, when the Zadokites finally purged the line of Eli from the official Aaronite genealogies and replaced it with their own. The old traditions of Numbers, Joshua and 1 Samuel, however, correctly associate the priesthood of Phineas, the son of Eleazar, the son of Aaron, in the Ephraimite hill country (Josh. 24.33) with the line of Eli at Shiloh.

In the last analysis, the connection of Eli with the line of Aaron was not the result of post-exilic reconstruction. The post-exilic Jews, in fact, excised the house of Eli from the official line of Aaron. Only the link between Zadokites and the line of Aaron is demonstrably a product of the post-exilic community.

6.4 Samuel, Saul and Shiloh

6.4.1 Samuel and Saul in 1 Samuel 1-7

The princial issue in the narratives of 1 Samuel 1-7 is the relationship of Samuel to Shiloh and the priesthood of Eli. The dominant figure in these chapters is Samuel, whose character is developed against the backdrop of the corrupt sons of Eli. 1 Samuel 1 narrates the birth of Samuel to Hannah, wife of the Ephraimite Elkanah, a woman who up to that time had been barren. Out of her thankfulness for the birth of a male child, Hannah names the child Samuel (šĕmû'ēl), 'Because I asked him from Yahweh' (kîmēyhwh šĕ'iltîw 1 Sam. 1.20b), and dedicates him to Yahweh, saying, 'All the days which he lives, he is lent to Yahweh' (kol-hayyāmîm 'ăšer hāyāh hû' šā'ûl laYhwh, 1 Sam. 1.28b).[26] The motif of the one asked from Yahweh, and the one lent to him, continues in 1 Sam. 2.20, where Eli the priest blesses Elkanah with the words: 'May Yahweh establish for you seed from this woman in place of the loan (šĕ'ēlāh) which she lent (šĕ'al/hš'yl[h] to Yahweh'. The boy Samuel, dedicated to Yahweh by his mother, grows up under Eli's supervision at Shiloh (1 Sam. 2-3).

A second tradition is introduced into these narratives in 1 Sam. 2.12-17, 22-25, 27-36. There Eli's two sons, Hophni and Phineas, are found abusing the sacrificial ritual for their own gain. Although Eli remonstrates with his sons, they do not listen. Therefore, an anonymous 'man of God' is sent to pronounce judgement upon Eli and his house (1 Sam. 2.27-36). This judgment is reaffirmed when the word of Yahweh comes to Samuel in 1 Samuel 3. Then, in 1 Sam. 4.1, Samuel succeeds to prophetic office at Shiloh. The prophesied judgment upon Eli is fulfilled in 1 Samuel 4, where the ark is lost in battle to the Philistines and the sons of Eli slain. Eli himself, upon hearing the news of the disaster, falls over and breaks his neck. The story of the captivity of the ark among the Philistines and its miraculous deliverance from its captors follows in 1 Samuel 5-6. The conclusion of this section is the account of Samuel's deliverance of Israel from the Philistine oppression.

Evidence indicates, however, that the entire body of tradition in 1 Samuel 1-7 has been composed and edited into its present form to superimpose the figure of Samuel upon the pre-existing Elide and ark traditions, and to create of Samuel an ideal figure similar to Moses. The first indication that the authenticity of the account of Samuel's boyhood at Shiloh is doubtful comes from 1 Samuel 1-2. The traditions of Samuel's birth and dedication to the priests of Shiloh always have been problematic on account of the aetiology of Samuel's name, which uses the verb *šā'al*, 'to ask, to loan', as the incongruous explanation of the name *šĕmû'ēl* (Samuel). In fact, *šā'al* is used seven times in the account of Samuel's birth and childhood at Shiloh (1 Sam. 1.20b, 27 [2×], 28b [2×]; 2.20 [2×]). 1 Sam. 1.28b actually reads, *hû' šā'ûl laYhwh* ('he is [one] lent to Yahweh').[27] The aetiology thus suggests an original reference to Saul, not Samuel.

The chief obstacle to interpreting the story of Samuel's birth and dedication to the cultus at Shiloh as an originally Saulide tradition is that the names of Samuel's parents, Hannah and Elkanah, and not those of Saul, 'the son of Kish', are found in this story. One may easily surmount this difficulty, however, by positing not only the substitution of Samuel's name for Saul in v. 20, but also the replacement of the names of Saul's parents with those of Samuel's parents as well. This thesis is supported by the fact that the play upon the root of Saul's name is integral to the birth story, and would not have been easily expunged, whereas the names of the parents could be interchanged with little trouble. Thus, the introduction to the story in 1 Sam. 1.1-2 may also have supplanted an original Saulide introduction, while the home of Samuel has replaced that of Saul. McCarter has argued similarly (in agreement with Dus) that the birth story of Samuel has borrowed elements of an older tradition of the Nazirite origins of Saul's birth, and that the identification of Saul's father Kish may originally have stood at the beginning of the Nazirite birth narrative.[28]

At the same time, both Dus and McCarter have argued for the independence of the Shiloh and Eli elements of the story from the Saulide and Nazirite features. This position, however, seems rather arbitrary, as there is no exegetical reason for such a move. That Shiloh is a secondary element in the birth story in 1 Samuel 1 can be maintained only as long as the birth story is held to have referred to Samuel originally.[29] The same is not true, however, if 1 Samuel 1 at one time referred to Saul. Indeed, Saul's connection to Shiloh emerges in 1 Sam. 14.3, where the priest Ahijah, of the line of Shiloh, is found in camp with Saul, with an ephod. In 1 Sam. 14.18, the same priest inquires of *the ark* for Saul, without any hint that the ark had been lost to the Philistines (1 Sam. 4). Thus, 1 Sam. 14.3 and 18 link

Saul to both the Shilonite priesthood (v. 3) and the ark (v. 18), even though the narratives in 1 Samuel 4–7 indicate that by Saul's day, the priests of Shiloh had been long dead, and the ark in captivity under the Philistines. 1 Sam. 14.3 and 18 would therefore seem to preserve a tradition of a connection between Saul and Shiloh. Because of the discord between the presence of the ark in Saul's camp and the narrative sequence in 1 Samuel 4–7, one cannot lightly dispense with this evidence.[30]

Dus, however, claims that the priest and the sanctuary in 1 Samuel 1 were originally anonymous:

> At the time that Saul was born, Shiloh would already have lain in ruins: Saul was a contemporary of a great-great-grandson of the last priest of Shiloh (cf. 1 Sam. 14.3). Shiloh and Eli evidently were introduced into the story by the author of the 'youth-tradition' in 1 Samuel 1–3, for whom Shiloh as well as Eli were essential, from the beginning to the end of his account.[31]

Dus's argument rests upon two assumptions: that Shiloh was destroyed in the mid-eleventh century, and that the genealogy connecting the priests of Shiloh to those at Nob is accurate. The dubious reliability of the genealogy of Ahijah (1 Sam. 14.3) has been demonstrated above; the alleged destruction of Shiloh in the mid-eleventh century is hardly certain. For now it is necessary only to point out that no scholar has yet cited any convincing traditio-historical evidence that Shiloh and Eli are secondary to the text of 1 Samuel 1. Indeed, that the word play on *šā'al* is found in the mouth of Eli in 1 Sam. 2.20 suggests that the connection between Eli and Saul was original to the birth story.

Therefore, there is no compelling reason to excise Eli and Shiloh from the traditions in 1 Samuel 1–2. In all likelihood, the birth story in 1 Samuel 1 originally tied Saul to Eli and Shiloh, until the figure of Saul was displaced by that of Samuel. The writer who introduced Samuel into the story probably did so in order to break Saul's connection to Eli and Shiloh, and to replace it with the Samuel-Shiloh connection. This particular editorial activity aimed at discrediting Saul's ties to the prestigious northern shrine, and at establishing the legitimacy of the call of Samuel. This change was most likely the product of the pro-Davidic redaction evident in the anti-Elide passages mentioned above (e.g. 1 Sam. 2.27-36).

Therefore, the originality of Shiloh and Eli to the traditions of

1 Samuel 1-2 is not to be doubted, but rather, the connection of Samuel to both. As Noth correctly observed, Samuel was tied to Shiloh in order to bridge the gap between the pre-monarchical and monarchical orders.[32] Moreover, a deliberate foil has been created by the juxtaposition of the young, faithful Samuel, growing up before Yahweh, and the evil and corrupt sons of Eli.[33] While Dus has reckoned to the original Saulide tradition the statement in 1 Sam. 3.19, 'And Samuel [Saul] grew, and Yahweh was with him',[34] the other notations about Samuel's growth before Yahweh (1 Sam. 2.26; 3.1; 4.1) are secondary to the tradition, accenting the contrast between Eli's corrupt sons and the boy Samuel.

The motif of Samuel's dedication to Yahweh, begun in 1 Samuel 1, reaches its climax in 1 Sam. 3.19-4.1a. The ark Narrative in 4.1b-7.2 interrupts this theme, which only re-emerges in the story of Israel's deliverance from the Philistines under Samuel in 1 Sam. 7.3-14. While vv. 3-12 seem to reflect an older tradition of Samuel as a judge-delverer figure, the motif of Samuel's rise from temple servant to prophet of Yahweh at Shiloh culminates in 1 Sam. 7.13-14. The theme of Samuel as prophet differs both from that in 7.3-12, where Samuel is depicted as a deliverer figure, and that in 7.15-8.3, which assume that Samuel was a judge, according to the order found in the book of Judges. The real question, then, concerns the authenticity of these two respective treatments of Samuel.

In this regard, it seems that 1 Sam. 7.3-12 may be a story originally associated with Samuel the judge-deliverer. The account of Samuel's judgeship includes fairly precise information as to Samuel's sphere of activity, which accords with what is recorded elsewhere of Samuel's origins (1 Sam. 1.9; 2.11a; 25.1) and does not depend upon the figure of Samuel developed in 1 Samuel 1-3. Indeed, 1 Sam. 7.3-12 and 7.15-8.3 seem to comprise the only genuine Samuel traditions in 1 Samuel 1-7. The rest of the picture of Samuel in these chapters, from his birth and dedication to Yahweh at Shiloh to his emergence as a prophet, has built upon expropriated Saulide traditions. These the editors have expanded into a significant literary stratum making Samuel the dominant presence in Israel on the eve of Saul's monarchy. The figure of Samuel developed in this literary stratum plays the key role in the subsequent account of Yahweh's rejection of Saul and his election of David. Therefore, it is logical to conclude that this treatment of Samuel is the work of the Davidic editors of the traditions of David's rise, in whose interest it was to supplant the figure of Saul with that of Samuel.

The secondary nature of the motif of Samuel's growth to the stature of a prophet to 'all Israel' means that the prophecy against Eli attributed to Samuel (1 Sam. 3.11-14) is also secondary.[35] Indeed, this prophecy presupposes that in 2.27-36 when Yahweh says, 'On that day I will fulfill all that I have spoken concerning his house, from beginning to end'. Moreover, 1 Sam. 3.11-14 adds nothing to 2.27-36, but only stresses that Eli's punishment will be forever, and that neither sacrifice nor offering will expiate the iniquity of Eli's house. Samuel's prophecy against Eli, then, intensifies the judgment against Eli, just as the redactional motif of Samuel's growth to the status of prophet heightens the tension between the traditions of the fidelity of Samuel's family to Yahweh and those regarding the iniquity of the Elides.

Given the secondary nature of the figure of Samuel in 1 Samuel 1-3, the entire tradition of Samuel at Shiloh appears to have been theologically formulated rather than historically based. The actual traditional materials related to Samuel in 1 Samuel 1-2 belong to an original body of Saulide traditions and preserve a memory of Saul's close association with the Elide priesthood at Shiloh. There are, in fact, no reliable traditions which tie Samuel to Shiloh. Samuel is identified, rather, with the shrine at Mizpah (1 Sam. 7.5), as well as with those at Bethel and Gilgal (1 Sam. 7.16), while his home was at Ramah (1 Sam. 25.1). 1 Sam. 1.1, 19; 2.11, which assume that Samuel's parents came from Ramah, are based on traditional lore regarding Samuel, but have been secondarily inserted into their present context. Finally, the oldest traditions regarded Samuel as a judge (1 Sam. 7.15-8.3), a seer (1 Sam. 9-10), and a lawgiver (1 Sam. 11.25), and not as a prophet.[36]

6.4.2 *Conclusions*

In sum, 1 Samuel 1-4 includes three old traditions relating to the priests of Shiloh: the birth of Saul and his dedication to the sanctuary at Shiloh, perhaps as a Nazirite; the corruption of the sons of Eli, and the demise of the Shilonite priesthood and the loss of the ark to the Philistines. These traditions, in turn, have been overlaid with the motif of Samuel's birth to Hannah, his service under Eli, and his emergence as a prophet to all Israel (1 Sam. 3.19–4.1a), who led his people in their struggle against the Philistines (1 Sam. 7). Of these Samuel narratives, only 1 Sam. 7.3-13 actually has a basis in old tradition; the rest are part of a broader literary development of the figure of Samuel which sought to magnify Samuel's role in the foundation of the monarchy, and to minimize that of Saul, as well as Saul's connection to Shiloh.

The importance of Samuel to the cause of David in the subsequent narratives of David's rise led to Samuel's eventual displacement of Saul, and his succession to the authority of Shiloh in the current narratives. The elevation of Samuel to the stature formerly held by the priesthood of Shiloh made him the protagonist in the establishment of the monarchy. At the same time, the pro-Davidic redactors used Samuel to legitimize David's controversial claim to the throne first held by Saul. The aim of the present text, then, was to provide sacral legitimation for David's throne, while simultaneously wiping away Saul's traditional link to the pre-eminent shrine and priesthood in pre-monarchic Israel.

6.5 *The Capture and Exile of the Ark*

1 Samuel 4 reports a great Israelite disaster where the ark was lost to the Philistines, and the priests of Shiloh slain. This story fulfills the prophecy by the anonymous man of God against Eli and his house in 1 Sam. 2.27-36 and introduces the traditions of the ark's captivity (1 Sam. 5–7.2). These traditions relate the effects of the ark upon the Philistines, and its return from Philistine territory. A key verse in this complex is the historian's redactional conclusion in 1 Sam. 7.2: 'And it came to pass from the day that the ark dwelt in Kiriath-Jearim, that the days were many, and they were twenty years; and all the house of Israel lamented after Yahweh'. Furthermore, Samuel's story (1 Sam. 7.3-14) concludes with the statement:

> The Philistines were subdued and did not again enter the territory of Israel. And the hand of Yahweh was against the Philistines all the days of Samuel. The cities which the Philistines had taken from Israel were restored to Israel, from Ekron to Gath; and Israel rescued their territory from the hand of the Philistines. There was peace also between Israel and the Amorites (1 Sam. 7.13-14).

1 Samuel 4–7 thus depicts the ark as having been lost to the

Philis:ines under the Elides and concludes with the resurgence of
Israelite fortunes under Samuel. The related text in 2 Samuel 6
recounts the return of the ark to Jerusalem under David. According
to the present account, then, the ark could not have been in the
possession of the Israelites at any time during the reign of Saul.

Certain factors, however, cast doubt upon this order of events.
First, Samuel's expulsion of the Philistines stands in open contradiction
to the situation elsewhere in 1 and 2 Samuel. Yahweh describes Saul
to Samuel as the 'prince over my people Israel' (1 Sam. 9.16) and
says to him, 'He shall save my people from the hand of the
Philistines, for I have seen the affliction of my people, because their
cry has come to me'. This verse *assumes* that the Philistines
oppression continued down to the time of Saul, and that Saul was
Israel's true deliverer from the Philistines. Moreover, this assumption
knows nothing of the period of peace and freedom depicted in 7.13-
14. Indeed, a garrison of the Philistines is said to be in *Gibʿat-
hāʾēlōhîm* in 1 Sam. 10.5, where *Gibʿat-hāʾēlōhîm* must be in Israelite
territory, as the other geographical referents, Bethel, the tomb of
Rachel in Benjamin, and Gilgal, are in Benjamin. The only referent
which appears out of place is the 'oak of Tabor'. Again, Jonathan, the
son of Saul, is said to have defeated a garrison of the Philistines at
Gebaʿ (1 Sam. 13.30), probably identical with Gibeah.[37] Finally, 1
Sam. 13.19-23 describes a situation in which the Philistines have
effectively prohibited the Hebrews from working iron. Such circumstances could have been possible only at a time when the Israelites
were in forcible subjugation to the Philistines.

Therefore, the claims made in 1 Sam. 7.13-14 concerning the
results of Samuel's victory over the Philistines at Ebenezer are
fictional. They do no belong to the tradition of the victory at
Ebenezer itself, but to the redactional overlay, written to contrast the
ignominious end of the corrupt house of Eli with the glorious reign of
faith under Samuel, and to allow the figure of Samuel to overshadow
that of Saul. Thus, the claims made for Samuel in 1 Sam. 7.13-14
have no value for the reconstruction of the history of Samuel's
career, and derive from the same literary stratum which is responsible
for the idealization of Samuel elsewhere in 1 Samuel 1-7.

Just as the Philistine domination of Israel in 1 Samuel 9-13 casts
doubt upon the redactional notice in 1 Sam. 7.13-14, the Saulide
narrative in 1 Samuel 14 casts doubt upon the present order of events

which places the capture of the ark and the annihilation of the priests of Shiloh prior to the reign of Saul (1 Sam. 4). In fact, 1 Sam. 14.2-3 describes Saul as having with him 'about six hundred men, and Ahijah, the son of Ahitub, the brother of Ichabod, the son of Phineas, the son of Eli, the priest of Yahweh in Shiloh, bearing an ephod'. As has been shown above, this genealogy is the result of a pro-Zadokite *Tendenz* tying the Aaronite line of Eli to the independent line of Ahitub at Nob. In its original form, Ahijah's genealogy probably read, 'Ahijah, the son of Phineas, the son of Eli, the priest of Yahweh at Shiloh'. Moreover, 1 Sam. 14.3 betrays no knowledge of either the curse on Eli's line in 1 Sam. 2.27-36, or its fulfillment.[38] The Saulide narrative in 1 Sam. 14.18 increases the difficulty posed by 14.3: 'And Saul said to Ahijah, "Bring hither the ark of God". For the ark of God went at that time with the people of Israel'. This verse stands in direct conflict with the present scheme of 1 Samuel, in which the ark is captured long before Saul's acclamation as king (1 Sam. 11).

The usual solution to this difficulty is to prefer the reading of the LXX[BL] for v. 18, which reads *ephoud* instead of *'ărôn*.[39] Indeed, Saul's command to Ahijah, 'Withdraw your hand', might best be understood as referring to the pockets of the oracular ephod, in which the Urim and the Thummim were carried. The importance of the oracular ephod which stood in Nob, and which Abiathar carried to David (1 Sam. 23.6, 9; 30.7), may be connected to this text as well.

Nonetheless, the presence of the ark in Saul's camp in 1 Sam. 14.18 is introduced so incidentally, and with such plain innocence of the events of 1 Samuel 4, that it is unlikely that it is a secondary intrusion into the text. The explanatory phrase in 1 Sam. 14.18b— 'for the ark of God went at that time with the people of Israel'— knows nothing of the captivity of the ark in 1 Samuel 4-6,[40] and it is difficult to see why a later editor would have introduced so problematic a reading. Furthermore, since the ephod has already been introduced in 14.3,[41] it is logical to conclude that 14.18b was written specifically to account for the presence of the ark, which had not yet entered the narrative. The use of *ephoud* in the LXX[BL] of 14.18 (2×) represnts a harmonization of the original Hebrew text with the mention of Ahijah as 'bearing an ephod' (or 'wearing an ephod'?) in 14.3, with the traditions in 1 Samuel 21-22, where the sanctuary of Nob houses an ephod, and with Samuel 4-7. Although this harmonization may reflect an older Hebrew *Vorlage*, that *Vorlage* was not as old as the MT.

The presence of the ark in the camp of Saul has wide-ranging ramifications for the history of the Shilonite priesthood, for the ark, and for the Saulide monarchy. Most importantly, Saul is portrayed as conducting his monarchy with the support of the Shilonite priesthood. This connection between Saul and Shiloh in 1 Sam. 14.3, 18 is in accord with the older tradition of Saul's dedication to Yahweh before Eli at Shiloh in 1 Samuel 1–2. Taken together, the traditional association of Saul with the sanctuary and priesthood of Shiloh, and the tradition of Saul's carrying of the ark on his campaigns, suggest that the events of 1 Samuel 1–4 did not occur *before* Saul's rise, but during Saul's own career. If this conclusion is correct, the logical place to look for the battle in which the ark was lost is at the end of Saul's life, on Mt Gilboa. It is of interest in this context that the Philistines are said to have gathered at Aphek in both 1 Sam. 4.1 and 1 Sam. 29.1.[42] Both engagements resulted in sweeping defeats for the Israelites. Indeed, on the heels of Gilboa, Saul's scattered forces could only regroup in the Transjordan.

6.5.1 *Summary*

To sum up, the story of the loss of the ark and the slaughter of the priests of Shiloh in 1 Samuel 4 most likely does not relate to events prior to the reign of Saul, but to the decisive battle at the end of Saul's life. That is, the engagement in which the Philistines captured the ark was probably one and the same with Saul's defeat on Mt Gilboa. This reconstruction has the advantage of accounting for a number of significant discrepancies in the present narrative sequence of 1 Samuel. First, it explains the conflict between the literary development of the figure of Samuel in Samuel 1–7 and the incidental assumptions about the circumstances surrounding Saul's elevation to the kingship. Second, by tying the capture of the ark and the slaughter of the priests of Shiloh to Saul's last battle, one can explain the now muted associations of Saul with the priesthood and sanctuary of Shiloh as well as the ark (1 Sam. 1–2; 14), which are incongruous in the present narrative sequence. Finally, this theory places the development of the present narrative structure of 1 Samuel in the context of an identifiable editorial *Tendenz*: i.e. the needs of the Davidic editors of the Saulide traditions to separate Saul's monarchy from its very real association with the sanctuary at Shiloh, the ancient Aaronite priesthood of Eli, and the ark.[43]

6.6 *The Expropriation of the Sacral Traditions of Shiloh under David*

The rewriting of the history of the early monarchy to give it a pro-Davidic flavor was made necessary by David's status as a usurper of the legitimate throne. Although David probably had enjoyed the support of Samuel, he lacked connections to Israel's traditional institutions. Saul, on the other hand, enjoyed a degree of support among the Israelites unknown to David,[44] and the persistent claims of Saul's house to the throne of Israel haunted David throughout his tenure. Very early in his reign, David attempted to overcome these disadvantages by appropriating Shiloh's cultic symbolism: he had the ark brought up from Kiriath-Jearim to be housed in Jerusalem (2 Sam. 6), and the name of the Shilonite Deity, Yahweh Seba'oth transferred to the Jerusalem cult as well.[45] The erection of the tent shrine at the great high place at Gibeon (1 Chron. 16.39; 21.29; 2 Chron. 1.3, 13; cf. 1 Kgs 3.4) may have been carried out for the same reason.[46] By such means, David sought to tie his claim to royal legitimacy to the religious traditions of Israel.

6.6.1 *The Shiloh Oracle* (Gen. 49.10-12)
David's appropriation of the sacral traditions of the Shiloh cult is found not only in the pro-Davidic redaction of the books of Samuel, but also in the Shiloh oracle in Gen. 49.10-12. This text reads:

> (10) The scepter shall not depart from Judah,
> Nor the ruler's staff from between his feet,
> Until he comes to Shiloh;
> And to him shall be the obedience of the peoples.
> (11) Binding his foal to the vine
> And his ass's colt to the choice vine,
> He washes his garments in wine,
> And his vestments in the blood of grapes;
> (12) His eyes shall be red with wine,
> and his teeth white with milk.

Although the reading of 'Shiloh' in v. 10 has given commentators no end of difficulty,[47] the plain reading of the MT makes good sense if interpreted in light of David's political need to appropriate the religious heritage of Shiloh.

Despite the objection that the MT reading is grammatically faulty, or even incomprehensible, the adverbial use of *šīlōh* without the aid of either of the *he locale* or a preposition, is attested elsewhere in the Hebrew Bible, most notably in Josh. 18.1: *wayyiqqāhălû kol-'ădat bĕnê-Yiśrā'ēl šilōh* ('and the whole congregation of the children Israel assembled *at* Shiloh'); and in Josh. 18.9: *'el-hammahăneh šilōh* ('unto the camp *at* Shiloh'). Thus, the present MT reading of Gen. 49.10 can stand as it is. Consequently, Lindblom's interpretation of this verse as applying to David's appropriation of the sacral authority of the Shiloh traditions, especially through the adoption of the ark into the Jerusalem cultus, is correct.[48] That is, this oracle should be understood against the background of David's attempt to bring unity to his kingdom, and more importantly, perhaps, a semblance of sacral legitimacy to his throne. 'Until he comes to Shiloh' would then refer to David's hoped-for attainment of the sacral and political unity and legitiamacy represented by the Shiloh sanctuary in the late premonarchic and early monarchic period.[49] The reference to the Judaean ruler coming to Shiloh probably implies David's political ambitions to move north from Hebron to take over Israel as well.

Indeed, the latter interpretation might help explain another important conundrum in this oracle. That is, if Gen. 49.10 is to be understood against the background of David's early attempts to secure his throne and to unite Israel both religiously and politically, v. 11, 'Binding his foal to the vine, and his ass's colt to the choice vine', would appear to be a veiled reference to Jerusalem. In support of this suggestion is the fact that the Jerusalemite prophet Isaiah consistently uses agricultural terminology for the cities of Jerusalem and Samaria, as well as for royal houses. Isa. 4.2 makes the clearest reference to Jerusalem using such language: 'In that day the branch of Yahweh shall be beautiful and glorious, and the fruit of the land shall be the pride and glory of the survivors of Israel'. Although Isa. 4.2 refers to Jerusalem as Yahweh's *ṣemah*, and Gen. 49.11 speaks of the *gespen*, the similarity in imagery cannot be mistaken: Gen. 49.11 refers to David's taking of Jerusalem as his sacral and political capital. Accordingly, this oracle celebrates David's selection of Jerusalem as his capital, his unification of Israel, and his appropriation of Shiloh's cultic heritage.

A precise date for this piece is, however, difficult to determine. The oracle could stem from David's days as king in Hebron, since the tone is forward-looking. With regard to Shiloh, the oracle expresses David's hopes for Judean dominance of Israel, and for appropriating to his own cause the sacral sumbolism of the ancient sanctuary of Shiloh. With regard to Jerusalem, David's selection of the city of the Jebusites as his capital is celebrated, along with the good fortune which this move is expected to bring to his throne and his line.[50] Thus, Gen. 49.10-12 bears witness to David's ambitions regarding Shiloh and Israel, and to the importance of Shiloh in both a political and religious sense in unifying David's nascent kingdom.

6.6.2 Conclusion

In conclusion, the traditions of 1 and 2 Samuel preserve the traces of a significant connection between Saul and the sanctuary and priesthood at Shiloh, and this tradition is born out indirectly by 1 Sam. 14.3, 18. Furthermore, there is considerable evidence that the current chronological arrangement of the traditions in 1 Sam. 4-6; 7; 29.1; 31 is unreliable. Indeed, the events of 1 Samuel 4-6 are best associated with Saul's defeat on Mt Gilboa and its aftermath.

The present arrangement of the traditions, moreover, which places the capture of the ark and the destruction of the ancient priesthood of Shiloh prior to Saul's reign, reflects a pro-Davidic redaction. This editorial activity has obscured the breadth of power wielded by the Shilonite priests and their strong affiliation with Saul's monarchy. Shiloh may even have served as the royal sanctuary of Saul, although Saul also had ties to the priests at Nob.[51] The Davidic editors, however, substituted Samuel for Saul in 1 Samuel 1-3 and elevated Samuel to the status of prophet to all Israel in place of the corrupt Elides of Shiloh. After David, similar steps were taken by Solomon's apologists to tie the line of Abiathar, the son of Ahimelech, the son of Ahitub, of the sanctuary at Nob, to the fate of the house of Eli, and thus to replace Abiathar's line with that of the upstart Zadok. That is to say, the Davidic and Solomonic editors of 1 and 2 Samuel had been more than willing to alter genealogies (cf. 1 Sam. 14.3; 2 Sam. 8.17), and to write certain figures out of the traditions pertaining to them (1 Sam. 1), to justify their heroes, just as the Chronicler wrote the line of Eli completely out of his history and replaced it with Zadok. In each instance, however, enough traces of the earlier order have remained to posit a plausible reconstruction, and to illumine the close relationship which once existed between Saul and Shiloh, and which David sought to displace.

Chapter 7

SHILOH IN THE LATER HISTORICAL BOOKS,
THE PSALMS, AND JEREMIAH

7.1 *Shiloh in 1 Kings 11-15*

After the long silence of the latter half of 1 Samuel, all of 2 Samuel, and the first ten chapters of the first book of Kings, Shiloh re-emerges in 1 Kings 11-15 as the domicile of a prophet, Ahijah the Shilonite. The name *'ăhiyyāh haššîlônî* occurs in 1 Kgs 11.29; 12.15; 15.29. The designation *'ăhiyyāh hannābî'* appears in 1 Kgs 14.2, 18; and *hannābî' 'ăhiyyāh haššîlônî* occurs in 11.29. Otherwise, Ahijah is referred to four times without further specification: 11.30; 14.4, 5, 6. In 1 Kgs 11.26-40, the initial reference is to *'ăhiyyāh haššîlônî*, the next two to *'ăhiyyāh*. 1 Kings 14 begins with a reference to *'ăhiyāh hannābî'*, who thereafter becomes merely *'ăhiyyāh*. *'Ăhiyyāh haššîlônî* is found as a single reference in 1 Kgs 12.15; 15.29, where it appears to be a traditional designation such as 'Uriah the Hittite', 'Do'eg the Edomite', or 'Ittai the Gittite'. The city of Shiloh receives mention as Ahijah's residence apart from the gentilic appelative to his name, in 14.2, 4. Thus, of a total of five references to Shiloh in these chapters, three occur in the gentilic appelative of the prophet Ahijah, and two refer specifically to the place where he resided.

In the narratives of Jeroboam the son of Nebat, Ahijah serves a function similar to that of Samuel in the narratives of Saul. It is Ahijah who anoints Jeroboam king over the northern tribes and promises him 'a sure house'[1] if Jeroboam does what is right by keeping the statues and commandments of Yahweh (1 Kgs 11.26-40). Later, however, Ahijah prophesies Yahweh's judgment upon Jeroboam for the erection of the calf images at Dan and Bethel (though Dan and Bethel are never specified, only the 'molten images'), as well as the destruction of Israel (1 Kgs 14.1-20). Thus, Ahijah first commissions the secession of the northern tribes under Jeroboam from the house of David but later condemns Jeroboam for his idolatry.

While Shiloh appears in 1 Kings 11-15 as the residence of the prophet Ahijah, it is difficult to assess what role Shiloh played at this time. The narratives of 1 Kings tell us only that Shiloh was the home of Ahijah. Caquot has argued that Ahijah first supported Jeroboam in the hope that Jeroboam would restore the old sanctuary to its former prominence.[2] However, when Jeroboam chose to honor Bethel and Dan, Ahijah turned against him, as he had turned against Solomon. While Caquot's thesis cannot be proven, it is interesting that Ahijah bears the same name as the Shilonite priest in the camp of Saul in 1 Samuel 14. This fact might suggest that Ahijah himself was a descendant of the Elide priests. The existence of a prophetic figure such as Ahijah at Shiloh is not unrelated to the oracular tradition of the Elides, who were 'oracular priests', as is implied in 1 Samuel 14. 1 Sam. 3.1b also alludes to the prophetic function of the Shilonite priesthood, albeit in a negative fashion,[3] and the rest of the narrative assumes that Eli himself was accustomed to receiving the word of Yahweh. One could thus hypothesize that Ahijah represents the continuation of the ancient oracular tradition at Shiloh. Inasmuch as that tradition was tied to the cult, it is also possible that Ahijah was a representative of the Elide priesthood. One could conclude on this basis that Ahijah represented the interests and claims of the ancient Shilonite cult and sought the restoration of the old Ephraimite sanctuary to the prominence it had held in pre-Davidic times.

That this thesis cannot be proven does not detract from its attractiveness. Any concrete connection between Ahijah the Shilonite and the Elides probably would have been suppressed by the dtr editors in accordance with the prophecy in 1 Sam. 2.27-36. Moreover, Ahijah does not function for the deuteronomists as a representative of a particular cultus. Rather, he has become one of those enigmatic 'men of God' who from time to time appear to cast Yahweh's judgment upon those disobedient to his will. Thus any connection between Ahijah and Shiloh in the dtr presentation is merely incidental and traditional.

In addition to the muted relationship between Ahijah the Shilonite and the old Josephide sanctuary at Shiloh contained in 1 Kings 11-15, the presence of Shiloh in these chapters at the very least indicates that Shiloh was not abandoned at the time of Jeroboam I, and that a memory of its cultic glory may have been maintained there. The presence of these narratives should in themselves have been enough to dispel the idea that Shiloh had been destroyed and had long lain deserted. 1 Kings 11-15 notwithstanding, the majority of scholars have continued to accept the theory that Shiloh was destroyed in the mid-eleventh century, and that for a long time thereafter the town lay deserted. Only the discovery of a considerable number of Iron II sherds at Tell Seilun by the Danish expedition of 1963 disproved the second part of the theory of Shiloh's destruction.

7.2 Shiloh in Ps. 78.60-72

One of the two most important texts invoked in support of the theory that Shiloh was destroyed in the mid-eleventh century is Ps. 78.60-72; the other is Jer. 7.12-15. Psalm 78 is part of a long historical psalm which deals with Israel's repeated rebellion against Elohim, despite the deity's continual demonstrations of mercy and kindness. This theme is somewhat reminiscent of the deuteronomistic theology of history in the book of Judges and presupposes a hexateuchal schema of Israel's pre-history.[4] Neverthelesss, Day is probably correct in arguing that this psalm belongs to pre-deuteronomistic tradition.[5] The psalm displays none of the fatalistic acceptance of kingship characteristic of the deuteronomistic history, but is instead related to the Zion psalms in its unabashed hallowing of the Davidic monarch and the holy city and in its use of the divine name Elohim.[6] Psalm 78 culminates in Elohim's wrathful judgment upon the tribes of Israel and Shiloh, their sanctuary, and his elevation of Judah and Zion in their stead. Elohim's rejection of Shiloh therefore forms the crux of Psalm 78, and it is this fact which has made Ps. 78.60-72 a key passage in the debate over Shiloh's destruction.

The crucial text reads thus:

56.   Yet they tested and rebelled against *'Elohim 'Elyon*
        And did not observe his testimonies.
57.   But they turned away and acted treacherously
        like their fathers;
        They twisted like a deceitful bow.
58.   For they provoked him to anger with their *bāmôth*;
        They moved him jealously with their graven images.

59.	Elohim heard, and he grew wroth,
	And he utterly rejected Israel.
60.	He forsook his *miškān* at Shiloh
	—the *'ōhel* he caused to dwell with mankind,
61.	and he gave his strength over to captivity
	—his glory to the hand of the foe.
62.	And he gave his people over to the sword
	And was wroth with his inheritance.
63.	Fire consumed his young men
	and his maidens were not praised.
64.	His priests fell by the sword
	And his widows did not lament.
65.	Then the Lord awoke, as from sleep;
	Like a warrior shouting from wine;
66.	And he drove his enemies back;
	He gave them everlasting reproach.[7]
67.	And he spurned the *'ōhel* of Joseph
	and the tribe of 'Ephraim he did not choose.
68.	But he chose the tribe of Judah,
	—Mt Zion which he loves.
69.	He built his *miqdāš* like the heights of heaven
	—like the earth, he established it forever.
70.	And he chose David his servant,
	and took him from the sheepfolds.
71.	From after the going up he took him
	To be shepherd over Jacob his people,
	—and over Israel, his inheritance.
72.	He shepherded them with the innocence of his heart,
	with skillful hand he led them.

It is clear from this reading that the rejection of Shiloh in Ps. 78.60 is the turning point of the entire psalm. Elohim repeatedly had shown his fidelity to the northern tribes, while these continually rejected him. Finally, he became outraged over their disloyalty and rejected both them and their tent sanctuary. In their stead, the tribe of Judah and the temple on Mount Zion were chosen and elevated to the leadership of Israel and Jacob.

The language of these verses is significant for understanding the cult at Shiloh and its history. In the first place, Elohim is said to reject the *miškan šilô* and the *'ōhel šikkēn bā'ādam*. These references clearly denote a tent shrine. Indeed, a striking distinction is made between the *miqdāš* which Elohim built (*bānāh*) on Mount Zion, which, 'like the earth', he founded forever (v. 69), and the *miškān* or *'ōhel* at Shiloh in the territory of Joseph which he rejected. The parallelism of *miškān*/*'ōhel* reflects the terminology of the priestly materials of the Pentateuch, where these two terms are used interchangeably for the tent sanctuary (cf. Josh. 18–22). At the same time, the *miqdāš* which Elohim built (*bānāh*) on Mount Zion refers to the Jerusalem temple and reflects the Zion theology, especially where the *miqdāš* is compared with the earth, which has been 'established forever' (v. 69). Ps. 78.60-72 thus assumes two cultic centers: the Jerusalem temple, which Elohim has chosen, and the Josephide tent shrine at Shiloh, which he has rejected.

The juxtaposition of Jerusalem's temple with Shiloh's tent therefore lends incidental support to the historicity of the tradition that the tent shrine stood at Shiloh. At the same time, the absences of any mention of a temple building at Shiloh, as depicted in 1 Samuel 1–3 and (probably) in Judg. 18.31, may derive from the desire to contrast the tent shrine, the traditional cultic symbol of the northern tribes, with the temple in Jerusalem. Thus, Ps. 78.60-72 supports the tradition otherwise known from priestly texts that the tent shrine had stood at Shiloh, but offers no insights on the existence of a temple at Shiloh.

The counterposing of the motifs of Elohim's rejection of Shiloh with his concommitant election of Mount Zion makes Ps. 78.60-72 a taunt song celebrating the emergence of a new Judean order (embodied in the elevation of the Davidic monarchy and in the building of the temple on Mount Zion), while mocking the fall of the old order of the northern tribes with their tent sanctuary and priesthood at Shiloh.[8] This celebration of the rise of the new order of the Davidic monarchy has as its closest parallel the redactional motif of Judges 17–21: the days when no king ruled in Israel, and affairs were badly conducted by the priests and the quasi-cultic council of the northern tribes. Moreover, just as Judges 17–21 is devoid of the fatalistic resignation to the monarchy characteristic of the Deuteronomistic History, Ps. 78.60-72 represents a similar departure from such attitudes and comprises one of those pre-dtr documents still flush with the confidence of the new Judean monarchy.

7.2.1 *The Destruction of Shiloh in Ps. 78.60-72*

While Ps. 78.60-72 focuses upon Shiloh's rejection, it says nothing of a destruction of Shiloh, and mentions no temple sanctuary, on the *miškān/'ōhel*.[9] The divine rejection of Shiloh and Joseph is expressed, rather, in the following events:

> (a) Elohim forsakes the *miškan šilô*—the tent he (Elohim) caused to dwell (*šikkēn*) with mankind (v. 60);
>
> (b) He (Elohim) gave over of 'his strength' to captivity, and his glory (*tip'artô*) to the hand of the foe (v. 61);
>
> (c) He (Elohim) gave over of his people to the sword (vv. 62-63); and let their priests to fall by the sword (v. 64);
>
> (d) He rejected the tent (*'ōhel*) of Joseph and refused to favor Ephraim (v. 67).

The events depicted here are probably to be identified with those of 1 Samuel 4; on this point there is widespread agreement.[10] If the Philistines did follow up their victory at Ebenezer by destroying Shiloh, however, Psalm 78 and 1 Samuel 4 are conspicuous for their silence on this count. In Ps. 78.60-72, Elohim's rejecton of the Josephide sanctuary at Shiloh is described in terms of three events:

> (1) a major military disaster (vv. 62-63);
>
> (2) the capture of the ark by the Philistines (v. 61);
>
> (3) the slaughter of the Shilonite priests (v. 64).

Indeed, Ps. 78.60-72 is consistent with 1 Samuel 4 in this threefold presentation of the defeat at Aphek, and neither passage mentions a destruction of Shiloh.[11] Nor does Day's claim hold up that the rejection of Shiloh implies the destruction of that sanctuary. As Ps. 78.67-68 shows, Elohim's rejection of Shiloh and Ephraim is a theological assertion which sets the stage for another theological assertion: the election of Judah and Mount Zion in their stead. In neither case is anything concrete suggested. Psalm 78 voices the theological claims of the Jerusalem cult to preeminence over the ancient Josephide shrine at Shiloh.

7.2.2 *Summary*

Ps. 78.60-72 thus alludes to the historical disaster depicted in 1 Samuel 4, but likewise mentions no destruction of the Shilonite sanctuary. Apparently, the disaster at Ebenezer, which resulted in the capture of the ark by the Philistines and the slaughter of the priests of Shiloh, was viewed by the Judeans as ample proof of

Yahweh's rejection of the northern tribes and their sanctuary. Had Shiloh actually been destroyed in connection with these events, one would have expected this fact to have been mentioned in Psalm 78, given the gloating tone of vv. 67-72. Instead, Ps. 78.60-72 is in agreement with 1 Samuel 4 in its silence regarding any destruction of Shiloh. While this evidence does not disprove the theory of a mid-eleventh-century destruction of Shiloh and its sanctuary, it does indicate that scholars' assumption of a destruction of Shiloh is no more than an inference into Psalm 78.

To sum up, Ps. 78.61-64 reveals no evidence that Shiloh was destroyed in connection with the events of 1 Samuel 4. That Elohim rejected the tent sanctuary at Shiloh does not imply a destruction of Shiloh, as Day has claimed, but functions instead as the foil for the theological claim that Elohim has elected Mount Zion, the tribe of Judah, and the Davidic king. Inasmuch as the rejection of Shiloh in Psalm 78 has a practical manifestation, this is described in the concrete terms of the capture of the ark, the slaughter of the soldiery and the priests, and the failure of the priests' widows to weep.

7.3 *Shiloh in Jer. 7.12-15 and 26.6-9*

Since the time of Hengstenberg, Jer. 7.12-15 and 26.6-9 have been used alongside Ps. 78.60-72 to argue that Shiloh was destroyed in the mid-eleventh century. It has already been shown, however, that Psalm 78 offers no evidence that Shiloh was destroyed as a result of the disaster at Aphek. In fact, the Bible preserves only three allusions to a possible destruction of Shiloh. The first of these, Judg. 18.30-31, has been treated above, and places the temporal expression, 'all the days that the house of God was at Shiloh', in parallel with another: 'until the day of the captivity of the land'. Judg. 18.30-31 thus appears to associate the end of the Shiloh sanctuary with the exile of the northern kingdom.[13] The other two allusions to a possible destruction of Shiloh are found in Jer. 7.12-15; 26.6-9. Jer. 7.12-15 reads:

> Go now, to my place that was in Shiloh,
> where I caused by name to dwell at first
> (*'ăšer šikkantî šĕmî šām bāri'šônāh*)
> and see what I did to it for the
> wickedness of my people Israel.

And now, because you have done all these things, says Yahweh,
and when I spoke to you persistently you did not listen,
and when I called you, you did not answer,
therefore I will do to the house which is called by my name,
(*wĕ'āśîtî labbayit 'ăšer niqrā' šĕmî 'ālāyw*) and in which you trust,
and to the place which I gave to you to your fathers,
as I did to Shiloh.
And I will cast you out of my sight,
as I cast out all of your kinsmen
—all the offspring of Ephraim.

This theme is taken up again in Jer. 26.6:

Then I will make this house like Shiloh,
and I will make this city a curse for all
the nations of the earth.

In response to Jeremiah's prophecy, the congregation laid hold of
him saying,

You shall die!
Why have you prophesied in the name of Yahweh saying,
'This house shall be like Shiloh,
and this city shall be desolate, without inhabitant'?
(Jer. 26.8b-9a)

Each of these passages relates to a single concern of Jeremiah:
namely, that Yahweh can destroy (or lay waste?) the temple in
Jerusalem, just as he had done earlier to the sanctuary at Shiloh.

Thus, just as Ps. 78.60-72 celebrates Jerusalem's displacement of
Shiloh, so also Jer. 7.12-15 works from the assumption that
Jerusalem had succeeded Shiloh as the place where Yahweh had
caused his name to dwell. Jeremiah takes this claim, however, and
turns it into a prophecy of judgment upon Jerusalem. In fact, the
prophecy in Jer. 7.12-15 derives its effectiveness from the irony
created by the deliberate reversal of the theological claims of the
Jerusalem cultus based on the Jerusalemite appropriation of Shiloh's
status. The cultic community in Jerusalem seems to have believed
that Mount Zion, in succeeding to Shiloh's position as the place
where Yahweh had caused his name to dwell, had attained to an
unparalleled status of glory and cultic eminence. This is the
implication of Ps. 78.60-72. In Jeremiah's prophecy, however,
Jerusalem's attainment to the status once held by Shiloh means that

Jerusalem had not only succeeded to Shiloh's former glory, but also to the judgment which had befallen Shiloh. This intentional use of irony aroused the ire of the Jerusalem community (Jer. 26.6-9) because this prophecy was grounded in accepted popular traditions (such as that expressed in Ps. 78.60-72). Indeed, the tradition that Shiloh had been 'the place where Yahweh caused his name to dwell' appears to have been an important ingredient of the theology of the cultic community in Jerusalem. The further claim that Jerusalem had succeeded to Shiloh's status formed the second member of this axiom. The belief that Jerusalem had succeeded to Shiloh's former status is precisely the substance of Ps. 78.60-72, and the prophecy in Jer. 7.12-15 is a play upon this belief.

7.3.1 *The Supposed Deuteronomistic Origin of Jer. 7.12-15*

Day has argued that Jer. 7.12-15 is deuteronomistic and that this oracle therefore presupposes that the destruction of Shiloh alluded to here occurred prior to the elevation of Jerusalem:

> Now, according to the Deuteronomists there was only one legitimate place where Yahweh caused his name to dwell (cf. Deut. xii 14) and from the 10th century B.C. onwards this was Jerusalem, specifically its Temple (cf. 1 Kings ix 3, xi 36, xiv 21; 2 Kings xxi 4, 7). In view of this, the reference to the destruction of Shiloh, the place where Yahweh caused his name to dwell, cannot refer to an 8th century destruction but only to one prior to the building of the Jerusalem Temple in the 10th century B.C.[14]

First let it be said that one cannot move directly from the dtr ideology of Jerusalem's exclusive legitimacy as the national sanctuary to any historical conclusions as to the manner of Jerusalem's attainment of that status. What the deuteronomists may perchance have believed about the sacral legitimacy of the cult in Jerusalem in the sixth century BCE in fact proves nothing about the history of Shiloh's eclipse by Jerusalem five centuries earlier. As has been shown with regard to the pro-Davidic narratives of 1 and 2 Samuel, quite a few liberties were taken to portray the Jerusalemite priesthood as bearing the same legitimate descent once claimed by the Elides. Thus historical traditions, and the perspectives by which later generations maintain them, possess a mutable quality that cannot be overlooked in discussing the connection between the dtr ideology of Jerusalem's succession to Shiloh's status, and the actual history of that succession.

Second, it is not at all certain that Jer. 7.12-15 reflects the dtr theology. To be sure, Jer. 7.12 uses the phrase *mĕqômî* ...*'ăšer šikkantî šĕmî šām* ('my place ... where I caused my name to dwell'), which is closely related to one found in Deut. 12.11: *hammāqôm 'ăšer-yibḥar Yhwh 'ĕlōhêkem bô lĕšakkēn šĕmô šām* ('the place which Yahweh your god will choose to cause his name to dwell there'; cf. also Deut. 14.23; 16.2, 6, 11; 26.2). This phraseology, however, never occurs in the books of Joshua–2 Kings. This striking discontinuity between the deuteronomic theology and that of the deuteronomists provides a key counterpoint to Day's sweeping claim that Jer. 7.12-15 is the product of deuteronomistic redaction. Given the signal importance of the theology of 'the place where Yahweh will cause his name to dwell' in Deuteronomy, the absence of this theology in the so-called Deuteronomistic History is remarkable. Indeed, one would have supposed that this *šēm* theology would have found its most poignant expression in the narrative of 1 and 2 Kings.[15] Properly speaking, however, the theology that Yahweh would 'cause his name to dwell' in a particular place in deuteronomic, not deuteronomistic. Since Jer. 7.12-15 reflects the deuteronomic rather than the deuteronomistic theology one must reject Day's claim that Jer. 7.12-15 presupposes a peculiarly dtr theology.

The theology of the divine dwelling place, and of the dwelling-place of the divine name, is also found outside of deuteronomic texts. For instance, that Yahweh dwells in the temple on Mount Zion is presupposed in genuine Isaianic texts such as Isa. 18.4, 7. Thus, Isa. 18.4 says that Yahweh will look from his dwelling, and Isa. 18.7 calls Mt Zion *mĕqôm šēm-Yhwh Ṣĕbā'ōt* ('the place of the name of Yahweh Seba'ot'). Moreover, the tent sanctuary in P is alternately designated the *'ōhel mô'ēd* or the *miškan-Yhwh* ('dwelling-place'), using the same root, *šākan*, as is used in the typical formulation of the *šēm* theology of Deuteronomy. The priestly text of Jos. 22.19 even describes the setting of the *miškān* as the *'ereṣ 'ăḥuzzat Yhwh 'ăšer šākan-šām miškan Yhwh* ('the land of Yahweh's possession where dwells the tabernacle of Yahweh'). Nor is it insignificant that the location of the tent sanctuary in this text is Shiloh. The priestly text of Jos. 18.1 reads: *wayyiqqahălû kol-'ădat bĕnê-Yiśrā'ēl šiloh wayyaškînû šām 'et-'ōhel mô'ēd* ('And the whole congregation of the Israelites assembled at Shiloh and erected [or "caused to dwell"!] there the tent of meeting'). The usual translation of *wayyaškînû* here as 'and they set up' may in fact miss the real point, namely that 'they caused the tent of meeting to dwell there'. This reading is in fact borne out by Jos. 22.19, where the *miškān* is said to 'dwell' (*šakan*) in the land of Yahweh's possession.

A subsidiary point which deserves mention here is the direct coupling of the verb *šakan* in these instances with the adverbial particle *šām*. The place where Yahweh's tent dwells must be specified by the referent of the *šām* particle, since this location is not taken for granted. This usage suggests that the priestly phrase, *šakan-šām*, may reflect a certain openness regarding the site where Yahweh's sanctuary dwells. A similar fluidity prevails as well in Deuteronomy, where the place where Yahweh's name will dwell is only specified as 'the place'—*hammāqôm*. While scholars have traditionally taken this phrase as implicitly referring to Jerusalem, there is no proof of this assumption. In fact, Deuteronomy may itself preserve a non-Jerusalemite tradition of Yahweh's autonomy in selecting the place where his shrine, or his name, would dwell.

Moreover, the real distinction between D and P on this count is that the priestly usage centers on Yahweh's dwelling-place, the *miškān*, while the dtn usage focuses upon the *māqôm*—the actual place where Yahweh will cause his name to dwell. The common thread which unites these two distinctive theological concerns is that Yahweh will *dwell* in the Promised Land, and that he will cause either his name or his *miškān* to dwell there. This fact suggests that the priestly traditions and Deuteronomy give divergent expression to a similar theology of Yahweh's dwelling. In the priestly tradition, this theology finds concrete expression in Yahweh's dwelling-place, the *miškān*. Deuteronomy, in focusing on the dwelling of Yahweh's name (as is found in Isa. 18.7), preserves a theology which emphasizes Yahweh's transcendence.

As Mettinger has shown, the difference between the theology of Yahweh's dwelling in P and D, on the one hand, and the Deuteronomistic History, on the other, is that Dtr avoided the belief that Yahweh actually caused his name to dwell in a specific place, whereas in D and P, the ideal of Yahweh's dwelling among men is crucial. The apparent reason for Dtr's avoidance of this idea was that the Deuteronomistic History was written in full awareness of the calamity which befell Jerusalem and its temple in 586 BCE. In the Jerusalem cult, however, the *šēm* theology was particularly associated with the temple and the Zion theology.[16]

For its own part, Jer. 7.12-15 constitutes an attack upon a fundamental premise of the Zion form of the *šēm* theology, that Jerusalem enjoyed a special status above other sanctuaries that would secure the holy city against the misfortunes of history. Jeremiah, in making use of the *deuteronomic* phraseology, appeals to the pre-Zion form of the tradition and Yahweh's freedom to choose the place where he will cause his name to dwell. Thus, he argues that just as Yahweh rejected his chosen dwelling-place at Shiloh, so can he also reject Jerusalem. By citing the example of Shiloh, moreover, Jeremiah has reversed the meaning which his comtemporaries seem to have attributed to the idea that Jerusalem was the 'place where Yahweh caused his name to dwell'. That is, Jerusalem was not only heir to the glory which had once been Shiloh's; the holy city would also inherit the desolation which Yahweh had brought upon Shiloh.

Thus, in employing the terminology of *hammāqôm 'ăšer šikkēn Yhwh šĕmô-šām* ('the place where Yahweh [has] caused his name to dwell'), Jeremiah drew upon deuteronomic rather than deuteronomistic theological tradition. At the same time, there are sharp parallels between Jeremiah and the language of the Deuteronomistic History. For instance, 2 Kgs 22.19 contains a reference by Huldah the prophetess to an earlier threat by Yahweh to make Jerusalem 'a desolation and a curse' (*lihyôt lĕšammāh wĕliqlālāh*—Jer. 26.6, 9). This fact shows that both Jeremiah and the dtr editors of 1-2 Kings drew on common traditions in formulating their respective messages. Therefore, the use of deuteronomic language by Jeremiah does not mean that that passage was composed by the dtn/dtr school, as Day has argued. On the contrary, just as Jeremiah drew upon the technical terminology of the priests,[17] he also employed the theology and terminology of the deuteronomic tradition.[18]

To conclude, the oracle in Jer. 7.12-15 stands midway between the dtn and dtr theologies, and its language reflects that of dtn rather than dtr. That is, Jeremiah appeals to the dtn *šēm* theology to prophesy the coming of events which would bring about the reformulation of that theology as found in the Deuteronomistic History. Rather than a deuteronomistic text, Jer. 7.12-15 is, technically speaking, a pre-dtr appeal to dtn theology. Consequently, one cannot equate the historical assumptions behind this oracle with those of Dtr or the dtr theology.

7.3.2 *The Destruction of Shiloh in Jer. 7.12-15*

Despite Yahweh's threat to 'do to the house which is called by my name . . . as I did to Shiloh' (Jer. 7.14), the connection between this threat and the theory of a destruction of Shiloh in the mid-eleventh century is doubtful at best. Thus, exactly what Yahweh will do to Jerusalem, or what he did to 'my place where I caused my name to dwell at first' (*mĕqômî . . . 'ăšer šikkantî šămî šām bari'šônah*), is not specified in Jer. 7.12-15. Apart from the analogy drawn between that which he did to Shiloh and what he will do to Jerusalem, nothing else is said except that Yahweh will 'cast out' the Judeans from his sight (*wĕhišlaktî 'etkem mē'al pānāy*) as he cast out their kinsmen, the Ephraimites.

Jeremiah's association of Yahweh's 'casting out' of the Judeans with the exile of 'all the offspring of Ephraim' is a critical factor in identifying the desolation of Shiloh spoken of in Jer. 7.12-15 and 26.6-9. Historically speaking, the state of Israel ceased to exist as a political entity at the end of the reign of Jeroboam II. Thereafter, the northern kingdom was limited to Samaria and the central hill country of Palestine, that is, to the territory of Ephraim. Israel's loss of territory had begun during the expansion of the Syrian ruler, Rezin of Damascus, who had apparently taken Galilee and the Israelite regions of the Transjordan. With the Assyrian conquest of Damascus in 732 BCE, the Israelite territories lost to Damascus were incorporated into the Assyrian empire as separate provinces, and the territory of Israel reduced to the hill country of Ephraim. Had Jeremiah wished to refer to a destruction of Shiloh in conjunction with events of the eleventh century, he likely would have referred to Israel, rather than Ephraim. Ephrain became the political designation for the north only after the Syrians and later the Assyrians had seized those Israelite regions outside the central hill country of Palestine.[19] The same principle, in fact, applies to Psalm 78. There, the Ephraimites are twice mentioned as a particular tribe, but the psalm is more generally concerned with Israel, which is the object of the divine wrath manifested in the rejection of the sanctuary at Shiloh. Jeremiah, however, did not associate the exile of Judah and the desolation of the temple on Mount Zion with Israel's fall, but with that of Ephraim. Therefore, it would seem that Jeremiah had in mind the actual events surrounding the Assyrian exile of Samaria when he likened Jerusalem's coming destruction to that of Shiloh, and the coming exile of Judah with the exile of 'all the offspring of Ephraim'.

The parallel between the destruction of Shiloh and the exile of the northern kingdom is given additional weight by the similar parallel in Judg. 18.30-31 (above, 5.2). Indeed, it is hardly coincidental that that destruction is set in parallel with the fall of the northern kingdom in two of the three biblical texts which imply a destruction of Shiloh.

7.3.3 *The Destruction of Shiloh in Jer. 26.6-9*

Besides the implicit reference to a possible destruction of Shiloh in Jer. 7.12-15, a destruction of Shiloh is mentioned in more specific language in Jer. 26.6-9. This language casts further light on the probable historical events with which Jeremiah associated Shiloh's fall. Jer. 26.6-9 mentions a prophecy by Jeremiah that Jerusalem and its temple will be made like Shiloh: 'a curse for all the nations of the earth' (*liqlālāh lĕkol gôyê hā'āreṣ*). The theme that Yahweh will make a place a 'curse' (*qĕlālāh*) occurs no less than eight times in Jeremiah (24.9; 25.18; 26.6; 42.18; 44.8, 12, 22; 49.13). Of these instances, all but the last occur in connection with Jerusalem and its inhabitants. Jer. 49.13 employs the same language and motifs as the other instances, but applies these to Bozrah, the Edomite capital. In Jeremiah, the term *qĕlālāh* is coupled regularly with several other parallel expressions: *šammāh* ('desolation/horror', Jer. 25.18; 42.18; 44.12, 22; 49.13); *'ālāh* ('execration', Jer. 42.18; 44.12);[20] *ḥerpāh* ('taunt', Jer. 42.18; 44.8, 12; 49.13). The individual parallelisms between these terms do not, however, lead to any clear interpretation of *qĕlālāh*. Only the word *šammāh* ('desolation, horror') gives some concrete indication of the specific content of the threat.

Nevertheless, the oracle against Jerusalem is further illuminated by the oracle against Edom in Jer. 49.7-22. There, the fate foreseen for that land is similar to that prophesied for Jerusalem in 26.6-9:

> For I have sworn by myself, it is the pronouncement of Yahweh,
> that Bozrah will become a *desolation*, a *taunt*, and a *curse*.
> And all her cities will become ruins forever.

This judgment is further spelled out as follows:

> As when Sodom and Gomorrah and their neighbor cities were overthrown, says Yahweh, no man shall dwell there, no man shall

> sojourn in her . . . even the little ones of the flock shall be dragged away; surely their fold shall be appalled at their fate (Jer. 49.18, 20b).

This text describes the desolation and depopulation of Edom. The analogy drawn with the fate of Sodom and Gomorrah is all too clear to be ignored: the total destruction of Edom and its cities (and the exile of its population) is what is foretold. That the same is meant for Jerusalem in Jer. 26.6-9 is made clear in v. 9, where the people quote Jeremiah as having said, 'This house shall be like Shiloh, and this city shall be desolate: without inhabitant'.

The language of exile and devastation used in Jer. 26.6-9 to describe the parallel fates of Shiloh and Jerusalem would seem to indicate that the destruction of the northern kingdom by Assyria and not the theoretical devastation by the Philistines is what is meant in Jer. 7.12-15. Indeed, this conclusion is borne out by the parallel between Yahweh's threat to do to Jerusalem as he once did to Shiloh and his subsequent threat to 'cast you out of my sight, as I cast out all your kinsmen, all the offspring of Ephraim'. This parallel strengthens the connection between Jer. 7.12-15 and the destruction of the northern kingdom during the last quarter of the eighth century. Similarly, the end of the Shiloh sanctuary in Judg. 18.31 stands in parallel with 'until the day of the captivity of the land'. The evidence of Jer. 7.12-15 and 26.6-9 thus supports the claims of Karl Heinrich Graf, Frants Buhl, Marie-Louise Buhl and Svend Holm-Nielsen, that the desolation of Shiloh in Jeremiah occurred at the time of the fall of the northern kingdom.

The evidence of 1 Kings 11–15, that Shiloh continued as an inhabited place during the later years of the united monarchy and the first years of the divided monarchy, at least demonstrates that the desolation of Shiloh to which Jeremiah calls the attention of his audience cannot be identical with the theoretical destruction of that place as a result of the disaster in 1 Samuel 4. The challenge,

> Go now to my place that was in Shiloh, where I caused my name to dwell at first, and see what I did to it for the wickedness of my people Israel . . .

refers to the concrete results of a judgment still painfully visible to the people of Jerusalem in the last years of the seventh century. Since no desolation of Shiloh is mentioned in 1 Samuel 4 (to which Jer.

7.12-15 has all too often been made to refer), and Shiloh remained an inhabited place in the early chapters of the books of Kings, it is unlikely that the ruins alluded to by Jeremiah are those which resulted from a destruction of Shiloh after the disaster at Ebenezer. Instead, the actual physical evidence to which Jer. 7.12-15 refers would most likely have stemmed from the Assyrian invasion and exile of the northern kingdom, as Graf and his successors have argued.

7.3.4 *Summary*

On the basis of the evidence of Jer. 7.12-15 and 26.6-9, then, the conclusion that Shiloh was laid waste at the time of the fall of Samaria is inescapable. The parallel in Jer. 7.14-15 between the fall of Shiloh and the casting off of 'all the offspring of Ephraim', supported by that in Judg. 18.30, 31, between 'the day of the captivity of the land' and 'all the days that the house of God was in Shiloh', suggests that Shiloh's abandonment coincided with the exile of the northern kingdom. There is no 'natural' way to make this evidence point to the events in 1 Samuel 4. The language of the related passage in Jer. 26.6-9, which points to the desolation and depopulation of Shiloh, confirms this analysis.

At the same time, Jeremiah does not argue that the desolation of Shiloh was a pre-condition to Jerusalem's status as 'the place where Yahweh has caused his name to dwell'. The point of Jer. 7.12-15, in fact, has nothing to do with the order of events by which Jerusalem supplanted Shiloh. Rather, this prophecy aims at reversing the effect of the Jerusalemite claim to have attained to Shiloh's status. Whereas the Jerusalem community had viewed this status as entirely positive, Jeremiah's proclamation claims that just as Jerusalem is heir to Shiloh's glory, the holy city likewise will be heir to Shiloh's demise. Thus, Jer. 7.12-15 naturally assumes that Shiloh once was the place where Yahweh had caused his name to dwell, while Jerusalem is not that place. But nothing is said of the time at which Jerusalem came to this status, or the process by which this status was attained. The matter of the succession does not even arise. The real concern of Jer. 7.12-15 is to establish the syllogism: Shiloh was the place where Yahweh caused his name to dwell at first; Shiloh was destroyed. Yahweh likewise has caused his name to dwell at Jerusalem; Jerusalem likewise can be destroyed. This analogy focuses upon the real effects of the status of a city being 'the place where Yahweh has caused his name to dwell', not upon the transfer of this status from one city to another. In making Jerusalem's *succession* to Shiloh's special status the key issue of Jer. 7.12-15, Day has missed the central concern of the text.[21]

7.4 *Shiloh in Jer. 41.5*

If the fall of Shiloh is associated with that of the northern kingdom by Jeremiah, the city had been re-occupied by the exilic period, since Jer. 41.5 depicts Shiloh as an inhabited place:

> And it came to pass, on the day after the killing of Gedaliah, when no man knew, that men came from Shechem, Shiloh, and Samaria—eighty men (with) shaven beards and rent garments and gashed bodies, and cereal offerings and incense to bring to the house of Yahweh.

This text suggests that the history of biblical Shiloh was more complex than has been assumed by historians. Whereas the traditional theory has presupposed a single destruction, and that in the mid-eleventh century, the evidence provided by Jeremiah is that Shiloh may have been destroyed or abandoned, and then re-inhabited a number of times during the Israelite period.

7.5 *Conclusions:*
The Destruction of Shiloh in Psalm 78 and Jeremiah

In conclusion, the references to the destruction of Shiloh in Jeremiah do not point to a *destruction* in the Early Iron Age, but to a desolation of the site in conjunction with the exile of the northern kingdom. On the other hand, Psalm 78, which has likewise been used as a key passage in the formulation of the theory of an eleventh-century destruction of Shiloh, mentions no destruction at all. In fact, Jeremiah's allusions to Shiloh's end have been brought together with the rehearsal of the events surrounding the loss of the ark in Psalm 78 in order to create a connection between the tradition of the capture of the ark and the tradition that Shiloh was destroyed (or abandoned), where none existed before. The truth is that Ps. 78.60-72 refers to events quite distinct from those alluded to in Jeremiah. Jer. 7.12-15 and 26.6-9 refer to the laying waste of Shiloh, probably in the late eighth century BCE. Conversely, Ps. 78.60-72 recalls the military catastrophe in 1 Samuel 4 in some detail but mentions no destruction of Shiloh or its sanctuary. Like 1 Samuel 4, Ps. 78.60-72 is notable for its silence regarding the fate of Shiloh and its sanctuary when the ark was lost. Thus, the outstanding feature of the theory that Shiloh was destroyed by the victorious Philistines in the wake of their capture of the ark is the remarkable dearth of biblical evidence for such a theory.

The lack of solid, exegetical evidence for a destruction of Shiloh in the mid-eleventh century, moreover, has led to considerable weight being placed upon the archaeological excavations at Tell Seilun. Nevertheless, if the excavators have uncovered an Iron I destruction (and the preliminary reports make this claim)[22] one must conclude that reference to this destruction was never preserved in the biblical traditions. In any event, the earliest interpretation of 1 Samuel 4 in terms of a destruction or abandonment of Shiloh was offered from by Moses Maimonides, the great twelfth-century philosopher and physician to the sultan Saladin, some two millennia after the presumed events.[23]

Furthermore, if Jeremiah did allude to a destruction of Shiloh which he associated with the events of 1 Samuel 4, and if, moreover, he pointed to the ruins of his day as proof, the historical veracity of his testimony must be questioned. That is to say, since 1 Kings 11-15 depict Shiloh as an inhabited town, the ruins visible to Jeremiah must have stemmed from a time later than that of Ahijah the Shilonite. A further consequence of interpreting the oracles of Jeremiah as references to the battle where the ark was lost is that serious doubt is thereby cast upon the notion that events placed in parallel with one another by the biblical writers are mutually interpretive. Indeed, when Day overlooks the connection between Yahweh's casting off of Judah and Jerusalem and his casting off of Ephraim (Jer. 7.14-15) and explains away the parallel between the 'day of the captivity of the land' and 'all the days that the house of God was in Shiloh' (Judg. 18.30-31), he rejects the clear associations made in the biblical traditions in favor of a theory about them. In short, considerable damage must be inflicted upon the biblical text and its historical testimony if one is to argue for a destruction of Shiloh in the mid-eleventh century on the basis of Ps. 78.60-72 and Jer. 7.12-15.

It may well be that Shiloh was burned to the ground in the wake of the defeat at Ebenezer; the current Israeli excavations at least seem to have identified an Iron I destruction layer.[24] It is nonetheless strange that a destruction of Shiloh is never mentioned in connection with the battle where the ark was lost, and conversely, that in those texts which actually mention the end of the Shiloh sanctuary (Jer. 7.12-15; 26.6-9; Judg. 18.30-31), there is a similar silence concerning the loss of the ark. These facts suggest that if Shiloh was destroyed in connection with the disaster at Ebenezer, this destruction has, for whatever reasons, gone unmentioned in the biblical traditions.

Chapter 8

THE TRADITIONS AND HISTORY OF BIBLICAL SHILOH

8.1 *The Traditions*

8.1.1 *Categories of Traditions*

Before moving to the reconstruction of Shiloh's history, it is first necessary to survey the traditions of biblical Shiloh, the respective periods which they represent, and their corresponding relationships to one another. In general, the traditions of Shiloh can be grouped under two broad headings: those of priestly or independent cultic provenance, and those bearing the distinctive impress of the Jerusalem cultus.

8.1.1.1 *Priestly and Independent Cultic Traditions about Shiloh*

The largest of these two categories is comprised of priestly traditions (i.e. traditions bearing the distinctive impress of the priestly language and style known from the Hexateuch) and of independent traditions focusing upon cultic places, events, and issues. The specifically priestly traditions include the account of the distribution of tribal inheritances at Shiloh, which is found in the lists of tribal allotments in Joshua 14–21, and specifically in Josh. 18.1-10; 19.51; 21.1-3. Josh. 22.9-34, which is related to the traditions of Phineas in Num. 25.6-13; 31.1-12, belongs to this category as well, as does the burial notice of Eleazar, the son of Aaron (Josh. 24.33). The tradition of the Benjaminite war (Judg. 20.1–21.15) is also related to the priestly traditions of the Hexateuch, though it is not part of the Priestly corpus. Among the independent cultic traditions which are not distinctively priestly are the story of 'the rape of the Shilonite maidens' (Judg. 21.16-24) and the traditions of the Elides at Shiloh (1 Sam. 1–4; 14). The traditions of Ahijah the Shilonite (1 Kgs 11–15) are not expressly cultic but, rather, prophetic. Nonetheless, these may be grouped together with other independent traditions which focus upon cultic concerns. Judg. 18.30-31 is not formally a tradition, but a historian's notation. Inasmuch as this notation reflects independent traditions of the Danite and Shilonite cults which are otherwise lost, however, it may classed with the independent cultic traditions.

Certain elements, moreover, are common to both the priestly traditions and those of independent origin. Among these common elements, a general focus upon northern shrines is to be noted, including Shiloh (Josh. 18–22; Judg. 18.31; 21.12, 16-24), Mizpah (Judg. 20.1; 21.1, 8), Bethel (Judg. 20.18, 26-28), and Dan (Judg. 18.30). Second, these traditions revolve around northern cultic figures such as Eleazar, buried in the hill country of Ephraim (Josh. 24.33), Phineas, his illustrious son (Josh. 22.9-34; Judg. 20.27-28), the Elides, probable descendants of Eleazar and Phineas (1 Sam. 1–4, 14), and Ahijah the Shilonite (1 Kgs 11–15). This evidence suggests a northern, non-Jerusalemite provenance for the priestly tradition.

With specific regard to Shiloh, there are several recurrent motifs. These include Shiloh as the site of the tent shrine (Josh. 18.1-10; 19.51; 22.9-34), Shiloh as the site of the war camp (Josh. 18.9; Judg. 21.12), Shiloh as located 'in the land of Canaan' (Josh. 21.2; 22.9; Judg. 21.19), Shiloh as the cultic center in early tribal wars (Josh. 22.9-34; Judg. 20.1-21.15), and Shiloh as a shrine of the Aaronite priesthood (Josh. 21.1-3; 22.9-34; 1 Sam. 1-4; 14). From these common elements and motifs, one may make the preliminary observation that in the cultic lore of northern Israel, Shiloh enjoyed a special, but by no means exclusive, status (cf. Gen. 35.9-15).

8.1.1.2 *The Jerusalemite Traditions about Shiloh*
In contrast to these largely northern cultic traditions of Shiloh, a group of distinctly Jerusalemite traditions about Shiloh exists as well. This group is decidedly smaller than that stemming from the north; it includes Gen. 49.10-12; Ps. 78.60-72; Jer. 7.12-15; 26.6-9; 41.5. Whereas the traditions of Shiloh stemming from northern lore treat Shiloh in a positive light and assume its special status, the traditions of Shiloh which derive from Jerusalem are competitive at best, and downright derogatory at worst. Thus, Ps. 78.60-72 is a Jerusalemite taunt song which celebrates Elohim's rejection of Shiloh and his concomitant choice of the sanctuary on Mount Zion. While Gen.

49.10-12 does not take an expressly negative attitude towards Shiloh, this oracle probably reflects David's appropriation of Shiloh's cultic heritage to Jerusalem. The Shiloh oracle (Gen. 49.10-12) casts light upon the reasons for Jerusalem's eclipse of Shiloh and upon the tradition, preserved in Jer. 7.12-15, that Jerusalem had succeeded to Shiloh's former status as 'the place where Yahweh had caused his name to dwell'.

The Jerusalemite traditions of Shiloh thus offer the reverse side of those preserved in the north. Instead of hallowing Shiloh as the site of the wilderness shrine, the cultic community in Jerusalem looked upon Shiloh as the rejected sanctuary, its tent as having been surpassed by the temple on Mount Zion. Gen. 49.10-12, which apparently views Shiloh's religious heritage in a positive light, celebrates above all the wedding of David's line to the ancient city of Jerusalem (see above, Chapter 6). Jer. 7.12-15 and 26.6-9 constitute an ironic play on the tradition of Jerusalem's superiority over Shiloh. Jeremiah apparently took the accepted tradition that Jerusalem had replaced Shiloh as the place where Yahweh had caused his name to dwell and interpreted this tradition in light of the common belief that Shiloh had been desolated in connection with the Assyrian dissolution of the northern kingdom. Therefore, Jeremiah argued, Yahweh could destroy the Jerusalem temple and cast off the Judaeans, just as he earlier had destroyed Shiloh and cast out 'all the offspring of Ephraim' (see above, Chapter 7). While Jeremiah shared with the other Jerusalemite witnesses to the Shiloh tradition the belief that Shiloh had been rejected by Yahweh, and replaced by Jerusalem, his real departure from the standard view in Jerusalem was not in his treatment of Shiloh, but in his treatment of Jerusalem, which he saw as the object of the same divine wrath that had previously fallen upon Shiloh.

In addition to those traditions of Shiloh which were handed down within the cultic community of Jerusalem, a number of the independent cultic traditions of probably northern origin were reworked from a pro-Davidic stance. These traditions include the story of Samuel's birth and dedication to the priests of Yahweh at Shiloh (1 Sam. 1.1-28; 2.11, 18-21; 3.19-21), which, because of the otherwise incongruous word-play on the root *šā'al*, probably originally referred to Saul, the one 'lent to Yahweh' (1 Sam. 1.28: *hû' šā'ûl laYhwh*). Similarly, the traditions of the Elides have been obscured by the artificial link created in 1 Sam. 14.3 between the house of Eli and the house of Ahitub, probably in the interests of the Zadokite priesthood in Jerusalem. Finally, the capture of the ark was secondarily associated with the years prior to Saul's reign. The purpose of these revisions of the traditions of Shiloh was in the first place to break the connection between Saul and Shiloh. Thus, Saul was depicted as having ruled apart from the official sanction of the Shilonite cultus, during a time when the ancient tribal war-palladium, the ark, was outside Israel. Such a portrayal gave the appearance that Saul's monarchy was not really legitimate. In the second place, these changes replaced Saul's ties to Shiloh with the theme of Samuel's succession to the prophetic office at Shiloh (1 Sam. 3.1, 19-21) in place of the Elide priesthood, thus supporting the legitimacy of David's claim to the throne through Samuel.

8.1.1.3 *Summary*
In summary, two broad categories of traditions regarding biblical Shiloh exist: those deriving from northern cultic circles, and those stemming from the Jerusalem community. The northern traditions depict Shiloh in a positive light and generally assume its special status above the other Israelite shrines. These northern traditions include those belonging to the priestly stratum of the Hexateuch as well as the independent cultic traditions of Judges and 1 Samuel.

The traditions about Shiloh which represent the perspective of the Jerusalem cult are found in Gen. 49.10-12 and Ps. 78.60-72. In contrast to the northern traditions, these portray Shiloh and its sanctuary as rejected for the wickedness and infidelity of the northern tribes. Of the Jerusalemite traditions, only Gen. 49.10-12 casts Shiloh in a positive light, and even this text has as its final word the celebration of David's selection of Jerusalem as his capital. The pro-Davidic revision of the Shiloh traditions in 1 Samuel, moreover, illustrates the need of both the Davidic monarchy and the cultic community in Jerusalem to denigrate the religious heritage of Shiloh and to arrogate to Jerusalem the prestige which formerly had been Shiloh's. This appropriation is reflected in Gen. 49.10-12, celebrated in Ps. 78.60-72, and assumed by Jeremiah.

8.1.2 *The Historical Periodization of the Traditions*
There are thus two bodies of traditions pertaining to Shiloh, the one

northern in origin, the other Jerusalemite. A rough periodization of these traditions is possible if one works from the principle that those which are held to be earliest must be those which fit more poorly with later custom and usage. On the basis of this consideration, those traditions focusing upon northern shrines and cultic figures, as well as upon institutions which had no place in the late period of Israelite history, must be assumed to be the earlier. According to these criteria, the northern traditions must be the earlier, since they refect a time before the Jerusalem cult had succeeded in establishing its claim to an absolute and unique superiority vis-à-vis the other shrines of the land. Conversely, the traditions which reflect the ascendancy of Jerusalem must be later, since Jerusalem's dominance in the history of the cult is a demonstrably late phenomenon. The argument that Shiloh's special status is a late fiction retrojected into the distant past by the post-exilic community in Jerusalem is refuted by the bitter antagonism in the Jerusalem community toward Shiloh and its priesthood, attested in Ps. 78.60-72, which culminated in the deletion of Eli and his sons from the official Aaronite genealogies. Conversely, in the non-Jerusalemite traditions about Shiloh, the special status of Shiloh reflects a positive assumption about the sanctuary there, without the least hint that Shiloh had been replaced by Jerusalem (cf. especially, Josh. 18–22). These traditions offer such a stark contrast to the attested Jerusalemite theology (Ps. 78.60-72; Jer. 7.12-15; 26.6-9) that it is unlikely that they derive from the post-exilic community or from any other period in Jerusalem's history as an Israelite cultic center. In their present form, then, traditions of Shiloh which are of northern provenance reflect a period in Israel's history before David had made Jerusalem the sacral center of the land.

Within the northern traditions, moreover, a further periodization of traditions is possible. The earliest of these traditions is that of Shiloh as a possibly non-Israelite, possibly Yahwistic shrine (Judg. 21.16-24), whatever the date of the present form of that story. This conclusion is based on the tension between this tradition and all other facets of the Shiloh tradition, whether Jerusalemite or northern Israelite. After this episode there are a number of traditions in the books of Joshua and Judges which may reflect conditions during the early pre-monarchic period. These include the account of the distribution of the land at Shiloh (Josh. 18.1-10; 19.51; 21.1-3) and

those of the early tribal wars (Josh. 22.9-34; Judg. 20.1-21.15; cf.
Num. 25.6-13; 31.1-12, which seem to presuppose a similar set of
conditions). The reason for this early dating is that neither the
division of the tribal inheritances, nor the early tribal wars has any
convincing parallel in the history of Israel after the rise of the
monarchy. The late pre-monarchic era is attested above all in the
Elide traditions (1 Sam. 1-3), despite the subsequent redaction of
these traditions by pro-Davidic editors in Jerusalem. The account of
Saul's campaign against the Philistines, in which Ahijah of the
priests of Shiloh serves as oracular priest before the ark (1 Sam. 14),
and the account of the battle of Aphek, where the ark was lost and
the priests of Shiloh slain (1 Sam. 4; compare 1 Sam. 31; 2 Sam. 1),
reflect the early years of the Israelite monarchy under Saul. 1 Kings
11-15 stems from the beginning of the divided monarchy.

The Jerusalemite traditions about Shiloh can be arranged according
to their respective historical periods as well. The Shiloh oracle (Gen.
49.10-12) is the earliest of these and stems from the beginning of
David's reign, perhaps in Hebron, but most likely in Jerusalem (see
above, Chapter 6). Ps. 78.60-72 is later than the Shiloh oracle, as is
clear from the celebration of the building of the sanctuary on Mount
Zion. A more precise identification of the date of this song is
impossible, except to say that it appears to have come from a time
before the northern kingdom had been reduced by the Assyrians (see
above, Chapter 7). Finally, Jeremiah's oracles concerning Shiloh
come from the last, desperate years of the Judean kingdom. The final
mention of Shiloh in Jer. 41.5 presumably was written sometime
during the exile, after the assassination of Gedaliah.

8.1.3 *Synopsis*
On the basis of the historical circumstances reflected in the various
traditions of Shiloh, and by analyzing and comparing the respective
concerns of these texts, one may arrive at a rough periodization of
the Shiloh traditions which may then provide the basis for the
reconstruction of Shiloh's history. The traditions themselves,
however, do not yield a consistent, running account of Shiloh's
history. Instead, when arranged from the earliest to the latest, the
traditions of Shiloh preserved in the Bible offer fleeting, successive
glimpses into Shiloh's role at various stages of Israelite history.
Certain lines of development within Shiloh's history may be

reconstructed from this evidence, although quite a few gaps will in any event remain to be filled by speculation or imagination.

8.2 *The History of Biblical Shiloh*

8.2.1 *The Earliest Period: Shiloh as the Site of a Non-Israelite Shrine*

The earliest period in the history of biblical Shiloh lies outside the ken of written sources and can be ascertained only on the basis of archaeological evidence. According to the Israeli excavators currently working at Tell Seilun, the accepted location of ancient Shiloh (see above, 1.2.5), the place was a walled city with a sanctuary during the late Middle Bronze Age (MB IIC). In the Late Bronze Age, the inhabitants of the region around Seilun appear to have continued worshipping at the site of the old Middle Bronze Age shrine, which they may have rebuilt. These people appear to have been largely unsettled and nomadic in culture, as the archaeological evidence indicates only sparse settlement of the surrounding territory during this period (see above, 3.5). The beginnings of the Early Iron Age saw Seilun re-occupied, not as a settlement, but as the site of a *temenos*, or sacred precinct.

The biblical traditions offer only the story of 'the rape of the Shilonite maidens' as evidence of Shiloh's existence as a non-Israelite cultic center and this tradition could fit into any of the earlier archaeological periods attested at Seilun. The Late Bronze and Early Iron Ages are both possible settings. This tradition, therefore, is of little help in establishing a definite period for the presence of Israel in the central hill country. The most Judg. 21.16-24 allows one to conclude is that before Shiloh became an Israelite shrine, it had been the site of an old Canaanite cultic center. As this story suggests, the early Israelite tribes may even have worshipped together with non-Israelites at the shrine at Shiloh, before the Ephraimite hills fell totally into Israelite hands.

8.2.2 *The Early Pre-Monarchic Period: Shiloh as the Site of an Israelite Shrine*

Given the ambiguous and controversial nature of the biblical traditions relating to the Israelite occupation of Palestine, and the concomitant problems of establishing either a chronology or a logical

progression of verifiable events by which one might define the
Israelite settlement of the central hill country, it is impossible to say
when or how Shiloh became an Israelite shrine. What is clear from
the biblical traditions is that Shiloh very early in the pre-monarchic
period served as an important cultic center. Shiloh was the site of the
war-camp in early tradition (Josh. 18.9; Judg. 21.12), and the locus of
the tent shrine (Josh. 18.1; 19.51; ww.9-34; cf. also Ps. 78.60, 67).
During these early years, Shiloh was administered by the Aaronite
priesthood of Eleazar (Josh. 21.1-3) and his son, Phineas (Josh. 22.9-
34), who was renowned for his cultic zeal during the early tribal wars
(Num. 25.6-13; 31.1-12; Josh. 22.9-34; cf. also Judg. 20.1-21.15). At
one time Shiloh even may have claimed an exclusive right over the
other sanctuaries of the land (Josh. 22.9-34; see above, Chapter 4),
although shrines such as Mizpah and Bethel eventually gained
recognition. Indeed, Bethel seems to have been administered by
Aaronite priests, just as Shiloh was (see above, Chapter 6).

A problem of special significance is that of the historical
relationship of Shiloh to the wilderness cultus, with which Shiloh
had special connections through the tent shrine, and the priesthood
of Aaron. The resolution of the conflict between the traditional
evidence that the Israelite tribes were active in the central hill
country before Shiloh became the site of an Israelite shrine (cf. Judg.
21.16-24), and the traditions that the Israelite tribes under Joshua
first erected the tent of meeting at Shiloh, poses like difficulties. So
little is known of the origin of the wilderness cultus, or of the
connection of that cultus to tribes which may have been settled in
Palestine long before its introduction, that no conclusion can here be
ventured on this subject. The biblical traditions and the archaeological
evidence yield only this: that Shiloh at one time had been the site of a
non-Israelite shrine; that it later became an Israelite shrine and for a
time served as the pre-eminent Israelite sanctuary. During this latter
phase, tradition associated Shiloh with the war-camp, the early tribal
wars, and the wilderness cultus, especially the tent of meeting.

8.2.3 *The Late Pre-Monarchic Period: Eli and his Sons*
8.2.3.1 *The Aaronite Priesthood of Eli*
Shiloh's role in Israelite history during the late pre-monarchic period
is attested only in 1 Samuel 1-3, where the priest Eli and his sons
Hophni and Phineas are found ministering in the shrine at Shiloh.

These priests are apparently descendants of the earlier Aaronite priesthood of Eleazar and Phineas, as is suggested by the recurrence of the name of Phineas in the line of Shiloh. That these priests were Aaronite is shown by the consistent identification of Eleazar as the son of Aaron, and Phineas as the son of Eleazar, the son of Aaron. Indeed, the corruption of the sons of Eli stands in sharp contrast to the tradition of the earlier Phineas, who on several occasions acted with violent zeal to preserve the purity of the Yahwistic cultus.

Nevertheless, the classical position formulated by Wellhausen held that the Shilonite priesthood was Mushite (i.e. Mosaic), and that the priesthood of Aaron was actually the later invention of the Zadokite priests of Jerusalem. The fallacy of this formulation, however, is seen in the strong condemnation of the Aaronite priests of Bethel by the cultic community in Jerusalem, which was indisputably Zadokite, and by the traditional association of the Aaronite priests with both Shiloh and Bethel, the two shrines from which Jerusalem felt the strongest competition. Other evidence indicates, moreover, that the Zadokites from the beginning sought not to identify with the Aaronites, but to replace them (cf. 1 Sam. 2.27-36). Finally, Moses was not traditionally the *Urpriester* of Israel's cult, but a trans-historical prophetic figure who commissioned Israel's basic institutions, including the priesthood. Only Aaron appears in the hexateuchal traditions exercising the technical duties of the priesthood. The only cultic center which in fact can be shown to have claimed legitimate Mushite ancestry was that at Dan (Judg. 18.30).

8.2.3.2 *The Shiloh Sanctuary*

1 Sam. 1.9, 24; 3.3, 15 depict Shiloh as the site of a temple at the time that the Elides were ministering there; this possibility may also be implied by the reference to the 'house of God' at Shiloh in Judg. 18.31. Nevertheless, the dominant tradition remains that of the tent shrine. Although the reference to the tent of meeting in 1 Sam. 2.22b may be secondary and late, the Jerusalemite text of Ps. 78.60-72 recalled Shiloh as the locus of a tent sanctuary, and made much of the tent-temple dichotomy between Jerusalem and Shiloh. 2 Sam. 7.6, moreover, claims that Yahweh had never dwelt in a house since his bringing of the Israelites up out of Egypt. Thus it may not be incorrect to understand the reference to a temple in 1 Samuel 1-3 as anachronisms from the time of the monarchy. Both Ps. 78.60-72 and

2 Samuel 7 refer to the pre-Jerusalemite sanctuary using the parallel terms *'ōhel* and *miškān* and lead one to believe that at the time of the demise of Shiloh's priesthood (1 Sam. 4), the chief shrine there had still been the tent of meeting. Nevertheless, the evidence of Judg. 18.30-31 cannot be so easily dismissed, so that the existence of a temple at Shiloh alongside the tent shrine remains a possibility.

Besides the enigmatic references to a Shilonite temple, 1 Samuel 1-3 places the ark there and makes Shiloh the site of an annual pilgrimage (1 Sam. 1.3, 24) as well. The presence of the ark at Shiloh is mentioned in 1 Sam. 3.3; 4.3-11, 17, 22. Ps. 78.61 also seems to provide a veiled reference to the ark at Shiloh. As with the temple, very little is said regarding either the ark or the annual pilgrimage to Shiloh, though certain scholars have wanted to make the pilgrimage the annual Passover feast (see above, 1.3.1).

8.2.4 *Shiloh and the Rise of the Monarchy*
8.2.4.1 *Saul, Samuel and Shiloh*

The traditions of 1 Samuel 1-4 attest not only the cultic role of Shiloh in the life of Israel during the late pre-monarchic era, but also in the rise of the Israelite monarchy. Thus, while 1 Samuel 1-2 on the face of it deals with Samuel's birth and service before the priests of Shiloh, Eli and his sons, this tradition seems originally to have referred to Saul, instead of Samuel. Indeed, the story of the birth and dedication of a child to divine service in 1 Samuel 1-2 is built around a play upon the root *šā'al*, which would best refer to Saul (*šā'ûl*), and not Samuel. The presence of Samuel in these chapters does not appear to be grounded in tradition. Rather, the figure of the prophet Samuel, dedicated to Yahweh at Shiloh, who ultimately supplants the authority of the ancient priesthood of Eli (1 Sam. 3.1-4.1), is the product of the pro-Davidic recension of the narratives of 1-2 Samuel (see above, Chapter 6). The substitution of Samuel for Saul in 1 Samuel 1-2 was meant to replace the traditional connection of Saul to the sanctuary at Shiloh with that of Samuel, who supported the usurper David against his Benjaminite lord Saul. In fact, Samuel had traditional ties not to Shiloh, but to Ramah, Mizpah, Gilgal and Bethel (1 Sam. 1.1-2; 7.15-17; 25.1).

Because the narratives of 1 Samuel 1-2 have been extensively re-edited to eliminate the figure of Saul, Saul's historical connection to Shiloh is difficult to determine. Even assuming that the story of

Saul's birth and his dedication to Yahweh at Shiloh was not true, however, the existence of such a tradition provides evidence that Saul had had a strong bond with the Shilonite sanctuary and priesthood. The nature of this bond comes to light in 1 Sam. 14.3, 18, where Saul is depicted as being accompanied on one of his Philistine campaigns by Ahijah, apparently a younger priest of Shiloh, who serves as oracular priest of the ark. This account suggests that Saul served as king with the open sanction and support of the Shilonite priests. In view of the antiquity of Shiloh's cultic tradition in Israel and its association with the wilderness cultus, support from this quarter would have lent an enormous measure of support to Saul's nascent monarchy.

The incongruous presence of the ark in Saul's camp (1 Sam. 14.18) further suggests that the ark did not fall into the hands of the Philistines long before Saul's monarchy, but that the catastrophe at Aphek must be dated later, to Saul's reign, or after. This difficulty is best resolved by postulating that Saul's defeat on Mt Gilboa (1 Sam. 31; 2 Sam. 1.1-10), for which the Philistines are said to have gathered at Aphek (1 Sam. 29.1; cf. 1 Sam. 4.1), was one and the same as the defeat described in 1 Samuel 4. Thus, the battle in which Saul lost his life was probably the same as that in which the ark was captured.

In sum, the biblical traditions relating to Shiloh's role in the rise of Israel's monarchy originally preserved the memory of the Shilonite priesthood's support of Saul, and of Saul's close association with the Shilonite cult. While he was king, Saul went into battle accompanied by the ark and a representative from the priests of Shiloh. Saul's last battle therefore witnessed not only the slaughter of the priests of Shiloh, but also the capture of the ancient Josephide war-palladium, the ark.

The defeat of Saul on Mt Gilboa had far-reaching consequences. The central hill country fell under Philistine domination once more, and Saul's family fled to Mahanayim in the Transjordan, where Abner, Saul's uncle, attempted to continue the Saulide monarchy under Saul's son (grandson?), Ish-bosheth. The Shilonite priesthood was shattered, and only Phineas's son Ichabod appears to have continued the line. As for the Shilonite sanctuary, the resounding defeat of its protege, Saul, and the exile of the ark to Philistia resulted in a corresponding loss of cultic prestige, which Shiloh apparently never recovered.

In may even be that Shiloh was destroyed at this time, burned to the ground by the victorious Philistines. Nevertheless, nothing is ever said of such a destruction in either Ps. 78.60-72 or 1 Samuel 4, the only two texts to deal explicitly with the events surrounding the capture of the ark. Nor does the claimed archaeological evidence for a massive destruction of the site during Iron I necessarily prove a destruction of Shiloh in conjunction with the events reported in 1 Samuel 4 and Ps. 78.60-72. Indeed, Iron I extends from the end of the thirteenth century BCE to the middle of the tenth, and an Iron I destruction layer theoretically could occur at any time during this period. The 1050 BCE date for this destruction originally proffered by Albright (see above, 3.3) and accepted by the current excavators (see above, 3.4) was based not on stratigraphic evidence, but upon the hypothetical chronology of the events depicted in 1 Samuel. Inasmuch as the order of events in 1 Samuel (esp. chs. 1-7) has been shown to be unreliable (see above, 6.1), any chronology based upon the face-value acceptance of that order of events is likewise dubious. Therefore, in spite of the evcavations at Tell Seilun, the destruction of Shiloh by the Philistines in the mid-eleventh century remains no more than an unconfirmed hypothesis. Indeed, the end of the sanctuary at Shiloh is reported in the biblical traditions only in connection with the fall of the northern kingdom (Judg. 18.30-31; Jer. 7.12-15; 26.6-9).

Thus it is not at all evident from the biblical sources that Shiloh was destroyed by the Philistines in the wake of the disaster at Aphek. It is more likely, in fact, that it was Saul's defeat on Mt Gilboa which brought an end to Shiloh's pre-eminence among the old northern shrines and opened the way for David to establish a new sacral center in Jerusalem.

8.2.4.2 *Summary*

To sum up, the Shilonite sanctuary and priesthood played a key role in the rise of the Israelite monarchy. Shiloh's importance in this development came through Eli and Saul, not through Samuel, and is attested in muted verses in 1 Samuel 1-2 and 14. In the current narratives of 1 Samuel, pro-Davidic editors have masked Saul's association with Shiloh and the Elides with that of Samuel, and seem to have re-arranged the traditions to place the capture of the ark and the slaughter of the Elides before the reign of Saul. The depiction of

Saul's reign as having fallen during a period when the tenure of the Elides was past and the ark was in captivity in Philistia gave the appearance that Saul had reigned without real sacral legitimacy. In all probability, it was the death of Saul and his men on Gilboa, the slaughter of the priests of Shiloh, and the capture of the ark which brought a decisive end to Shiloh's pre-eminence as an Israelite shrine. Nowhere, however, is a destruction of Shiloh or its sanctuary mentioned in connection with these events.

8.2.5 David, Jerusalem, and the Eclipse of Shiloh
8.2.5.1 David's Rise to Power after the Death of Saul
The sudden collapse of Saul's kingdom left the way open for Saul's bitter long-time rival, the Judean condottieri David, to establish his own rule. Nevertheless, it was some time before David was in a position to replace the Saulide monarchy with his own. Not only was Saul's successor, Ish-bosheth, able to maintain his position for some time with the able guidance of Saul's uncle, Abner, but David was able to establish himself only as King of Judah in Hebron (2 Sam. 2.1-4a). The timely deaths of Abner and Ish-bosheth, however, expedited David's quest for Saul's throne (2 Sam. 3.6-4.12).

8.2.5.2 The Eclipse of Shiloh under David
David's elevation to the throne of Israel led to a profound reshaping of the Shiloh traditions in the books of Samuel. Specifically, pro-Davidic editors recast the traditions of 1 Samuel to depict David as the legitimate successor to Saul, anointed by the prophet Samuel, who had replaced the authority once held by the oracular priests of Shiloh (1 Sam. 3.1-4.1a). This recasting of tradition entailed above all the replacement of Saul by Samuel in the birth and youth traditions of 1 Samuel 1-3, a step which broke the traditional connection between Saul and the priests of Shiloh. Nevertheless, hints of Saul's connection to Shiloh are still evident in the word-play on šā'al in 1 Samuel 1-2. At the same time, the Davidic editors of the Samuel narratives appear to have restructured the order of events which resulted in the capture of the ark by the Philistines (1 Sam. 4), so that the priests of Shiloh and the ark no longer appear to be operative during the reign of Saul. 1 Sam. 14.3 and 18, however, still yield traces of the close relationship which Saul enjoyed with the Elides, and of the importance of the ark on his campaigns.

The reasons for this massive revision of the Saulide traditions by pro-Davidic editors are as follows. Like most royal usurpers in the ancient Near East, David came to the throne in desperate need of some form of sacral legitimacy. Although there had been no precedent for Saul's acclamation as king of Israel, the legitimacy of Saul's rule was provided by the ancient Aaronite priesthood of Shiloh. These priests not only lent Saul their official sanction, they accompanied him on his campaigns and consulted the ark for him. David, however, faced a more severe handicap than Saul had: he usurped the throne of a popular warrior-king and did not enjoy the support of Israel's traditional sacral institutions. Instead, David had enjoyed the support of only two religious figures: the priest Abiathar, a junior member of the line of Ahitub of Nob, and the seer Samuel. The latter apparently had condemned Saul and (perhaps) anointed David, thus inaugurating a long history in which reigning monarchs were challenged, and often killed, by prophetically designated or instigated pretenders.

Himself a usurper, David set about to fill for his monarchy the political and sacral void left by the loss of the ark and the demise of Shiloh and its priesthood. His first step in this direction was the selection of his own sacral and political capital. For this purpose, David selected the Jebusite stronghold near Judah's northern border with Benjamin. His troops, led by his lieutenant Joab, probably took the city by slipping up the water shaft (1 Chron. 11.4-9). Most likely Jerusalem was not sacked, but simply subdued. David took pains to preserve the sacral integrity of the ancient fortress city, promoting to priest Zadok, the probable head of the Jebusite cult of El Elyon, alongside the Israelite Abiathar (see above, Chapter 6). Next, David was somehow able to secure the return of the ark from Kiriath-Jearim. He had the ancient tribal war-palladium brought up into his new capital (2 Sam. 6.1-19; cf. 2 Chron. 1.4), thereby appropriating one of the most important north-Israelite cultic symbols to his regime. The ancient tent shrine from Shiloh also may have found its way to the non-Israelite high place of Gibeon during David's reign (1 Chron. 16.39-40; 21.29; 2 Chron. 1.3). Thus, David was able to unify his realm through the establishment of a new sacral and political center, not only for him and his supporters, but for all Israelites who were still moved by their ancestral cultic heritage.

These abrupt changes effected by David are variously reflected in the Shiloh oracle (Gen. 49.10-12) and in Ps. 78.60-72. Gen. 49.10-12 celebrates David's appropriation of the sacral traditions of Shiloh and his choice of Jerusalem as his new capital, a choice on which he hung his hopes for successs and prosperity (cf. esp. vv. 11-12). Ps. 78.60-72 stems from the period after Solomon's construction of the temple on Mount Zion and celebrates Jerusalem's replacement of Shiloh as the chief sanctuary of Yahweh. For this psalm, the sacral glory of Shiloh is past, having been rejected by Yahweh in favor of Jerusalem. David's sacral innovations allowed him to appropriate to his own monarchy the heritage which formerly had been resident at Shiloh, and to set in motion the ultimate eclipse of Shiloh and its sanctuary by Jerusalem.

8.2.5.3 *Summary*

In sum, David consolidated his territory and established his throne in a non-Israelite city with its own ancient sacral traditions. He then commandeered the ark—sacred symbol of Shiloh's sanctuary and ancient war-palladium of the northern tribes—and transferred the tent shrine to the non-Israelite high place at Gibeon (cf. 2 Sam. 21.1-9). Indeed, David appears to have had special ties to the Gibeonite shrine, which Solomon, his son and successor, seems to have shared (1 Kgs 3.4-9; 9.1-2). By this means, David displaced the cultic prestige once held by Shiloh and ensured the emergence of a new sacral order, at the center of which stood Jerusalem and its priesthood. The construction of the temple on Mount Zion by Solomon inaugurated Jerusalem's final eclipse of Shiloh.

8.2.6 *Shiloh During the Divided Monarchy and Exile*
8.2.6.1 *Shiloh and the Break-up of David's Kingdom*

Despite David's efforts to create a new and unified sacral and political order centered in Jerusalem, northern disaffection with his reign continued, and he was forced to put down two major revolts (2 Sam. 15-20). Solomon's reign was troubled by revolts in Syria and Edom, as well as by disaffection in the North, led by Jeroboam the son of Nebat (1 Kgs 11). Under Solomon's successor Rehoboam, the northern tribes finally broke away from Judah to form their own kingdom under Jeroboam.

Just as David had claimed prophetic anointing to succeed Saul, Jeroboam was anointed by the prophet, Ahijah the Shilonite, to rule over the northern tribes. Although the Deuteronomistic Historian saw the revolt of the North under Jeroboam as Yahweh's judgment upon Solomon for his idolatry, Ahijah may have had other motives for anointing Jeroboam. That Ahijah resided at Shiloh, and that he bore the name of the oracular priest who accompanied Saul on his campaigns (1 Sam. 14.3, 18) suggests that he may have been of the line of Eli, and thus the bearer of the hopes for the restoration of the ancient Josephide sanctuary. His anointing of Jeroboam, if it is indeed historical, might therefore have been motivated by the desire to see Shiloh re-established as the chief sanctuary of the North (see above, 7.1). Similarly, Ahijah's condemnation of Jeroboam after that king's elevation of Dan and Bethel as royal shrines (1 Kgs 14.4-16) may have arisen in part from his own disappointment that Shiloh had not been so favored.

8.2.6.2 *The Continuation of Shiloh During the Divided Monarchy*
The traditions which preserve the memory of Ahihjah's role in the secession of the northern tribes from the Davidic monarchy also have an important bearing on the problem of Shiloh's fate following the disaster at Aphek. That Shiloh appears as the domicile of the prophet Ahijah suggests that Shiloh, if indeed it had been destroyed earlier in the Iron Age, had been re-occupied and maintained at least the tradition of its former cultic heritage. The discovery of a large number of Iron II vessels and sherds by the Danish excavators in 1963 corroborates this biblical evidence that Shiloh had continued to be occupied during the period of the divided monarchy. There is no evidence at all for the older view that Shiloh had been destroyed after Aphek and had lain deserted until the time of Jeremiah.

8.2.6.3 *Shiloh During the Time of Jeremiah*
The biblical text is silent with regard to Shiloh from the time of Ahijah down to the last tortured years of the kingdom of Judah, when the old northern shrine re-emerges in the preaching of Jeremiah (see above, Chapter 7). According to Jer. 7.12-15 and 26.6-9, Shiloh was a deserted ruin on the eve of Jerusalem's fall. Jeremiah used this fact to prophesy a similar judgment upon Jerusalem, and claimed that as Jerusalem had inherited Shiloh's cultic glory, so would the holy city inherit Shiloh's desolation. The ruins to which Jeremiah alluded probably stemmed from the desolation of the northern kingdom in

the last quarter of the eighth century BCE (see above, Chapter 7), and not from a hypothesized destruction by the Philistines in the mid-eleventh century. By the time of the exile, however, Shiloh had been re-occupied, and was an inhabited place during Gedaliah's tenure at Mizpah (Jer. 41.5).

8.2.7 *Conclusion*

The history of Shiloh was long and complex. From the sanctuary's beginnings in the Middle Bronze Age, through the turbulent years of the Late Bronze and Early Iron Ages, when Shiloh made the transition from a non-Israelite shrine to the chief sanctuary of the tribes settled in the hill country of Ephraim, only brief and tantalizing glimpses of the role of Shiloh in the religious life of Palestine, and later, Israel, are available. The same is true for the subsequent years as well: the relationship of the Shilonite shrine and priesthood to Israel's first king, Saul, must be carefully gleaned from the heavily edited traditions of 1 Samuel. The mechanics of Shiloh's demise and ultimate eclipse by Jerusalem can be tentatively reconstructed in a similar manner, though the celebration of this development in Davidic and Jerusalemite circles makes it a matter of record.

Conversely, a destruction of Shiloh by the Philistines, if one ever did occur, has been preserved nowhere in the biblical traditions and was not regarded as the necessary pre-condition to Jerusalem's accession to Shiloh's earlier status in any biblical text. Shiloh's downfall and the subsequent elevation of Jerusalem were not the result of any Philistine destruction, but of several factors: (1) the collapse of the kingdom of Saul, with which Shiloh and its priesthood were identified; (2) the slaughter of the Shilonite priests; (3) the capture of the ark, and (4) David's deliberate policy of appropriating to his sacral capital of Jerusalem the cultic symbols and traditions which had once resided at Shiloh.

Despite the eclipse of Shiloh by Jerusalem, the place seems to have been occupied down to the fall of the northern kingdom, during which period it probably continued to nurture its ancient sacral traditons. After the desolation of the Ephraimite hill country by the Assyrians, Shiloh lay waste until it was re-inhabited during the Judean exile. Therafter, practically nothing is known of Shiloh's history, though its occupation continued down into the Hellenistic and Roman periods.

APPENDIX

Table 1: The Formal Arrangement of the List of Tribal Inheritances in Josh. 14.1–19.51 according to Superscription and Subscriptions

General Superscription:

Josh. 14.1: *we'elleh 'ăšer-niḥălû-bēnê-Yiśrā'ēl bē'ereṣ kĕna'an 'ăšer niḥălû 'ôtām*
'el'āzār hakkōhēn wîhôšua' bin-nûn wĕro'šê 'ăbôt hammaṭṭôt libnê Yiśrā'ēl

Superscription for the allotment (*gôrāl*) of Judah

15.1: *wayhî haggôrāl lĕmaṭṭēh bĕnê yĕhûdāh lĕmišpĕḥôtām*

Subscription for the boundary-territory (*gĕbûl*) of Judah

15.12b: *zeh gĕbûl bĕnê-yĕhûdāh sābîb lĕmišpĕḥôtām*

Superscription for the inheritance (*naḥălāh*) of Judah (according to cities)

15.20: *zō't naḥălat maṭṭēh bĕnê-yehûdāh lĕmišpĕḥôtām* (Note: was this transposed from after 15.62, to be used as a superscription for the city lists, following the insertion of 15.13-19?)

Second superscription for the cities of Judah

15.21a: *wayyihyû he'ārîm (miqṣēh) lĕmaṭṭēh bĕnê-yĕhûdāh*

(No final subscription for Judah)

Superscription for the allotment (*gôrāl*) of Joseph

16.1: *wayyēṣē' haggôrāl libnê yôsēp*

Superscription for the boundary/territory (*gĕbûl*) of Ephraim

16.5: *wayhî gĕbûl bĕnê-'eprayim lĕmišpĕḥôtām*

Subscription for the inheritance (*naḥălāh*) of Ephraim

16.8b: *zō't naḥălat maṭṭēh bĕnê-'eprayim lĕmišpĕḥôtām*

Superscription for the allotment (*gôrāl*) of Manasseh

17.1: *wayhî haggôrāl lĕmaṭṭēh mĕnaššeh*

(No subscription for Manasseh)

Superscription for the allotment (*gôrāl*) of Benjamin

18.11a: *wayya'al gôrāl maṭṭēh bĕnê-binyāmin*

Subscription for the inheritance (*naḥălāh*) of Benjamin (according to its boundaries)

18.20b: *zō't naḥălat bĕnê binyāmin ligbûlôtēhā sābîb lĕmišpĕḥôtām*

Superscription for the cities of Benjamin

18.21a: *wĕhayû he'ārîm lĕmaṭṭēh bĕnê binyāmin lĕmišpĕḥôtēhem*

Subscription for the inheritance (*naḥălāh*) of Benjamin

18.28b: *zō't naḥălat bĕnê-binyāmin lĕmišpĕḥôtām*

Superscription for the allotment (*gôrāl*) of Simeon

19.1: *wayyēṣē' haggôrāl haššēnî lĕšim'ôn lĕmaṭṭēh bēnê-šim'ôn lĕmišpĕḥôtām*

Subscription for the inheritance (*naḥălāh*) of Simeon

19.8b: *zō't naḥălat maṭṭēh bĕnê-šim'ôn lĕmišpĕḥôtām*

Superscription for the allotment (*gôrāl*) of Zebulun

19.10a: *wayya'al haggôrāl haššĕlîšî libnê zĕbûlun*

Subscription for the inheritance (*naḥălāh*) of Zebulun

19.16a: *zō't naḥălat bĕnê-zĕbûlun lĕmišpĕḥôtām*

Superscription for the allotment (*gôrāl*) of Issachar

19.17: *lĕyiśśākār yāṣā' haggôrāl hārĕbî'î libnê yiśśākār lĕmišpĕḥôtām*

Subscription for the inheritance (*naḥălāh*) of Issachar

19.12a: *zō't naḥălat maṭṭēh bĕnê-yiśśākār lĕmišpĕḥôtām*

Superscription for the allotment (*gôrāl*) of Asher

19.24: *wayyēṣē' haggôrāl hāḥămîšî lĕmaṭṭēh bĕnê-'āšēr lĕmišpĕḥôtām*

Subscription for the inheritance (*naḥălāh*) of Asher

19.31a: *zō't naḥălat maṭṭēh bĕnê-'āšēr lĕmišpĕḥôtām*

Superscription for the allotment (*gôrāl*) of Naphtali

19.32: *libnê naptālî yāṣā' haggôrāl haššiššî libnê naptālî lĕmišpĕḥôtām*

Subscription for the inheritance (*naḥălāh*) of Naphtali

19.39a: *zō't naḥălat maṭṭēh bĕnê-naptālî lĕmišpĕḥôtām*

Superscription for the allotment (*gôrāl*) of Dan

19.40: *lemaṭṭēh bĕnê-dān lĕmišpĕḥôtām*

Superscription for the inheritance (*naḥălat*) of Dan

19.48a: *zō't naḥălat maṭṭēh bĕnê-dān lĕmišpĕḥôtām*

General Colophon for the entire list

19.51a: *'ēlleh hannaḥălôt 'ăšer niḥălû*
*'el'āzār hakkōhēn wîhôšua' bin-nûn wĕro'šê hā'ābôt lĕmaṭṭôt bĕnê-
Yiśrā'ēl bĕgôrāl bĕšilōh lipnê Yhwh petaḥ 'ōhel mô'ēd*

Table 2: Subscriptions regarding the Cities and Villages of the Tribal Inheritances

Benjamin	Josh. 18.28a:	*'ārîm 'arba'-'eśrēh wĕḥaṣrêhen*
Zebulun	Josh. 19.15b:	*'ārîm šĕtêm-'eśrēh wĕḥaṣrêhem*
	Josh. 19.16b:	*he'ārîm hā'ēlleh wĕḥaṣrêhen*
Issachar	Josh. 19.23b:	*he'ārîm wĕḥaṣrêhen*
Asher	Josh. 19.31b:	*he'ārîm hā'ēlleh wĕḥaṣrêhen*
Naphtali	Josh. 19.39b:	*he'ārîm wĕḥaṣrêhen*
Dan	Josh. 19.48b:	*he'ārîm hā'ēlleh wĕḥaṣrêhen*

Table 3: The Arrangement of the Conquest Traditions in Joshua 14–19

14.6-15:	The tradition of Caleb's inheritance in Hebron
15.13-19:	Traditions of Caleb and Othniel
17.1b:	Tradition of Machir
17.14-19:	Tradition of Joseph's occupation of the hill country

Table 4: The Historical Expansions and Anecdotes to the List of Tribal Inheritances in Joshua 14–19

| 14.2-5: | Historical introduction to the distribution of the land as based upon the injunction in Num. 34.13-15. This pericope |

ties the list to the Priestly narrative of the Hexateuch.

15.63:   Historical anecdote over the Jebusite occupation of Jerusalem 'until this day'.

16.9:   Historical anecdote over the Ephraimite towns in the inheritance of Manasseh (cf. 17.11).

16.10:   Historical anecdote over the Canaanites in Gezer.

17.2:   The further descendents of Manasseh (P).

17.3-6:   The inheritance of the daughters of Zelophehad (P) (note: no connection between 17.1b and 17.3-6).

17.11-13:   Historical anecdote over the Manassehite towns in Issachar and Asher, and Manasseh's failure to drive out the Canaanites (cf. Judg. 1.27-28; Josh. 16.9).

18.1-10:   Bringing up of the *'ōhel mô'ēd* to Shiloh, and casting of lots for the remaining seven tribes.

19.9:   Explanation of Simeon's inheritance in Judah.

19.47:   Historical anecdote over the Danites' loss of their inheritance.

19.49-50:   Joshua's inheritance in Timnath-serah (P).

19.51b: Historical summary, appended to subscription.

Table 5: The Priestly Language of Josh. 22.9-34

'ereṣ kĕna'an: vv. 9a, 10a, 11, 32

šilōh: vv. 9a, 12b

'ăhuzzāh: vv. 9, 19 (with verb *'āḥaz*)

'al-pî Yhwh bĕyad-mōšeh: v. 9

wayyiqqāhălu kol-'ădat bĕnê-Yiśrā'ēl: v. 12
    (cf. Josh. 18.2)

kol-'ădat Yhwh: v. 15b

kol-'adat Yiśrā'ēl: vv. 18b, 20a

pînḥas ben-'el'āzār hakkōhēn: vv. 13b, 31a, 32a

pînḥās hakkōhēn: v. 30a

la'ăbōd 'ăbōdat Yhwh: v. 27

ṭĕmē'āh 'ereṣ 'ăhuzzatkem: v. 19a
    (cf. this cryptic question in light of Lev. 18.24-30; Num. 35.29-34)

zibḥê šĕlāmîm: v. 23

mered: v. 22

mārad: vv. 16, 18, 19, 29

mā'al ... ma'al: vv. 16, 20, 31

nāśî': vv. 14 (3×), 30a, 32a
    (cf. Num. 17.17, 21: Josh. 22.14a; Num. 4.34 : Josh. 22.30a)

hiṭṭharnû: v. 17

miškān [Yhwh]: vv. 19, 29

NOTES

Notes to Chapter 1

1. *De Templo Silonensi, commentatio ad illustrandum locum Iud. xviii 30, 31* (1855); see below (1.3.5).
2. *Geschichte Israels* (Berlin: G. Reimer, 1978); subsequently reprinted under the title, *Prolegomena zur Geschichte Israels* (Berlin: G. Reimer, 1883).
3. (2 vols.; Halle: ben Schimmelpfennig u. Co., 1806, 1807). For the most recent treatment of de Wette's general role in the nineteenth-century debate, see John Rogerson, *Old Testament Criticism in the Nineteenth Century: England and Germany* (London: Fortress, 1985), pp. 28-49. On the more technical aspects of de Wette's work, see Rudolf Smend, *Wilhelm Martim Leberecht de Wettes Arbeit am Alten und am Neuen Testament* (Basel: Helbing & Lichtenbahn, 1958).
4. De Wette, *Beiträge*, I, pp. 225-65.
5. De Wette recognized the importance of Joshua 22 in this debate, but considered this passage late, precisely because it assumed that only a single central sanctuary was lawful; cf. *Beiträge*, I, pp. 227-28.
6. Ibid., pp. 229-34.
7. Ibid., pp. 254-58.
8. Ibid., pp. 227-58.
9. Cf. 2 Kgs 23.21-23.
10. Ibid., pp. 258-61.
11. Ibid., pp. 259-61, 267-68.
12. Ibid., p. 261.
13. (3rd edn; Leipzig: Wilhelm Vogel, 1842), pp. 300-302.
14. Ibid., 301; *idem, Beiträge*, I, pp. 231-32.
15. Ibid., pp. 232-33.
16. De Wette, *Lehrbuch*, p. 302.
17. Ibid., p. 302 n. a; *idem, Beiträge*, I, pp. 110-12.
18. (Leipzig: Carl Heinrich, 1820), p. 637.
19. Ibid., pp. 669-72.
20. Ibid., p. 671.
21. (2 vols.; Berlin: Duncker und Humblot, 1929).
22. Ibid., pp. 12-15.
23. Ibid., p. 75; cf. de Wette, *Beiträge*, I, pp. 227-28.
24. Gramberg, *Religionsideen*, I, pp. 81-85.

25. Ibid., p. 75. The tent shrine is never mentioned in the book of Judges. Only in the references cited from Joshua, in 1 Sam. 2.22b, and in Ps. 78.60, 67 does one find mention of the tent sanctuary at Shiloh.

26. Ibid., p. 20.

27. Ibid., p. 25. See below, Hengstenberg (1.3.1), Saalschütz (1.3.6), and Bleek (1.3.8).

28. Ibid., pp. 28-29.

29. Ibid., p. 30.

30. See above, n. 27.

31. (Berlin: G. Bethge, 1835).

32. Ibid., pp. 263-65, 343-91.

33. Ibid., pp. 264-65.

34. Ibid., pp. 264-66.

35. Ibid., p. 272.

36. See above, nn. 30, 37.

37. Edward Robinson and Eli Smith, *Biblical Researches in Palestine, and in the Adjacent Regions: A Journal of Travels in the Year 1838* (2 vols.; 11th edn; London: John Murray, 1874).

38. Ibid., II, pp. 269-71; the final *nûn* found in the Arabic *Seilun* is preserved in the gentilic form of the Hebrew *šîlōnî*: 1 Kgs 11.29; 12.15; 15.29.

39. Ernst Wilhelm Hengstenberg, *Die Authentie des Pentateuches* (2 vols.; Berlin: Ludwig Oehmigke, 1839).

40. De Wette, *Beiträge* I, pp. 256-57. It is important to note that de Wette's arguments were based on the assumption that the pentateuchal cultus was *vaterländisch* in both origin and goal. That is, the laws ascribed to Moses had been patriotic in design and purpose. It is highly doubtful whether this assumption is correct. In fact, it reflects de Wette's own nineteenth-century Germanic attitude toward the role of religion in uniting *Volk und Staat*, more than it does the substance of the Pentateuch.

41. Hengstenberg, *Authentie*, II, pp. 2-8.

42. The greatest difficulty with Hengstenberg's critique was that while he could show *how* the narratives of Judges might be *interpreted* so as to avoid a contradiction of pentateuchal law on the issue of cultic centralization, he could not demonstrate his point simply on the basis of the narratives themselves. Much of his work was further characterized by a tendency to harmonize dissimilar accounts. Thus, for example, the writer of the story of Gideon regards the erection of an *'ēphôd* as heretical, even though the *'ēphôd* later plays an important role in the narratives of Saul (1 Sam. 14.3, 18) and David (1 Sam. 21.9; 23.6; 30.7), and is a central feature of the priestly cultus of the Pentateuch (cf. esp. Exodus 28, 39). Hengstenberg, however, made no mention of such discrepancies in the biblical narratives, and sought simply to explain them away.

43. Hengstenberg, *Authentie*, II, pp. 14-15.

44. Ibid., p. 41.

45. Cf. Gramberg, *Religionsideen*, pp. 22-23; Gramberg argued that Gideon had indeed erected a permanent cultus as 'Ophrah, noting that Judg. 6.24 states that Gideon's altar 'stands until this day at 'Oprah of the Abi'ezerites'. Further, this altar at 'Ophrah was probably to be identified with the *'ēphôd* erected by Gideon in his native city, for which act Gideon was reprimanded by the narrator in Judg. 8.27.

46. Hengstenberg, *Authentie*, II, p. 45.

47. Ibid., pp. 45-48, 52.

48. Ibid.

49. Ibid., p. 52; cf. Hengstenberg, *The Genuineness of the Pentateuch* (Vol. II; Edinburgh: T.& T. Clark, 1847), p. 43, improperly translated as '. . . and I am going to the house of the Lord'.

50. Hengstenberg, *Authentie*, II, p. 53.

51. Ibid., pp. 53, 79-85.

52. Ibid., p. 80.

53. Actually, he should have cited v. 3.

54. Ibid., pp. 82.83.

55. Ibid., pp. 53-56.

56. Ibid., p. 56. Hengstenberg also cited several instances from these chapters where institutions prescribed in the Mosaic law were given incidental mention.

57. (3rd edn; Göttingen: Dietrichsche Buchhandlung, 1864-1866). An eighth volume, *Die Alterthümer des Volkes Israel*, appeared as an appendix to the first and second volumes.

58. For a contemporary summary of the Ewald's 'Supplementary Hypothesis', see Friedrich Bleek, *Einleitung in das Alte Testament* (ed. J. Wellhausen; 4th edn; Berlin: G. Reimer, 1878), pp. 60-61. Good general summaries of Ewald's work can be found in John H. Hayes, 'The History of the Study of Israelite and Judean History', *Israelite and Judean History*, ed. John H. Hayes, and J. Maxwell Miller (Philadelphia: Westminster, 1977), pp. 59-61; and Rogerson, *Nineteenth Century*, pp. 91-103.

59. Ewald, *Geschichte*, I, pp. 125, 129.

60. Ibid., I, pp. 171-78.

61. Ibid., I, pp. 92-99.

62. Ibid., I, p. 129; cf. also n. 1. Cited from Ewald, *History of Israel* (Vol. I; London: Longmans, Green, and Co., 1876), p. 87.

63. Ibid., II, p. 493.

64. Ibid., II, p. 492, esp. n. 1.

65. Ibid., II, p. 494.

66. De Wette, *Beiträge*, I, p. 255.

67. Ewald, *Geschichte*, I, pp. 226-58.

68. Ibid., II, pp. 577-78, esp. n. 1.
69. Ibid., II, p. 392.
70. Cf. Hengstenberg, *Authentie*, II, p. 56.
71. Ewald, *Geschichte*, II, p. 392.
72. Ibid.
73. Ibid., II, p. 393.
74. Ibid., II, p. 344.
75. Ibid., II, p. 584.
76. De Wette, *Beiträge*, I, pp. 3-132.
77. Ewald, *Geschichte*, II, pp. 584-85.
78. 2nd edn, 1854/1855; 3rd edn, 1864/1866.
79. Cf. Ewald, *Geschichte*, I, pp. 528-30; Noth, *Das System der zwölf Stämme Israels* (Stuttgart: W. Kohlhammer, 1930), pp. 43, 46-47. While Ewald never used the term 'amphictyony', he developed the idea of the tribal confederacy, and supported it by reference to the sacral leagues of classical antiquity. Cf. Otto Bächli, *Amphictyonie im Alten Testament* (Basel: Friedrich Reinhardt, 1977), pp. 17-19, for a discussion of the development of the theory of the amphictyony in Old Testament studies.
80. (2nd edn; Berlin: Carl Heymann, 1853).
81. Ibid., pp. xxviii-xxx.
82. Ibid., p. xxxi: 'Mann' oder 'Versammlung'.
83. Ibid.
84. Ibid., pp. 303-306, esp. nn. 380, 381; also see Karl Christian Wilhelm Felix Bahr, *Die Symbolik des mosäischen Cultus* (Heidelberg: J.C.B. Mohr, 1837-1838).
85. See below, Bleek (1.3.8), von Haneberg (1.3.11), and Kaufmann (3.7).
86. (Gotha: Friedrich Andreas Perthes, 1854).
87. Riehm, *Gesetzgebung*, pp. vi-viii.
88. Ibid., p. 28.
89. Although Reuss shared Graf's views, he did not publish these until much later than Graf. Reuss laid out his synthesis first in his *Geschichte der heiligen Schriften Alten Testaments* (Braunschweig: C.A. Schwetschke u. Sohn, 1881).
90. Ibid., pp. 15-16.
91. Ibid., pp. 2-8.
92. Ibid., pp. 1, 33.
93. See below (1.3.10) for Graf's later views on the history of Shiloh, and (1.3.11) for von Haneberg's conservative critique of Graf's views as presented in *De Templo Silonensi*.
94. (Königsberg: Bornträger, 1855) and above (1.3.3).
95. Ibid., p. 234; cf. Hengstenberg (above, 1.3.1), who claimed that the terms *bēt-hā'ĕlōhîm* and *bēt-Yhwh* in Judges 17–18 denoted the tent of

meeting at Shiloh, and that *miqdaš-Yhwh* in Joshua 24 referred not to a temple, but to any sacred place. While the arguments of Hengstenberg and Saalschütz were not identical, they followed the same general lines.

96. Ibid., pp. 233-36.
97. Ibid., p. 330.
98. Ibid., p. 331.
99. Cf. Saalschütz (above, 1.3.3).
100. Ibid. A similar view was taken by Bleek (below, 1.3.8), and by Kaufmann (below, 3.7).
101. Saalschütz, *Archaeologie*, p. 331.
102. (2 vols.; Frankfurt am Main/Erlangen: Heyder und Zimmer, 1858, 1859).
103. Ibid., I, pp. 116-18.
104. Ibid.
105. Ibid., I, pp. 187-90.
106. Cf. 2 Sam. 8.17; 15.24, 35; 17.15; 1 Chron. 15.11.
107. See Graf (above, 1.3.5).
108. (Berlin: G. Reimer, 1860).
109. Ibid., pp. 188-90; Bleek's position here was almost identical to that taken by Riehm (above, 1.3.4) and is identical to that developed later by Kaufmann (below, 3.7).
110. Bleek, *Einleitung*, pp. 189-91.
111. Cf., for example, Exodus 25-31; Leviticus 10, 16; ibid., p. 193;
112. For this discussion in its entirety, see ibid., pp. 181-200.
113. Ibid., p. 322.
114. Ibid., pp. 321-23.
115. Ibid., p. 330.
116. Ibid., pp. 343-48.
117. (Berlin: Wilhelm Hertz, 1866).
118. Ibid., p. 199.
119. Ibid., pp. 195-201.
119. (Leipzig: T.O. Weigel, 1866).
120. It is important to note, however, that Graf did not revert to the 'fragmentary hypothesis' laid down by Vater and de Wette.
121. Graf, *Geschichtlichen Bücher*, pp. 95-96: esp. the later chapters of Joshua were seen by Graf as dependent upon Numbers and Deuteronomy.
122. See below, ch. 2.
123. 'Zur Geschichte des Stammes Levi', *Archiv für wissenschaftliche Erforschung des Alten Testamentes*, ed. Adalbert Merx (2 vols.; Halle: Buchhandlung des Waisenhauses, 1867, 1869), I, pp. 68-106.
124. Ibid., p. 88.
125. Ibid., pp. 78-79, and n. 3.
126. Ibid., p. 81.

127. Ibid., pp. 71-72, 79-80, 83-84.
128. (Freiburg/Leipzig: J.C.B. Mohr, 1896).
129. (München: J.G. Cotta, 1869).
130. Ibid., pp. 161-62.
131. Ibid., pp. 208-209.
132. *M. Zebah.* 14.4-8; *Meg.* 1.11. Further, *m. Zebah.* 14.6, describes the structure as being built of stone, with a tent roof; also, cf. Saalschütz, *Recht*, pp. 297-306.
133. Ibid., pp. 211-15.
134. Ibid., p. 212.
135. Ibid., p. 214.
136. Cf. the description of the ark in 1 Kgs 8.8: 'The poles were so long that the ends of the poles were seen from the holy place (*haqqōdeš*) before the inner sanctuary (*haddebîr*)... and they are there to this day'. It would seem that the ark and the other items from the pre-Jerusalemite cultus had been taken up into the temple and deposited there as *reliquiae*.
137. Von Haneberg, *Alterthümer*, pp. 165-69.
138. Ibid.
139. Ibid., pp. 208-13.
140. (Göttingen: Vandenhoeck & Ruprecht, 1871).
141. Ibid., p. 46.
142. (2 vols.; Tübingen: J.J. Heckenhauer, 1873, 1874).
143. Ibid., II, pp. 1-5.
144. Ibid., II, p. 6; see Saalschütz (1.3.6), Bleek (1.3.8).
145. See above, 1.3.1. Oehler followed Hengstenberg, and to a lesser extent, Ewald, in his historical reconstruction.
146. Oehler, *Theologie*, II, pp. 5-7.
147. Ibid., II, p. 13.
148. (2 vols.; Erlangen: Andreas Deichert, 1875, 1884).
149. Ibid., I, p. 364, and above (1.3.11).
150. Ibid., II, p. 13.
151. Ibid., I, p. 496.
152. Cf. Saalschütz (above, 1.3.6).

Notes to Chapter 2

1. See above (1.3.10).
2. =*The Origin and Composition of the Hexateuch* (London: Macmillan, 1886) = *Historisch-kritische Einleitung in die Bücher des Alten Testaments* (Leipzig: O.R. Reisland, 1890).
3. =*The Religion of Israel* (London: Williams and Norgate, 1882).
4. Cf. e.g. 'Critische Bijtragen tot de Gischiedenis van den Israelitischen

Godsdienst, IV: Zadok en de Zadokieten', *Theologisch Tijdschrift* 3 (1869), pp. 463-509; 'VII: De Stam Levi', 5 (1872), pp. 628-70.

5. Kuenen, *Hexateuch*, pp. xi-xl.

6. Ibid., pp. xxxiii-xxxiv. Kayser's work was strenuously opposed by Theodor Nöldeke and Eberhard Schrader. Nöldeke's major contributions to the debate (*Die alttestamentliche Literatur in einer Reihe von Aufsätzen dargestellt* [Leipzig: Quand & Handel, 1868], and *Untersuchungen zur Kritik des Alten Testaments* [Kiel: Schwer'sche Buchhandlung, 1869]) had already appeared in print by the time of Kayser's work. Schrader's initial work, *Studien zur Kritik und Erklärung der biblischen Urgeschichte* (Zürich: Meyer & Zeller, 1863), had been published a decade before that of Kayser. Schrader published a second volume, however, which ran through several editions, entitled *Die Keilinschriften und das Alte Testament* (Giessen: J. Ricker, 1872).

7. Ibid., pp. xxxv-xxxviii.

8. 1876-1877; republished in monograph form as *Die Composition des Hexateuchs und der historischen Bücher des Alten Testaments* (3rd edn; Berlin: Walter de Gruyter, 1963).

9. Reprinted under the title, *Prolegomena zur Geschichte Israels*.

10. See above, Saalschütz (1.3.3), and von Haneberg (1.3.11).

11. Wellhausen, *Geschichte Israels*, p. 44; idem, *Israelitische und jüdische Geschichte* (Berlin: G. 1897), p. 36.

12. Wellhausen, *Composition*, p. 233.

13. Wellhausen, *Geschichte Israels*, p. 42.

14. Ibid., pp. 130-34.

15. Ibid., pp. 146-53.

16. Ibid., p. 131.

17. Wellhausen, *Israelitische und jüdische Geschichte*, p. 52.

18. (2 vols.; Bielefeld/Leipzig: Velhagen & Klasing, 1884), II, p. 1566; cf. *idem, Einleitung in das Alte Testament* (Halle: Eugen Strien, 1889).

19. Ibid., II, p. 1476b; cf. Hengstenberg (1.3.1), Saalschütz (1.3.6), Köhler (1.3.14).

20. Karl Budde, *Die Bücher Samuel* (Tübingen/Leipzig: J.C.B. Mohr [Paul Siebeck], 1902), p. 23.

21. Wellhausen, *Composition*, pp. 236-40.

22. *Geschichte des Volkes Israel* (Vol. I; Berlin: G. Grote, 1887) pp. 197-202.

23. Ibid., pp. 202, 457.

24. Ibid., pp. 198-99.

25. *Lehrbuch der Alttestamentlichen Religionsgeschichte* (2nd edn; Freiburg: J.C.B. Mohr [Paul Siebeck], 1899), pp. 72-73.

26. Ibid., pp. 137-38.

27. Ibid., pp. 37-38 n. 2. Smend further considered 1 Sam. 1.27-36 to refer to Eli's Mushite descent (ibid., p. 72).

28. Ibid., p. 72.

29. *Geschichte des Volkes Israel* (2nd edn; Tübingen/Leipzig: J.C.B. Mohr [Paul Siebeck], 1904), pp. 44-45.

30. See above, 1.3.2.

31. *Die Lade Jahves* (FRLANT, 7; Göttingen: Vandenhoeck & Ruprecht, 1906). An extensive bibliography on the subject of the ark, which covers subjects such as the ark and the tent as well, is found in Rainer Schmitt's *Zelt und Lade* (Gütersloh: Gerd Mohn, 1972).

32. Ibid., p. 119.

33. Ibid., pp. 121-22.

34. See below, chapter 6.

35. Ibid., p. 122 n. 2. Cf. 1 Sam. 7.15-17. This is an important point—one which has been overlooked in subsequent treatments—and one to which the present discussion will return below, ch. 6.

36. *Hebräische Archaeologie* (Freiburg: J.C.B. Mohr [Paul Siebeck], 1894), p. 409.

37. *Die Israeliten und ihre Nachbarstämme* (Halle: Max Niemeyer, 1906).

38. Ibid., pp. 92-93.

39. Ibid., p. 93. Meyer attributed this view to *Redslobs*, but gave no other reference by which this author or his work might be identified.

40. Ibid., pp. 134-35.

41. Ibid., pp. 135-36.

42. Ibid., pp. 134, 135, 163.

43. Ibid., pp. 214-15.

44. Ibid., pp. 215-16.

45. See below, 2.5.2.

46. Cf. Gunkel's treatment of the results of pentateuchal criticism in his volume, *Die Urgeschichte und die Patriarchen* in *Die Schriften des Alten Testaments*, ed. H. Gressmann, H. Gunkel et al. (6 vols.; Göttingen: Vandenhoeck & Ruprecht, 1911) I.1, pp. 4-5.

47. *The Documents of the Hexateuch* (2 vols.; New York: G. Putnam's Sons, 1898), II, p. v.

48. A. Knobel, *Die Bücher Exodus und Leviticus*, ed. August Dillmann (2nd edn; Leipzig: s. Hirzel, 1880).

49. August Dillmann, *Die Bücher Numeri, Deuteronomium, und Josua* (2nd edn; Leipzig: S. Hirzel, 1886). Dillmann's appendix to this last commentary, 'Die Composition des Hexateuch', pp. 593-690, occupied the same status among the critics of the Graf-Wellhausen hypothesis which came to be assumed by Wellhausen's *Composition* and by his *Geschichte Israels* among proponents of that theory. The treatments by both scholars are crucial to an understanding of the historical debate.

50. Dillmann, *Numeri*, p. 607.

51. Cf. Exod. 33.7-11; Num. 11.16, 24ff.; 12.4; Deut. 31.14.

52. Dillmann, 'Composition', pp. 607-609.

53. Dillmann, *Numeri*, p. 294; Franz Delitzsch, 'Pentateuch-kritische Studien', *Zeitschrift für kirchliche Wissenschaft und kirchliches Leben* 11, pp. 562-67; cf. Rogerson, *Nineteenth Century*, pp. 104-20, for a general treatment of Delitzsch's work in biblical studies; Paul Kleinert, *Das Deuteronomium und der Deuteronomiker* (Bielefeld/Leipzig: Velhagen & Klasing, 1872), pp. 154-58.

54. Cf. Smend (2.3.2), Stade (2.3.1), Guthe (2.3.2), and Meyer (2.3.4).

55. 1 Chron. 24.1-6 traces Zadok from Eleazar and Ahimelech from Ithamar. Presumably then, Chronicles also traced the Elides from Ithamar, given the connection between these two lines in 1 Sam. 14.3; 1 Kgs 2.27.

56. Dillmann, 'Composition', p. 660.

57. Delitzsch, 'Pentateuch', I, pp. 57-66.

58. Ibid., I, pp. 57-66. On this issue, compare De Vaux, below, 3.7.

59. Delitzsch also cited 1 Sam. 1.9 in this connection, taking the reference to the *hêkal-Yhwh* in 1 Sam. 1.9 as refering to the *'ōhel-mô'ēd*, as had been done by certain scholars of the mid-century consensus, such as Hengstenberg (1.3.1, above), and Köhler (1.3.14, above).

60. Cf. above, Bleek (1.3.8).

61. Delitzsch, 'Pentateuch', V, pp. 223-34.

62. Ibid., p. 233; Delitzsch also included the pair Moses-Aaron in this scheme, but this inclusion is mistaken as Moses can hardly be described as a 'temporal ruler'.

63. 1 Sam. 4.18 records Eli as a judge.

64. *Geschichte der Hebräer* (2 vols.; Gotha: Friedrich Andreas Perthes, 1888, 1892); republished as *Geschichte des Volkes Israel* (2 vols; 2nd edn; Gotha: Friedrich Andreas Perthes, 1909, 1912).

65. Kittel, *Hebräer*, I, pp. 92-96.

66. Dilmann, *Numeri*, p. 644-47, 652. Dillmann developed many of these ideas before Kittel, but his own writing lacked the clear, concise style which characterized Kittel's work. The ideas which Dillmann pioneered were (a) that many of the individual law collections of the Priestly Code had originated in the monarchy, as the cultic regulations followed by the priests, and handed on in specifically priestly circles; (b) that these laws had been modified and aded to over time, until they had reached their final redaction during the exile; and (c) that similar phenomena were attested elsewhere in the ancient world, esp. in Babylonia, Syia, and Phoenicia. These arguments by Dillmann and Kittel anticipated the studies of the French scholar, René Dussaud, by nearly thirty years, but it was Dussaud's work which demonstrated the truth of Dillmann's observations, long after Dillmann's work had been forgotten; see below, 3.1, n. 1.

67. Kittel, *Hebräer*, I, pp. 100-101.

68. Wellhausen, *Composition*, p. 227.

69. Kittel, *Volkes Israel*, II, pp. 120-23.

70. Ibid., II, p. 273. In tracing the Elide genealogy from Moses, Kittel was in agreement with Wellhausen, Reuss, and other important representatives of that school; see above, Wellhausen, 2.1.

71. Kittel, *Volkes Israel*, II, p. 273.

72. Ibid., II, pp. 120-22; see Procksch (below, 2.5.2).

73. Kittel, *Volkes Israel*, II, p. 128.

74. Ibid., II, p. 273.

75. Ibid., II, pp. 273-74; against this see above, Wellhausen (2.2), whose work took seriously the Mushite descent of the Danite priesthood.

76. *Die Geschichte des alttestamentlichen Priesterthums* (Leipzig: S. Hirzel, 1889).

77. Ibid., pp. 272-80; *idem*, *Einleitung in das Alte Testament* (Leipzig: S. Hirzel, 1901), pp. 161-62; see above, Dillmann (2.4.1), and Kittel (2.4.3).

78. Baudissin, *Geschichte*, pp. 89-91.

79. Ibid., pp. 62-63, 137-39, 199, 272-73.

80. Ibid., pp. 195-98, 272.

81. Ibid., pp. 137-39.

82. Ibid., pp. 195-201; Baudissin also denied that Zadok's father, the enigmatic Ahitub (2 Sam. 8.17; 1 Chron. 6.8, 12; 18.16; Ezra 7.2), was one and the same with the Ahitub of the Elide line (1 Sam. 14.3). This view may be correct, after all. But the fact that Ahitub, the father of Zadok, bore the same name as the father of Ahimelech, the priest of Nob, made it that much easier for the Zadokites to tie themselves to the older genealogy of the priests of Nob (see below, ch. 6).

83. Ibid., pp. 199-201.

84. Ibid., pp. 201-202. While Baudissin did not cite Kittel (above, 2.4.3) at this point, their views on this subject were remarkably similar.

85. Baudissin, *Geschichte*, pp. 204-205.

86. (Freiburg/Leipzig: J.C.B. Mohr [Paul Siebeck], 1896).

87. Ibid., p. 178: Buhl cited Josh. 18.1; Judg. 21.19; 1 Samuel 1-4; 1 Kgs 11.29; Jer. 7.12-15; 41.5 in support of his conclusions.

88. Cf. Marie-Louise Buhl and Svend Holm-Nielsen, *Shiloh—The Danish Excavations at Tall Sailun, Palestine, in 1926, 1929, 1932, and 1963: The Pre-Hellenistic Remains* (Copenhagen: The National Museum of Denmark, 1969); see below, 3.3.

89. Procksch's views on Old Testament theology, which appeared posthumously (*Theologie des Alten Testaments* (Gütersloh: C. Bertelsmann, 1950), were the chief influences on the Old Testament theology of Walther Eichrodt, and had a major impact upon Gerhard von Rad's Old Testament theology as well; cf. John H. Hayes and Frederick Prussner, *Old Testament Theology: Its History and Development* (Atlanta: John Knox Press, 1985), p. 191.

90. (Leipzig: J.C. Hinrich, 1906). Noth's work on the amphictyony, for instance, showed some dependence on Procksch (*Das System*, pp. 8 n. 1, 30 n. 1). Otherwise, it is clear from Noth's other *traditionsgeschichtlich* work, especially on the patriarchal narratives in his *Geschichte Israels* (6th edn; Göttingen: Vandenhoeck & Ruprecht, 1966), pp. 9-151, that he was working with methodological presuppositions laid out in Procksch's 'Einleitung' to his work on the Elohist.

91. Ibid., p. 391.

92. Although Procksch went further on this score than Kittel, their views were similar; see above, 2.4.3.

93. Procksch, pp. 392-93.

94. Ibid., p. 230.

95. That the priestly court was meant was clear to Procksch from the fact that the Urim and Thummin were in the hands of Levi in Deut. 33.8. Procksch (ibid., p. 178) held Deuteronomy 33 to be Elohistic, and shared with Baudissin the view that Urim and Thummin had been associated with the priestly judicial function, which Baudissin (*Geschichte*, pp. 57-58) had seen as originally standing in connection with the oracular function of the priesthood. Meyer (*Die Israeliten*, pp. 95-97), on the other hand, had denied the judicial function of the Urim and Thummin, and held that this term designated merely the sacred oracular lots.

96. Cf. the argument by Wellhausen (*Geschichte Israels*, pp. 134-37) that the priests during the time of the monarchy had been largely royal administrators and servants of the king.

97. O. Eissfeldt, 'Silo und Jerusalem', *VTS* 4 (1956), pp. 138-47; J. Lindblom, 'The Political Background of the Shilo Oracle', *VTS* 1 (1953), pp. 73-87.

98. *Geschichte des Bundesgedankens im Alten Testament* (Münster i. W.: Aschendorfsche Buchhandlung, 1910).

99. G.E. Mendenhall, 'Law and Covenant in Israel and the Ancient Near East', *BA* 17 (1954), pp. 26-46 and 'Covenant Forms in the Israelite Tradition', *BA* 17 (1954), pp. 50-76; reprinted as *Law and Covenant in Israel and the Ancient Near East* (Pittsburg: Biblical Colloquium, 1955).

100. Karge, pp. 235-54.

101. Ibid., pp. 173-74, 196-99.

102. See above, Dillmann (2.4.1), Kittel (2.4.3), Baudissin (2.4.4).

103. Karge, pp. 1-32; this, in spite of the fact that Karge was fundamentally at odds with the developmental theory of the history of Israelite religion represented by the school of Wellhausen and Kuenen.

104. (Berlin: G. Reimer, 1912).

105. 'Mosiden und Aharoniden', ibid., pp. 352-60.

Notes to Chapter 3

1. *Le sacrifice en Israël et chez les Phéniciens* (Paris: E. Leroux, 1914).
2. (Paris: E. Leroux, 1921).
3. (2nd edn; Paris: P. Guethner, 1941).
4. See below, ch. 4. Similar arguments had already been advanced on historical and exegetical grounds by Dillmann, who also alluded to the ancient Near Eastern parallels to the priestly laws (*Numeri*, pp. 647, 652), whose work had been followed by Kittel; see above, 2.4.3.
5. See above, 1.2.5
6. P.J. Riis, 'Discussion remarks to the Jubilee Congress of the German Palestine Society in Tübingen', November, 1977, unpubl.
7. 'The Danish Excavations at Shiloh', *BASOR* 9 (1923), pp. 10-11.
8. 'The Site of Shiloh', *PEFQS* 57 (1925), pp. 162-63.
9. 'The Site of Shiloh', *PEFQS* 59 (1927), pp. 85-88.
10. 'The Danish Excavations at Seilun—A Correction', *PEFQS* 59 (1927), pp. 157-58.
11. H. Kjaer, 'The Danish Excavation of Shiloh. Preliminary Report', *PEFQS* 59 (1927), pp. 202-13.
12. H. Kjaer, 'Shiloh. A Summary Report of the Second Danish Expedition, 1929', *PEFQS* 63 (1931), pp. 71-88; *idem*, 'The Excavation of Shiloh, 1929. Preliminary Report', *JPOS* 10 (1930), pp. 87-174.
13. 'Seilun', *AJA* 34 (1930), pp. 95-96.
14. Cf. Riis, 'Remarks', who cited *Shiloh*, Pls. 13.14, Nos. 150-51, 158, 160, 168, 170, 171, 181-82 as evidence and noted that Iron II sherds had occurred elsewhere on the mound as well.
15. Cf. Buhl, *Shiloh*, p. 11.
16. See above, Dibelius (2.3.3.) and Meyer (2.3.4.)
17. Buhl and Holm-Nielsen, *Shiloh* (see above, ch. 2, n. 88).
18. Ibid., pp. 31-35, 51-55.
19. Ibid.
20. Ibid., Pl. 15-16; Pl. XXII-XXIII; cf. also p. 31 n. 161.
21. Ibid., pp. 56-59.
22. Ibid., p. 57.
23. See above, Dibelius (2.3.3) and Meyer (2.3.4).
24. J. van Rossum, 'Wanneer is Silo verwoest?', *NedTT* 24 (1970), pp. 321-32; R.A. Pearce, 'Shiloh and Jer. vii 12, 14 & 15', *VT* 23 (1973), pp. 105-108; W. Anderson, 'Shiloh', *HBD* (1974), pp. 676-77.
25. Pp. 822-23.
26. *IEJ* 21 (1971), pp. 67-69.
27. 'The Destruction of the Shiloh Sanctuary and Jeremiah vii 12, 14', *VTS* 30 (1979), pp. 87-94, esp. p. 93.
28. Ibid., p. 93.

29. 'Shiloh. 1981', *IEJ* 32 (1982), pp. 148-50; 'Shiloh. 1982', *IEJ* 33 (1983), pp. 123-26; 'Shiloh Yields Some, But Not All, of its Secrets', *BAR* 12/1 (1986), pp. 22-41. Fuller treatment of these issues is contained in Finkelstein's *Archaeology of the Israelite Settlement* (IES: Jerusalem, 1988) which did not appear until the completion of this manuscript.

30. Finkelstein (1982), p. 148; (1986), pp. 36-37.

31. Finkelstein (1982), p. 149.

32. Ibid., pp. 35-36.

33. Ibid., p. 40.

34. Ibid.

35. Ibid., p. 40: 'it is now clear that Yohanan Aharoni's view ... that Shiloh may furnish evidence for raising the beginning of Israelite settlement to the 14th and 13th centuries B.C., is no longer valid. Instead, Shiloh fits the pattern now emerging all over the country—there is no unequivocal *archaeological* evidence that Israelite settlement began as early as the 13th century B.C.'

36. Ibid., pp. 40-41.

37. Ibid.

38. Yigael Yadin, *Hazor* (3 vols.; Jerusalem: Magnes Press, 1958, 1960, 1961), II, Pl. CXXII, 1-6; Pl. CXXXII, 13, 14; Pl. CXXXIII, 2, 4, 5; Pl. CXLIV, 4; Pl. CXLV, 1-5.

39. Ibid., Pl. CXIV, 10, 11.

40. Moawiyah M. Ibrahim, 'The Collared-Rim Jar of the Early Iron Age', *Archaeology in the Levant. Essays for Kathleen Kenyon*, ed. R. Moorey and Parr (Warminster, England, 1978), pp. 116-26.

41. *Hazor*, II, Pl. XCV, 4.

42. Ibid., Pl. XCV, 3.

43. Unfortunately, the standard reference work on Palestinian pottery by Ruth Amiran (*Ancient Pottery of the Holy Land* [Jeruslaem: Masada Press, 1969]), contains no more than a passing mention of the problem of the continuity of the form of the 'collared-rim jar' in Palestine down to the later phases of Iron II; cf. p. 238.

44. Finkelstein (1986), pp. 23, 38-39.

45. Ibid., p. 35.

46. Ibid.

47. Cf. John Bimson, *Redating the Exodus and Conquest* (JSOTS, 5; Sheffield: JSOT, 1978). Bimson raises penetrating questions regarding the somewhat arbitrary dating of the end of the Middle Bronze Age to 1550 BCE, and suggests that this dating should be lowered to 1450 BCE, since the destruction of the Canaanite city-states at the end of this period can be related to the Egyptian conquest of Canaan in the middle of the fifteenth century BCE. No Egyptian incursions into Palestine proper in pursuit of the

Hyksos, in fact, can be dated prior to this time, yet the dating of the end of MB by Albright was tied to the hypothetical Egyptian invasion of Palestine immediately after the expulsion of the Hyksos.

48. Cf. J. Maxwell Miller, 'The Israelite Occupation of Canaan', *IJH*, pp. 213-84, for a thorough discussion of the problems relating to the Israelite occupation of Palestine.

49. Yohanan Aharoni, *The Land of the Bible* (2nd edn; Philadelphia; Westminster, 1979), p. 220.

50. Finkelstein (1986), p. 40.

51. *ANET*, pp. 376-78, esp. n. 18. The name 'Israel' in this text is writen with the determination element for 'people', in contrast to the other names in the list, which are written with the determination for 'land', 'country'. Israel at the time would thus appear to have been a non-settled group in Palestine, in contrast to other settled peoples such as Hatti and Ashkelon.

52. Finkelstein (1986), p. 40.

53. Martin Noth, *The History of Israel* (2nd edn; New York: Harper & Row, 1960), p. 47: 'As far as the Israelite period is concerned, Syrian-Palestinian archaeology is therefore almost wholly silent; and it is clear that under these circumstances the historical interpretation of archaeological discoveries is particularly difficult. The understandable enthusiasm with which, to begin with, unusually intensive excavations were carried out in Palestine, from purely Biblical motives, with the aim of finding positive and indisputable traces of Israelite history, has in many cases led to the drawing of over-hasty parallels between the discoveries and known events of history, which have turned out to be untenable; and although Syrian-Palestinian archaeology has long since developed from an auxiliary discipline of Biblical studies into an independent science with methods of its own and aims evolving from its own work, it has still not entirely overcome the improper search for direct Biblical connections.'

54. Albright (1923), pp. 10-11.

55. Noth, *System*, pp. 124-30.

56. Cf. Bächli (*Amphiktyonie*, pp. 17-20), who traces the roots of Noth's thesis back through several generations of Old Testament scholars, including Alt, Galling, Steuernagel, Weber, Ewald and, as the earliest, Spinoza.

57. Cf. Ewald, *Geschichte*, I, pp. 528-30, for his observation that the neighboring peoples known to the Israelites had also displayed the twelve-tribe organization principle, and ibid., pp. 530-31 n. 2, for Ewald's suggestion of the parallel between the Greek and Italian amphictyonies, and Israel's tribal confederacy. Still, Ewald never termed Israel's tribal organization an 'amphictyony', nor did he seek to explain all the workings of that confederacy by reference to the practice of the classical amphictyonies.

58. Noth, *System*, p. 56.

59. Ibid., pp. 62-65; also cf. pp. 74, 87.

60. Ibid., pp. 67-80.

61. Ibid., pp. 95-96.

62. Ibid.

63. Ibid.

64. S. Mowinckel, *Psalmenstudien* (6 vols.; Oslo, 1921-1924; reprinted, 2 vols.; Amsterdam: P. Schippers, 1961); *idem, The Psalms in Israel's Worship* (Oxford: Basil Blackwell, 1962).

65. *The Religion of Israel: From the Beginnings to the Babylonian Exile* (Chicago/London: University of Chicago Press/George Allen & Unwin, 1960).

66. Ibid., p. 183.

67. Ibid., pp. 180-82.

68. Ibid.

69. Ibid., pp. 183-87. Similar points had been stressed by the earlier critics of the Wellhausian school; see above ch. 2.

70. Kaufmann, *Religion*, p. 415.

71. (Philadelphia: Westminster, 1978) = *Histoire ancienne d'Israel: Des origines à l'installation en Canaan* (Paris: J. Gabalda, 1971) and *Histoire ancienne d'Israel: La période des Juges* (Paris: J. Gabalda, 1973). In his *Early History of Israel*, De Vaux argued along lines very similar to those of Wellhausen that the priestly materials of the Hexateuch were exilic, and that Shiloh only clearly emerged as a sanctuary toward the end of the period of Judges (cf. pp. 707-709 n. 47).

72. (2 vols., London/New York: Darton, Longman & Todd/Doubleday, 1961) = *Les institutions de l'Ancien Testament* (Paris: Les Editions du Cerf, 1957). De Vaux's bibliography on the ark and the tent (II, p. 571) is especially important.

73. Cf. the women who served at the door of the tent of meeting: Exod. 38.8; 1 Sam. 2.22b. Cf. more recently, Klaus Koch ('Ohel', *TWAT* I, pp. 127-42, esp. p. 133), who reiterates this evidence. In contrast to de Vaux's treatment, which identified the ark and the tent with Israel's wilderness cultus, von Rad ('Zelt und Lade', *Gesammelte Studien zum Alten Testament* [2 vols.; München: Chr. Kaiser, 1958], II, pp. 109-290) argued that the ark and the tent represented two different theologies: the ark had been the symbol of Israel as a settled people, whereas the tent derived from the nomadic period.

In fact, since Dibelius (above, 2.3.3) first argued that the ark had not originated in the wilderness, but in Canaan, a number of studies on the ark and its relationship to other features of the cult have been published. These include William R. Arnold, *Ephod and Ark: A Study in the Records and Religion of the Ancient Hebrews* (Cambridge, MA: Harvard University Press, 1917); Hugo Gressmann, *Die Lade Jahves und das allerheiligste des salomonischen Tempels* (Stuttgart: W. Kohlhammer, 1920); Julian Morgenstern,

The Ark, the Ephod, and the 'Tent of Meeting' (Cincinnati: Hebrew Union College Press, 1945); Marten H. Woudstra, *The Ark of the Covenant from Conquest to Kingship* (Philadelphia: Presbyterian and Reformed Publishing Company, 1965); and Johann Maier, *Das altisraelitische Ladeheiligtum* (BZAW, 93; Berlin: Alfred Töpelmann, 1965), and most recently, Rainer Schmitt's *Zelt und Lade* (see above, ch. 2, n. 31).

74. Cf. de Vaux, *Ancient Israel*, II, pp. 296-304, for this entire discussion.

75. Ibid., pp. 298-301.

76. Ibid., pp. 301-303.

77. *Temples and Temple Service in Ancient Israel* (Oxford: Clarendon, 1978).

78. Ibid., p. 11; see above, Kittel (2.4.3), and Baudissin (2.4.4). The origins of this idea in Dillmann's work are discussed under Kittel, who first used the expression *innerpriesterliche Privatschrift*. The importance of the work of Dillmann in the development of the thinking of Kaufmann and his students is, however, uncertain. M. Weinfeld, at least, has acknowledged Dillmann's key role in the nineteenth-century opposition to the Graf-Wellhausen hypothesis (*Getting at the Roots of Wellhausen's Understanding of the Law of Israel on the 100th Anniversary of the Prolegomena* [Jerusalem: Institute for Advanced Studies of the Hebrew University, 1978], pp. 1, 39-40). But it is significant for all aspects of this debate that the key arguments raised by Kaufmann, Haran, and Weinfeld, had been raised earlier by the *German* opposition to Wellhausen's synthesis.

79. Ibid., pp. 28-39. Among these temples were those at Dan, Bethel, Mizpah, Gilgal, Hebron, Bethlehem, Nob, Ophrah, Gibeath-Saul, Arad, and Jerusalem. To this list of temples Haran (pp. 48-49) added a number of open-air cultic sites: Shechem, Bethel, Beer-sheba, Hebron, Horeb, and Mount Gilead (= Mizpah of Gilead?).

80. Ibid., p. 27.

81. Ibid., pp. 84-86.

82. Ibid., p. 87

83. Ibid., pp. 198-99.

84. Ibid., p. 200. Haran regarded this verse as too slender a thread on which to hang the theory that P's Tabernacle in reality had been a figure for the Jerusalem temple.

85. Ibid., p. 201.

86. This position is similar to Ewald's contention that the Tabernacle was historical, but had been described according to the reality of the Jerusalem temple.

87. Ibid., pp. 273-75.

88. In fact, Haran's work has complicated the discussion of the nature of the tent sanctuary. If his distinction between the *miškān* and the *'ōhel-mô'ēd* is correct, there may be no small significance in the exclusive use of the term

'*ōhel-mô'ēd* in Josh. 18.1; 19.51, in contrast to Josh. 22.9-34, where only the *miškan-Yhwh* (22.19) or *miškanô*—'his tabernacle' (Josh. 22.29) receives direct mention.

The supposition that the '*ōhel-mô'ēd* was an institution of prophetic revelation alone at the earliest stage, however, is belied by the fact that the *petaḥ* '*ōhel-mô'ēd*—'the door of the tent of meeting'—is the center of activity in the priestly tradition as well as in JE (Exod. 33.7-11). Indeed, the term *petaḥ* '*ōhel-mô'ēd* is a priestly *terminus technicus* for the focus of the ritual and sacrificial functions of the tent shrine (e.g. Lev. 1.3, 5; 3.2; 4.4, 7, 18; 8.3, 4, 31; 12.6; 14.11, 23; 15.14, 29; 16.7; 17.4, 5, 6, 9; 19.21). These instances are all drawn from the technical sacrificial laws. On the other hand, the tradition of Phineas' valor (Num. 25.1-9) has the congregation weeping *petaḥ* '*ōhel mô'ēd*—'at the door of the tent of meeting—in a fashion which recalls the function of the tent in Exod. 33.7-11. The account of the division of the land by lot was also carried out by Joshua and Eleazar *petaḥ* '*ōhel-mô'ēd* (Josh. 19.51), in a way similar to Exod. 33.7-11. This evidence suggests not a combination of two different traditions, but a single institution with multiple functions. The door of the tent in Josh. 19.51 may have been chosen as the site of the distribution of the land by lot because the divine presence would have stood as a witness (v. '*wd*) to the process.

This suggestion raises the possibility that the term *mô'ēd* (v. *y'd*) actually carried a double meaning: not only was it the tent of 'meeting', but the tent of 'witness' as well, a meaning which may have been implied in the term *mô'ēd*, and which is certainly at work in Josh. 19.51. Thus, the '*ōhel-mô'ēd* carried with it several cultic functions. The tent of meeting (as distinct from the tabernacle, or *miškān*), was first and foremost the place of meeting with the deity. In addition, it was the place of 'witness', where acts were performed with the deity as witness (compare the similar role of the door of the shrine in the law of the Hebrew slave in Exod. 21.6). Finally, the tent of meeting was the place before which the altar stood, and consequently, where sacrifice was carried out. Of all of these functions, only the function of the door of the tent as the place of revelation is preserved in the fragmentary JE tradition (Exod. 33.7-11).

The term *miškān*, which sometimes occurs as a general designation for the tent shrine, as (apparently) in Josh. 22.9-34, also appears in the priestly laws as a *terminus technicus* for the smaller tent in which the ark was housed, and which was covered in red ram-skins (cf. Exod. 25-27, where reference is made exclusively to the *miškān*, with the lone exception of the mention of the '*ōhel-mô'ēd* in 27.21). Although the '*ōhel-mô'ēd* and the *miškān* seem, therefore, to have been the designations for two separate institutions, which were combined into one in later tradition, it is the '*ōhel-mô'ēd* which had the chief cultic role, while the *miškān* served chiefly as the 'dwelling-place' for the ark. The intricacies of this problem would entail a separate study in themselves, and so can only be outlined here. Cf. von Rad's distinction between the theologies of ark and tent (above, n. 69); Koch (*TWAT*, pp. 127-42) similarly distinguishes between two different versions of the tent tradition.

89. Eissfeldt (1956), pp. 138-47.

90. Ibid., p. 139.

91. Ibid., p. 140.

92. Lindblom (1953), pp. 73-87.

93. Against this view, see T.N.D. Mettinger, *The Dethronement of Sabaoth: Studies in the Shem and Kabod Theologies* (CBOTS 18; Lund: CWK Gleerup, 1982), pp. 121, 132; *idem*, 'YHWH SABAOTH—The Heavenly King on the Cherubim Throne', *Studies in the Period of David and Solomon*, ed. Tomoo Ishida (Winona Lake: Eisenbrauns, 1982), pp. 109-38, esp. 128-35. Mettinger shows that there is some, albeit muted, evidence for the worship of Yahweh Ṣeba'oth in premonarchic times, especially at Shiloh.

94. 'Jerusalem und die israelitische Tradition', *OTS* 8 (1950), pp. 28-46.

95. A. Cody, *A History of Old Testament Priesthood* (Rome: Pontifical Biblical Institute, 1969).

96. Ibid., p. 69.

97. Ibid., pp. 70-71.

98. Ibid., pp. 71-72.

99. Ibid., pp. 74-75.

100. Ibid., pp. 78-80.

101. 'The Priestly Houses of Early Israel', *Canaanite Myth and Hebrew Epic* (Cambridge, MA: Harvard University Press, 1973), pp. 195-215.

102. Ibid., pp. 195-96.

103. Ibid., pp. 196-98.

104. Cf. Mettinger ('Sabaoth', pp. 128-35), who argues that the cult at Shiloh had fostered the cherubim iconography, whereas Bethel had been devoted to the Canaanite god El, and his bull iconography.

105. An important objection to this theory is that the name Phineas is identified above all with Shiloh, in both the priestly strata of Joshua and in the narratives of 1 Samuel 1-4. Conversely, the reference which Cross cites in Judg. 20.27-28 is a redactional note, perhaps stemming from a time when the Aaronite priesthood at Bethel had eclipsed that at Shiloh.

106. Cf. Cross (*Canaanite Myth*, pp. 198-99); Procksch (*Sagenbuch*, pp. 391-92) had earlier made this claim, which is not unrelated to Kittel's contention that Shiloh had been the center for the preservation of the true tradition of the ('image-free') Mosaic religion (see above, 2.4.3). Both views may have their origin in Wellhausen's identification of Shiloh with the Mushite line of priests (see above, 2.2).

107. Ibid., p. 203.

108. Ibid., pp. 200-203.
109. Ibid., p. 211. This position was similar to that advocated by Haran (*Temples*, p. 85), who pointed out that the cities of the Aaronite priests were all found in Judah.
110. Contra Wellhausen, *Geschichte Israels*, p. 128-29.
111. Cross, *Canaanite Myth*, pp. 209-15.
112. See below, 6.3, for a thorough treatment of the problem of the Aaronites and Zadokites.
113. See above, n. 23.
114. Haran, *Temples*, pp. 84-87.

Notes to Chapter 4

1. The Septuagintal readings of 'Shiloh' for 'Shechem' in Josh. 24.1, 25 probably resulted from scribal alteration, to bring Joshua 24 into conformity with the emphasis placed on Shiloh in Joshua 18-22. Although certain points might support the view that Shiloh was the primary reading, the decisive factor is the mention of the 'oak which is in the sanctuary of Yahweh'. Nowhere is an oak associated Shiloh, but the tradition of the sacred oak at Shechem is attested in at least one other place (Gen. 35.4); cf. Alexander Rofé, 'The End of the Book of Joshua according to the Septuagint', *Henoch* 4 (1982), pp. 17-36.
2. J. Blenkinsopp ('The Structure of P', *CBQ* 38 [1976], pp. 275-92) has pointed out the linguistic similarities between the phrase, *wĕhā'āreṣ nikbĕšāh lipnêhem* ('And the land lay subdued before them') in Josh. 18.1b and the injunction in Gen. 1.28: *pĕrû ûrĕbû ûmil'û 'et-hā'āreṣ wĕkibšuhā* ('Be fruitful, and multiply, and fill the earth, and subdue it'). Moreover, he has noted the importance of the motif of dividing the land to P, a fact which has considerable implications for the identification of the basic source in Josh. 18.2-10 (see below).
3. A. Alt, 'Israels Gaue unter Josia', *Palästinajahrbuch* 21 (1925), pp. 100-16; M. Noth, *Überlieferungsgeschichtliche Studien* (Tübingen: Max Niemeyer, 1943) = *The Deuteronomistic History* (JSOTS, 15; Sheffield: JSOT, 1981).
4. Noth has been followed in this by Aharoni (*Land*, pp. 248-55).
5. *Zur Frage nach den dokumentarischen Quellen in Joshua 13-19* (Oslo: Jacob Dybwad, 1946); idem, *Tetrateuch-Pentateuch-Hexateuch* (BZAW 90; Berlin: Alfred Töpelmann, 1964).
6. *Tetrateuch*, p. 56. When Noth had argued that neither Num. 33.50-34.29 nor Joshua 13-19 stemmed from P, Mowinckel suggested that, in reality, Noth, for the sake of his theory, could not *allow* these passages to stem from P.
7. Ibid., pp. 57, 68-70.

8. Support for the hexateuchal schema also came from the work of Gerhard von Rad, *Das formgeschichtliche Problem des Hexateuch* (BWANT, 6/26; Stuttgart: W. Kohlhammer, 1938) = *The Problem of the Hexateuch and other Essays* (New York; McGraw-Hill, 1966), pp. 1-78; and more recently, from Blenkinsopp, 'The Structure of P'.

9. Although the overarching claims of Noth's theory are not accepted here, many of his literary-critical observations about the nature of the dtr editing of Joshua–2 Kings nonetheless hold true, especially his observation that the 'deuteronomistic historian' (Dtr) had provided an historical framework for the materials he edited, and which most often appeared in the form of speeches by the major characters (e.g. Josh. 1; 1 Sam. 12) or long historical-theological digressions (Judg. 2.6-23; 2 Kgs 17).

10. These latter sections were designated by the nineteenth-century source-critics as R^d: i.e. stemming from the 'deuteronomistic redactor'.

11. This change may have been occasioned by the insertion of the traditions of Caleb and Othniel in Josh. 15.13-19. In the original list, the boundary description ending in Josh. 15.12 was probably followed directly by the city-list beginning in 15.21, so that the subscription in 15.12 immediately preceded the superscription in 15.21a.

12. Mowinckel, *Zur Frage*, pp. 8-10.

13. The depiction of Ephraim and Manasseh as the tribal offspring of Joseph, and the exclusion of Joseph from tribal status, may in fact have been the result of efforts to reconcile this ambivalence.

14. A. Alt, 'Judas Gaue unter Josia', *PJ* 21 (1925), pp. 100-16 = *KS* II, pp. 276-88; *idem*, 'Das System der Stammesgrenzen im Buche Josua', *Beiträge zur Religionsgeschichte und Archäologie Palästinas. Festschrift Ernst Sellin* (Leipzig: A. Deichert, 1927), pp. 13-29 = *KS* I, pp. 193-203; cf. further, Aharoni (*Land*, pp. 248-55).

15. Cf. esp. Mowinckel (*Zur Frage*, p. 19), who considered at least some elements in these lists fictional.

16. Cf. Aharoni (*Land*, pp. 67-77, 248-55); along the same lines, cf. M. Weinfeld, 'The Extent of the Promised Land—the Status of Transjordan', *Das Land Israel in biblischer Zeit*, ed. Georg Strecher (Göttingen: Vandenhoeck & Ruprecht, 1983), pp. 59-75.

17. Wellhausen, *Composition*, p. 128.

18. Mowinckel, *Tetrateuch*, p. 61.

19. Cf. Wellhaussen, *Composition*, p. 131.

20. Cf. Eissfeldt, *Hexateuch-Synopse*, pp. 236-37; Rudolph, *Der Elohist*, pp. 228-32.

21. Mowinckel, *Tetrateuch*, p. 45. Mowinckel disputed the existence of an 'Elohistic' source altogether. For him, 'E' was merely a Judean expansion of the Yahwistic tradition, which nonetheless contained more North Israelite material than did J. Thus, Mowinckel gave to E the designation 'J^v' (ibid., pp. 6-8).

22. Noth, *Studien*, pp. 182-89.
23. Wellhausen, *Composition*, p. 128; Mowinckel (1964), p. 61.
24. Wellhausen (ibid., p. 129) drew the same conclusion.
25. Cf. Ps. 78.60-72, below, Chapter 7.
26. Blenkinsopp, 'The Structure of P', p. 290.
27. The phrase *lābô' lārešet 'et-hā'āreṣ* occurs in this and its most similar forms in the parenetic framework of the book of Deuteronomy, and in passages which are either deuteronomistic, or stand under that influence. Thus, the exact phrase occurs in Deut. 11.31, Josh. 1.11; Judg. 18.9. Those most nearly related are found in

Deut. 1.8:   *bô'û ûrĕšû 'et-hā'āreṣ.*
Deut. 9.4:   *hebî'anî Yahweh lārešet 'et-ha'āreṣ hazzō't;*
Deut. 9.5:   *'attāh bā' lārešet 'et-'arṣām;*
Deut. 10.11:   *wĕyābō'û wĕyiršû 'et-hā'āreṣ;*
Judg. 2.6:   *wayyēlĕkû bĕnê-Yiśrā'ēl 'îš lĕnaḥălātô lārešet 'et-hā'āreṣ.*

Other similar instances are found in Deut. 2.31; 4.1, 22; 6.18; 8.1; 9.23; 11.8; 16.20; 17.14; 18.9; 26.1; 31.7; 32.52; Josh. 1.15.

In passages which are not expressly deuteronomistic, similar phrases occur five times: in Lev. 20.24 (H); Num. 33.53 (P); Amos 2.10; Neh. 9.15, 23. The instances in Nehemiah can easily be attributed to the standardization of this stereotypical phraseology at a later time. The occurrences in P and H, however, as well as that in Amos, suggest that this phraseology had its root in old conquest traditions. The deuteronomic school then adopted this phrase and made it a central motif and expression of their own theology of the land.

28. This expression has an origin similar to that of the aforementioned phrase. The designation *Yhwh 'ĕlōhê 'ăbōtêkem* occurs in the literature of the Hexateuch and the historical books just three times outside of the book of Deuteronomy, all of these in the story of Yahweh's revelation to Moses. Two of these instances are found in a clearly Elohistic context, in Exod. 3.13, 15. The other stands in the Yahwistic parallel to this text, in Exod. 3.16. These instances suggest that the expression *Yhwh 'ĕlōhê 'ăbōtêkem* had its origin in the ancient hexateuchal traditions of Israel. This phrase, and its theology, were subsequently taken over by the writers of the deuteronomic school, and given their peculiar impress. Consequently, this phrase, along with its derivatives, occurs in some of the most important and familiar passages in the book of Deuteronomy: Deut. 1.11; 4.1: *Yhwh 'ĕlōhê 'ăbōtêkem*; Deut. 1.21; 6.3; 12.1; 27.3: *Yhwh 'ĕlōhê 'ăbōtêkā*; Deut. 26.7: *Yhwh 'ĕlōhê 'ăbōtênû*; Deut. 29.24, Judg. 2.12: *Yhwh 'ĕlōhê 'ăbōtām*. The plethora of occurrences in the books of Ezra and Chronicles comes from the standardization of this phraseology within the later Jewish faith.

29. Cf. Wellhausen, *Composition*, p. 132: This verse reflects 'die Hand des Deuteronomisten, der überall die drittehalb Stämme und die Leviten nachträgt'.

30. The priestly list in Joshua 14–19 includes the following twelve tribes, without including the superscription for Joseph:

Joshua 13:	*Joshua 16–17:*	*Joshua 18–19:*
Reuben	Ephraim	Benjamin
Gad	Half-Manasseh	Simeon
Half-Manasseh		Zebulun
		Issachar
Joshua 14–15:		Asher
		Naphtali
Judah		Dan

31. With the exception of Deut. 18.1-8, Cf. Dillmann, *Numeri*, pp. 324-28, who recognizes the distinction made in this dtn text between the priests (*hakkōhănîm*: v. 3) and the Levites (*hallēwî*: v. 6), in contrast to Wellhausen (*Geschichte Israels*, pp. 150-51) *et al.*, for whom Deuteronomy served as the basis for the theory that the special status of the Aaronites vis-à-vis the Levites had been a late development.

32. Mowinckel, *Tetrateuch*, p. 45.

33. Although Wellhausen (*Composition*, pp. 116-34) made the absence of a dtr redaction of P in Joshua a primary proof of his relative dating of the hexateuchal sources, Josh. 18.1-10 offers positive evidence to the contrary. Josh. 21.43-45 offers further evidence to this effect (see below). Rather than an independent account of the settlement, Dtr contributed largely parenetic and interpretive expansions, expressed via the stereotypical, rhetorical language of the book of Deuteronomy. Josh. 18.3b, in fact offers a clear instance of the subtle interpolations made by Dtr into received traditions and documents. The phrase *lābô' lārešet 'et-hā'āreṣ* in Josh. 18.3b and Judg. 18.9b is a good example of the more subtle interpretive method of these editors.

34. Cf. Noth, *Josua*, pp. 108-109.

35. Eissfeldt, *Hexateuch-Synopse*, pp. 236-37. Eissfeldt's division of Josh. 18.1-10 according to the hexateuchal sources was as follows: E = 2-4, 7ba, 8, 10a; J = 5-7a, 7bb, 9, 10b; v. 1 = E[1].

36. Contra Mowinckel (*Tetrateuch*, p. 45), who regarded 18.1 as the Priestly annotation to the deuteronomistic report of the distribution of the land by lot. As a result, he treated the Shiloh references as secondary to vv. 2-9. This is even true in v. 9, where he regarded Gilgal as the logical and original site of the camp in this passage, an assertion which he supported via reference to v. 5b. Nonetheless, Mowinckel's views, like those of nearly every other heir to the New Documentary Hypothesis, were founded upon the assumption that there was a non-priestly *Grundlage* here which had been modified by a priestly editor.

37. How Eissfeldt (*Hexateuch-Synopse*, p. 236) is able to ascribe v. 10b to J, and v. 10a to E, when 10b is clearly dependent upon 10a, is a mystery! As the evidence of LXX indicates, if a particular part of this verse is secondary, it is more likely 10b.

38. See Blenkinsopp, 'The Structure of P', for an overview of the relationship between the priestly account of the commissioning and construction of the tabernacle on the one hand, and the occupation of the land on the other.

41. According to Mowinckel (*Tetrateuch*, p. 68) and Noth (*Studien*, p. 46) this piece belongs to a secondary expansion of the dtr conquest and land-distribution reports, and has been influenced by Deut. 19.1-13; 4.41-3. Several factors, however, speak against this claim. First, Josh. 20.1-9 follows Num. 35.6-34 nearly verbatim through Josh. 20.3. Second, these two passages share important elements of formulaic language and legal concepts. Third, both Num. 35.6-34 and Josh. 20.1-9 assume the appointment of six cities of refuge, whereas Deut. 19.1-13 commands only three. Finally, there is in Josh. 20 no trace of the distinctive dtr parenesis. On the contrary, the language of the chapter is decidedly priestly.

42. Mowinckel, *Tetrateuch*, pp. 67-69.

43. Using the singular of *miṣwāh*, the phrase *miṣwat Yhwh 'ĕlōhêkem* occurs only once in dtr literature, in 1 Sam. 13.13. Otherwise, it is found most often in the plural: *miṣôt Yhwh*: Lev. 4.2, 13, 27; 5.17; Num. 15.35; Deut. 10.13; Judg. 2.17; 3.4; 1 Kgs 18.18; 2 Kgs 17.16; *miṣôt Yhwh 'ĕlōhêkem/ka*: Deut. 4.2; 6.17; 8.6; 11.27, 28; 28.9, 13. The plural forms are also found, albeit infrequently, in Ezra, Nehemiah, and Chronicles, since for those books both priestly and dtn/dtr usage had become stereotypical.

44. The occurrences of *'ăḥuzzāh* are not widely distributed, the heaviest concentration falling in Leviticus (19×).

45. E.g. Lev. 8.35; Num. 1.53; 3.7, 8, 28, 32, 36, 38; 4.31, 32; 8.26; 9.19, 32. Of special note is the phrase *mišmeret Yhwh* in Lev. 8.35; Num. 9.19, 23, which may have been brought into closer conformity with dtr usage by the insertion of *miṣwat*, though this is uncertain. The coupling of *mišmeret* with some form of the verb *šāmar*, as in Josh. 22.3, occurs frequently in P, once in Deuteronomy (11.1), and several times in the dtr literature, where it is found in 1 Kgs 2.3—*wĕšāmartā 'et-mišmeret Yhwh 'ĕlōhêkā lāleket bidrākāyw lišmor ḥuqqōtāyw miṣôtāyw ûmišpāṭāyw wĕ'ēdôtāyw kakkātûb bĕtôrat mōšeh* ('Any you shall keep the charge of Yahweh your god to walk in his ways, to keep his statutes and his ordinances and his testimonies as it is written in the law of Moses'), 2 Kgs 11.5, 6, 7. Deut. 11.1 and 1 Kgs 2.3 reflect a broader usage than that in P, apparently with reference to the whole law, as is clear from 1 Kgs 2.3. In Josh. 22.3 the technical priestly sense of *mišmeret* has been expanded by the (perhaps dtr) addition of *miṣwat*.

46. Cf. Wellhausen, *Composition*, p. 132; also cf. the source-critical tables in H. Holzinger, *Einleitung in den Hexateuch* (Freiburg/Leipzig: J.C.B. Mohr [Paul Siebeck], 1893): Wellhausen regarded vv. 1-6 as JE, but attributed v. 7 to D or R^d.

47. Ibid., Wellhausen considered these verses P; Kuenen and Driver, a later redaction of P.

48. Cf. Holzinger, tables; Wellhausen regarded this passage as priestly, whereas Kuenen considered it the work of a later priestly redactor (P^8).

49. Wellhausen, *Composition*, p. 227.

50. The JE account in Num. 25.1-5 only associates Moab with the events at Ba'al-Pe'or, whereas in the priestly accounts (Num. 25.6-13; 31), the Midianites have the central role.

51. See below, Chapter 5.

52. The exclusive cultic sanctity ascribed to Shiloh here may also confirm Fretheim's thesis that P is anti-temple ('The Priestly Document: Antil-Temple?', *VT* 18 [1968], p. 313-29).

Notes to Chapter 5

1. See above, 1.3.5.

2. *De Templo Silonensi*, pp. 1-2. Graf had originally interpreted the time reference, 'all the days that the house of God was in Shiloh' (Judg. 18.31) as denoting the destruction of the northern kingdom by the Assyrians, by reading this verse in parallel with the aforegoing, 'until the day of the captivity of the land' (above, 1.3.5). While Graf later reversed this opinion (above, 1.3.10), the exegetical merit of his initial observations still stands (see above, Buhl, 2.4.1). Noth's essay ('The Background of Judges 17-18', *Israel's Prophetic Heritage: Essays in Honor of James Muilenburg* [ed. B.W. Anderson and Walter Harrelson; New York: Harper & Brothers, 1962], pp. 68-85), however, assumes the standard reconstruction of Shiloh's history, and thus considers the temporal qualifications in Judg. 18.30, 31 intrinsically different. Therefore, he drops out the initial reference ('until the day of the captivity of the land'), then argues that the graven image of the Danites had stood in Dan only as long as the house of God had stood in Shiloh, i.e. according to the standard reconstruction, until the destruction of city by the Philistines in the mid-eleventh century BCE.

3. Budde, *Das Buch der Richter* (Freiburg: J.C.B. Mohr, 1897), p. 123: 'The doubled source is "plain as day" ("mit Händen zu greifen")'.

4. So Graf, *De Templo Silonensi*, pp. 2-5; Graf had stressed the sharp distinction made in 2 Samuel 7 between *'ōhel* and *bayit*.

5. E.g. Saalschütz, *Archaeologie*, pp. 234-35; Riehm, *Handwörterbuch*, p. 255; Bleek (1860), pp. 347-48.

6. See above, 1.3.5.

7. As Graf (above, 1.3.5) originally argued; and as Buhl (above, 2.4.1) later contended as well. A different possibility altogether is raised by 1 Kgs 15.20, which records the campaign of Ben-hadad of Syria against the cities of the kingdom of Jeroboam I, at the behest of Asa, king of Judah. According to this text, Ben-Hadad smote 'Ijon, Dan, Abel-beth-ma'acah, and all Chinneroth *'al* (?) all the land of Naphtali'. If the cities named in this text were burned, and their inhabitants carried off, Judg. 18.30 could possibly refer to this event in the reign of Jeroboam I. However, the verb *nākāh* (hiph., 'to smite') is not further qualified, so that one ought not to make too much of this passage.

8. Cf. Haran, *Temples*, p. 26; also Exod. 21.6.

9. The affinity between Judg. 20.26-28 and 1 Sam. 14.3, 18, where the ark is the focus of the oracle, attests an historical milieu in which the ark served as an oracular means, despite the secondary nature of Judg. 20.27b-28a.

10. See below, Chapter 6.

11. Cf. Ps. 78.60-72, below, Chapter 6.

12. Buhl/Holm-Nielsen, p. 57. First Dibelius (above, 2.3.3) and later Eduard Meyer (above, 2.3.4) suggested that Shiloh had originated as a non-Israelite sanctuary.

13. Buhl/Holm-Nielsen, p. 58.

14. See above, 3.1.

15. Finkelstein (1986, p. 34) terms the MBA site a *temenos*—a site, often containing a sanctuary, which was marked off and set apart to a deity. For the huge MB IIC fortifications Finkelstein offers the explanation that Seilun may have been a well-defended stronghold where the inhabitants of the small villages from this period found refuge.

16. Ibid., p. 35.

17. Cf. Theodore Gaster, *Myth, Legend and Custom in the Old Testament* (New York/Evanston: Harper & Row, 1969), pp. 444-46, for a treatment of the folkloristic background to Judg. 21.16-24; ibid., n. 2, for the references to the 'Rape of the Sabine Women', and other similar tales in classical lore.

Notes to Chapter 6

1. So Graf (above, 1.3.5) and Wellhausen (above, 2.2).

2. So Cross (above 3.8.3), developing Wellhausen's line of argument.

3. Cf. Wellhausen (above, 2.2) and Dibelius (above, 2.3.3).

4. See Haran (above, 3.7.3) on the anachronistic nature of the references to the temple at Shiloh in 1 Samuel.

5. *M. Zebah.* 14.6.

6. See Hengstenberg (above, 1.3.1); Saalschütz (1.3.6); Bleek (1.3.8); Köhler (1.3.14).

7. Cf. 2 Sam. 7.6, as well.

8. See Haran's treatment of this subject (*Temples*, ch. 15), where he argues that the ark and other ancient cult objects had been destroyed by Manasseh.

9. Ibid., p. 201. Haran argues to the contrary that the references to a temple at Shiloh (Judg. 18.31; 1 Sam. 1-3) are merely anachronisms.

10. That the tent of meeting was associated with the Elides is suggested by 1 Sam. 2.22b, but the authenticity of this verse is controversial. Cf. McCarter (*I Samuel* [AB; Garden City: Doubleday, 1980], p. 81), who takes this verse as secondary, apparently on textual grounds. Still, the best evidence that this half-verse has been interpolated is not textual (i.e. the reference is missing in 4QSama and in the LXX, but cf. Josephus, *Antiquities*, 5.339 and LXX^L), but rather literary. As Wellhausen (*Text*, p. 46) pointed out, there is no allusion to this crime either in the preceding narratives, or in the anonymous prophecy in 1 Sam. 2.27-36. At the same time, however, the priestly language of this verse does not prove its late, post-exilic origin. The similarities of this half-verse with the language of Exod. 38.8; Num. 25.6-10 derives from the fact that each of these texts reflects the traditional as well as technical terminology of P, which can be shown to have been early (esp. Exod. 38.8; Num. 25.6-13: How do these traditions fit into post-exilic life?). The use of priestly language here could have arisen just as easily from the incorporation of an old priestly tradition into the present text, as from a mere gloss. Finally, 1 Sam. 2.22b merely makes explicit what was already implicit in the narrative anyway: the juxtaposition of the corrupt sons of Eli with their illustrious forebear. This fact shows the priestly tradition of Num. 25.6-13 to have pre-dated that of the currupt Elides.

11. See Cody (above, 3.8.2).

12. Wellhausen, *Geschichte Israels*, pp. 146-47; Reuss, *Geschichte*, pp. 137-38; Cross, *Canaanite Myth*, p. 198.

13. See above, 2.4.4.

14. Baudissin, *Geschichte*, pp. 107-10.

15. Reuss, *Geschichte*, p. 138.

16. The abrupt appearance of the Elides on the scene in 1 Samuel 1 led Wellhausen and Budde, among others, to suggest that an older introduction had been broken off. A better explanation for the same phenomenon is that Eli and his sons were well-known traditional figures, who needed no further introduction. That Eleazar apparently was pre-empted in status by his son Phineas in Josh. 24.33 similarly sugests that Phineas was a better-known traditional figure than his father.

17. Num. 31.6; Josh. 22.13, 31, 32 refer to this figure simply as Phineas, the son of Eleazar the priest, while Josh. 22.30 calls him Phineas the priest.

18. In point of fact, Eleazar is a common enough name in the Old

Testament, so that such an arbitrary identification of Eliezer, the son of Moses with Eleazar, the son of Aaron is really a circular argument, designed to support the pre-conceived conclusion that the line of Eleazar was Mushite, and not Aaronite.

19. Wellhausen (*Geschichte Israels*, p. 147) argued that Aaron did not occur at all in the original form of J.

20. The non-Israelite pedigree of Zadok has been the subject of a long discussion in Old Testament studies. See Cody (*History*, pp. 88-93) for a summary of the various theories of Zadok's origins. Cody (ibid., p. 91 nn. 12, 13) also gives an extensive bibilography of the position taken by Rowley, Hauer, and others, that Zadok actually had been the high priest of the city of the Jebusites prior to David's annexation of the city as his capital.

21. Cf. Ezek. 40.46; 43.19; 44.15; 48.11; cf. Baudissin (*Geschichte*, pp. 107-10) on this material.

22. The proper interpretation of 1 Sam. 2.27-36 is not that it refers to the supposed cultic reforms carried out by Josiah (which view has been arbitrarily imposed upon the text, not derived from it), but that it seeks to discredit the ancient Aaronite priesthood of the North, and to justify the new line of Zadok in Jerusalem; contra McCarter (*I Samuel*, pp. 91-93), who represents the view of Wellhausen as developed by Cross.

23. Ibid., pp. 239, 349.

24. Ibid., p. 93 n. 2.

25. Cf. Fretheim, 'Anti-Temple', p. 317: from Jer. 1.1 it may be postulated that Abiathar's family maintained their priestly status down to the time of Jeremiah, who may have been a direct descendant of Abiathar. Nevertheless, the possible descent of Jeremiah from Abiathar, which Fretheim also maintains, does not prove Jeremiah's descent from Eli.

26. Reading *ḥet* for *hē*, in accordance with some other Hebrew MSS, the LXX, Syriac, Targum, and Old Latin.

27. See Jan Dus, 'Die Geburtslegende 1 Sam. 1. (Eine traditionsge-schichtliche Untersuchung zu 1 Sam. 1-3)', *Revista Degli Studia Orientali* 43 (1968), pp. 163-94. Dus is the first to advance a full blown traditio-historical theory for the development of 1 Samuel 1 from a Saulide tradition to the story of the birth of Samuel. Others, however, have drawn similar conclusions, among them Hylander and Lods; cf. Dus, p. 163 n. 1, 167 n. 2, for a bibliography of the view that Saul, rather than Samuel, had been the original figure in this tradition. Wellhausen (*Geschichte Israels*, p. 139) makes the interesting suggestion that Samuel's name is the result of a word play from *mwš'l*, but does not explain the statement *hû' šā'ûl laYhwh* in light of this word play, or vice versa, and leaves the unraveling of this mystery to the reader.

28. *I Samuel*, pp. 62, 63-66.

29. Noth, 'Samuel und Silo', pp. 391-92. Noth contends that the connection

between Samuel and Shiloh was 'a secondary unhistorical piece of the Samuel tradition . . . which perhaps had the aim of creating a bridge between the pre-monarchical, pan-Israelite history, represented by Shiloh, and the newly emergent monarchy in the time of the young Samuel'. That the purpose of the Samuel-Shiloh connection was to create a bridge between Samuel and the pre-monarchical history of the tribes is probably correct. The question, however, is not *whether* the Samuel-Shiloh link in the tradition is correct, but rather, *which* of the members of this link is secondary. The evidence at hand suggests that Samuel, and not Shiloh, is actually the secondary element.

30. Cf. Arnold, *Ephod and the Ark*, pp. 12-23.

31. Dus (1968), p. 168.

32. Noth, 'Samuel und Silo', p. 391.

33. McCarter, *I Samuel*, pp. 84-85.

34. Dus (1968), p. 167.

35. Cf. R.K. Gnuse, *The Dream and Theophany of Samuel: Its Structure in Relation to Ancient Near Eastern Dreams and its Theological Significance* (Lanham, MD: University Press of America, 1984).

36. Although the Hebrew Bible often equates the functions of seer and prophet, the old traditions, such as those in 1 Samuel 9-10, seem to preserve the memory of an office of seer which is different from that of prophet. On the one hand, the seer seems to have been one possessed of a special gift of 'seeing' into hidden matters, whether past, present, or future. As such, a seer would be consulted by local people on all matters of concern which might be closed to normal means of inquiry. In this office, the seer probably was accustomed to receiving 'gifts' for his services. In fact, the office of seer is explained in just these terms in 1 Sam. 9.8-9; note that Saul's servant assumes that payment of the seer for services rendered was customary (v. 8). Moreover, 1 Sam. 9.9 treats the 'seer' as an office no longer extant in Israel, which has been supplanted by that of prophet. Although this verse claims that the later prophet was the same as the earlier seer, there is no representation of a prophet elsewhere in the Hebrew Bible in the same terms as the seer in 1 Samuel 9 is depicted. Thus, despite the equation of prophet with seer (cf. 1 Sam. 9.9b), the prophet seems to have been primarily the mediator of the 'word of Yahweh'. Samuel is found in the latter role in the secondary stratum of 1 Samuel 3-4.

If Samuel's traditional role was not that of prophet, neither was he remembered as a priest. Cody (*History*, pp. 72-80) makes this same point and further notes (ibid., pp. 74-75 n. 33) that the word *na'ar* in 1 Sam. 2.13 refers to the servant of the priest, and that in Phoenicia, *na'ar* was a technical term for a lower temple servant. This interpretation might also have some bearing on the interplay between the terms *lēwî* and *na'ar* in Judges 17-18.

37. J.M. Miller, 'Geba/Gibeah of Benjamin', *VT* 25 (1975), pp. 145-66.

38. See above, 6.4.
39. McCarter, *I Samuel*, p. 237; but cf. P.R. Davies, 'Ark or Ephod in 1 Sam. xiv 18?, *JTS* 26 (1975), pp. 82-87, for a contrary opinion.
40. Reading from the MT. The LXX at this point reads *ephoud*, in conjunction with v. 18a.
41. In both the MT and the LXX.
42. In addition, the site of the mustering of the Israelite forces in 1 Samuel 4 is given as Ebenezer, a place which is assumed in 1 Samuel 4, but which is first explained in 1 Samuel 7, where the tradition of Yahweh's deliverance of Israel under Samuel serves as an etiology for the place-name *'Ében hā'ēzer*, that is 'the stone of help' (1 Sam. 7.12).
43. See above, 6.4.1.
44. Cf. 2 Sam. 16.5-8.
45. Cf. A. Alt, 'Die Staatenbildung der Israeliten in Palästina', *KS*, II, pp. 21-22; Mettinger, *Dethronement*, p. 132; *idem*; 'Sabaoth', pp. 109-33, esp. 129-31.
46. David apparently made a policy of incorporating non-Israelite holy places into Israelite life, probably as a means of integrating the non-Israelite elements of Palestine with the Israelites. The selection of Gibeon, which had been hard-pressed during Saul's tenure, was an important step in this policy. In this regard, the pitching of the sacral tent at Gibeon would have had a twofold purpose: to graft the non-Israelite sanctuary at Gibeon into Israel's sacral tradition, and to legitimize David's policy towards non-Israelite Palestinians; cf. 2 Sam. 21.1-9; 1 Chron. 16.39; 21.29; 2 Chron. 1.3, 13. David also made a policy of promoting non-Israelite persons into his service; cf. Cody (*History*, pp. 87-97) for a bibliography and thorough discussion of this issue; also T.N.D. Mettinger, *King and Messiah: The Civil and Sacral Legitimation of the Israelite Kings* (CB OTS, 8; Lund: CWK Gleerup, 1976), pp. 92-95.
47. What is meant by 'until he comes to Shiloh' is nowhere specified. Early commentators, attempting to deal with this problem, appealed to the LXX reading of *hō apokeitai* (= Hebrew *šelô*), which would alter the translation of the last line to 'until he comes to that which is his'; cf. O. Procksch, *Die Genesis* (*KAT* 1; Leipzig: A. Deichert, 1913), pp. 264-70. E.A. Speiser (*Genesis* [AB; Garden City: Doubleday, 1982], pp. 362-66) reads, however, 'to the end that tribute be brought to him', but he also suggests rearranging the consonantal breaks in the Hebrew to read 'his foes shall come fawning to him', in parallel with the following 'and the peoples' homage shall be his'.
48. Lindblom (1953), pp. 73-87. Supported more recently by J.A. Emerton, 'Some Difficult Words in Genesis 49', in *Words and Meanings. Essays presented to David Winton Thomas* (ed. Peter R. Ackroyd and Barnabas Lindars; Cambridge: Cambridge University Press, 1968), pp. 81-94.
49. Cf. also Eissfeldt (1956), pp. 138-47 (above, 3.8.1).

50. The use of the imagery of the vine for Jerusalem in both Gen. 49.11 and Isa. 4.2 suggests that both Isaiah and this oracle drew on a specifically Jerusalemite tradition of imagery. This conclusion is supported by the existence elsewhere of a separate Jerusalemite tradition onto which the Davidic monarchs seem to have grafted the fortunes of their line. At any rate, Jerusalem was venerated for its own sake, and as a separate entity within the Davidic realm, as is illustrated by passages such as Ps. 78.60-72 and 1 Kgs 10.26-29 (esp. 10.27).

51. There is no reason to doubt the veracity of the traditions in 1 Samuel 21-22. Indeed, it is the sympathetic portrayal of Ahimelech and the priests of Nob in relation to David's rise which casts suspicion upon the originality of the connection of the judgment oracle against Eli (1 Sam. 2.27-36) to the extermination of the priests of Nob by Saul (1 Sam. 22). Most probably, the tradition in 1 Samuel 22 was incorporated into the narratives of David's rise in order to lend a formal cultic legitimacy to the Judean usurper's cause. The oracle in 1 Sam. 2.27-36 had no original connection to the fate of the priests of Nob in 1 Samuel 22, but a connection was made later, on the strength of Solomon's banishment of Abiathar.

Notes to Chapter 7

1. Cf. the promise to David in 2 Sam. 7.16.

2. 'Ahiyya de Silo et Jeroboam 1er', *Semitica* 11 (1961), pp. 17-27.

3. 1 Sam. 3.1b: 'And the word of Yahweh was rare in those days; there was no frequent vision.

4. Cf. H. Gunkel, *Die Psalmen* (HKAT II/2; Göttingen: Vandenhoeck & Ruprecht, 1926), pp. 340-41. H.J. Kraus (*Psalmen* [BKAT 15/1; Neukirchen-Vluyn: Neukirchener Verlag, 1966], p. 540) adds to Gunkel's observations the recognition of a connection between this psalm and the deuteronomistic circles. Nevertheless, the strongest parallels seem to be with the Yahwistic tradition of the Hexateuch: vv. 12-14 = the crossing of the Red Sea; vv. 15-16, 20 = the waters of Meribah; vv. 18-19 = the people's demand for meat; vv. 21-30 = God's provision of quail and manna; vv. 42-51 = the plagues upon the Egyptians.

5. Cf. Day (1979), p. 91. n. 15. That this psalm is pre-dtr is borne out by the parallels with the Yahwistic traditions of the Hexateuch (above, n. 4). Along the same lines see, more recently, J. Day, 'The Pre-Deuteronomic Allusions to the Covenant in Hosea and Psalm lxxviii', *VT* 36 (1986), pp. 1-12.

6. Cf. Psalms 46; 48; 76; 84; 87; 122; esp. Pss. 48.1.-3; 122.1-5, for the theology of Zion and the Davidic King. Among these psalms, the divine name of Elohim predominates in Psalms 46; 48; 76; 78. This name is found to

a lesser extent as a proper divine name in Psalms 84 and 87, and coupled with Yhwh in the appelation *Yhwh 'ĕlōhîm/'ĕlōmênû* in Psalms 84 and 122.

7. Verses 65-66 constitute a later insert into the text, breaking the development of the theme of judgment with a statement of Yahweh's deliverance of his people. The original Psalm proceeded from v. 64 directly to v. 67, so that the judgment theme reached its climax in the rejection of the tent sanctuary, with which the election of the tribe of Judah over the northern tribes and their sanctuary was then juxtaposed.

8. Cf. the old tradition that Eli was a judge, 1 Sam. 4.18. As far as the dating of Psalm 78 goes, Kraus, appealing to Noth (*Studien*, pp. 171-80), places the authorship of this psalm close to 'den deuteronomistischen Verfasserkreisen des chronistischen Geschichtswerkes' (*Psalmen*, p. 540). C. Westermann (*Praise and Lament in the Psalms* [Atlanta: John Knox, 1981], pp. 236-38) considers Psalm 78 to be probably late. Nonetheless, the psalm has close ties to the Zion songs, which most likely date from the period of the first temple, prior to the catastrophe in 587-586 BCE, and Psalm 78 itself reflects a view of Jerusalem's statics unbesmirched by that humiliation.

9. That Ps. 78.60-72 refers only to an *'ōhel* and a *miškān* confutes the argument that Judg. 18.30-31 (*bêt-hā'ĕlōhîm*) refers to the same event as that described in Ps. 78.60-72.

10. Day (1979), pp. 87-94.

11. Contra Day, ibid., p. 91. Day further claims that the departure of the divine glory in Ps. 78.61 is symbolic of impending destruction, and he cites Ezek. 11.22-23 to support this interpretation. Ezek. 11.22-23 occurs in the context of a vision, in which the cherubim and the glory accompany the prophet when he is taken up from the city. This vision, however, is not one of the impending destruction of the city, but of restoration to the exiles (cf. Ezek. 11.16-21).

12. Ibid.

13. See above, Chapter 5.

14. Day (1979), p. 89.

15. See Mettinger (*Dethronement*, pp. 46-52) for an analysis of this problem.

16. Ibid., pp. 91-97; Mettinger clarifies the differences between the priestly and Zion versions of the *šēm* theology.

17. As in his use of the expressions *nātan 'ālāh* and *'ālāh hāyāh*, below, n. 20.

18. These observations call into question the dtr origins of the prose oracles in Jeremiah, and suggest that a broader theory is needed to explain the use of dtn/dtr language in this prophetic literature.

19. See J. Maxwell Miller and John H. Hayes, *A History of Ancient Israel and Judah* (Philadelphia: Westminster, 1986), pp. 323-32, for a thorough

discussion of the political developments in the northern kingdom after the death of Jeroboam II.

20. The expression *lĕ'ālāh hāyāh* in these two verses occurs only in one other instance, in Num. 5.27, a priestly text. The similar expression, *nātan lĕ'ālāh*, occurs only twice: in Jer. 29.18, and in the priestly text of Num. 5.21.

21. Day (1979, p. 89) makes the succession issue the focus of his analysis of Jer. 7.12-15 on the basis of his claim that the language of 'the place where Yahweh will cause his name to dwell' marks this passage as deuteronomistic. He then infers the concerns of the deuteronomistic author of Kings into his treatment of Jer. 7.12-15. I have tried to show that this special theological concept occurs in this form nowhere in the books of the Deuteronomistic History, but only in Deuteronomy itself (and there only in chs. 12–26, while not at all in the framing chapters). The *šēm* theology may be found in a less concrete form in dtr texts such as 1 Kgs 8.27, 30, 48 (cf. Mettinger, *Dethronement*, pp. 46-52), but cannot be made identical with the dtr concerns. If Mettinger's treatment is in fact correct, the forms of this theology in P and Deuteronomy, in which, respectively, Yahweh or his name actually dwells in the *miškān* or temple, this language is pre-dtr, and reflects the era before the destruction of the temple, while the dtr readings of 1 Kgs 8.27, 30, 48, reflect the consequent crisis in the theology of the deity's dwelling among men. Therefore, just as the succession issue obscures the real focus of this passage for Day and others who wish to tie it to a mid-eleventh-century destruction of Shiloh, the doubtful equation of the phraseology of 'the place where Yahweh will cause his name to dwell' and the dtr theology ignores the real differences in the theology of Deuteronomy and Jeremiah on the one hand, and that of dtr on the other. There is, in fact, nothing in Jer. 7.12-15 to suggest that the peculiar dtr theme of Jerusalem as the only legitimate sanctuary is at work in this passage. Therefore, Day's inference of this dtr theme into the analysis of Jer. 7.12-15 is just that, and nothing more.

22. Finkelstein (1986), pp. 36-37, 39.

23. Cf. de Wette, *Lehrbuch*, p. 302.

24. Finkelstein (1986), pp. 24, 36-38. Nevertheless, a destruction layer from Iron Age I hardly pinpoints a date for this destruction in the mid-eleventh century. Indeed, the famous 1050 BCE date for this layer depends not upon empirical data, but upon the hypothetical reconstruction of the history of the events in 1 Samuel 1–7.

BIBLIOGRAPHY

Abba, R., 'Priests and Levites', *IDB* III, pp. 876-89.

Addis, W.E., *The Documents of the Hexateuch* (2 vols.; New York: G. Putnam's Sons, 1898).

Aharoni, Yohanan, *The Land of the Bible* (2nd edn; Philadelphia: Westminster, 1979).

Albright, W.F., *The Danish Excavations at Shiloh'*, *BASOR* 9 (1923), pp. 10-11.

—'The Danish Excavations at Seilun—A Correction', *PEFQS* 59 (1927), pp. 157-58.

—'Shiloh', *BASOR* 48 (1932), pp. 14-15.

Anderson, W., 'Shiloh', *HBD* (1974), pp. 676-77.

Anonymous, 'Did the Philistines Destroy the Israelite Sanctuary at Shiloh?—The Archaeological Evidence', *BAR* 1 (1975), pp. 3-5.

Bächli, O., *Amphictyonie im Alten Testament* (Basel: Friedrich Reinhardt, 1977).

Bähr, K.C.W.F., *Symbolik des mosäischen Cultus* (Heidelberg: J.C.B. Mohr, 1837-1839).

Baudissin, W.W.G., *Die Geschichte des alttestamentlichen Priesterthums* (Leipzig: S. Hirzel, 1889).

—*Einleitung in das Alte Testament* (Leipzig: S. Hirzel, 1901).

Benzinger, J., *Hebräische Archaeologie* (Freiburg: J.C.B. Mohr [Paul Siebeck], 1894).

Bimson, J., *Redating the Exodus and Conquest* (JSOTS, 5; Sheffield: JSOT Press, 1978).

Bleek, F., *Einleitung in das Alte Testament* (Berlin: G. Reimer, 1860).

—*Einleitung in das Alte Testament* (ed. J. Wellhausen; 4th edn; Berlin: G. Reimer, 1878).

Blenkinsopp, J., 'The Structure of P', *CBQ* 38/3 (1978), pp. 275-92.

Budde, K., *Das Buch der Richter* (KHAT, 7; J.C.B. Mohr [Paul Siebeck], 1897).

—*Die Bücher Samuel* (KHAT, 8; Tübingen/Leipzig: J.C.B. Mohr [Paul Siebeck], 1902).

Buhl, F., *Die Geographie des alten Palästinas* (Freiburg/Leipzig: J.C.B. Mohr [Paul Siebeck], 1896).

Buhl, M.-L. and S. Holm-Nielsen, *Shiloh—The Danish Excavations at Tall Sailun, Palestine, in 1926, 1929, 1932, and 1963: The Pre-Hellenistic Remains* (Copenhagen: The National Museum of Denmark, 1969).

Caquot, A., 'Ahiyya de Silo et Jeroboam 1er', *Sem* 11 (1961), pp. 17-27.

Clifford, R.J., 'The Tent of El and the Israelite Tent of Meeting', *CBQ* 33 (1971), pp. 221-27.

Cody, A., *A History of Old Testament Priesthood* (AnBib, 35; Rome: Pontifical Biblical Institute, 1969).

Cohen, M.A., 'The Role of the Shilonite Priesthood in the United Monarchy of Ancient Israel', *HUCA* 36 (1965), pp. 59-98.

Cross, F.M., 'The Tabernacle', *BA* 10 (1947), pp. 45-68.

—'The Priestly Tabernacle', in *Old Testament Issues* (ed. Samuel Sandmel; New York: Harper & Row, 1968), pp. 39-67.

—*Canaanite Myth and Hebrew Epic* (Cambridge: Harvard University Press, 1973).

Curtiss, S.I., *The Levitical Priests. A Contribution to the Criticism of the Pentateuch* (Edinburgh/Leipzig: 1877)

—*De Aaronitici sacerdotii atque Thorae elohisticae origine dissertatio historico-critica* (Leipzig: 1878)

—*Primitive Semitic Religion Today* (New York/Chicago: Fleming H. Revell, 1902) = *Ursemitische Religion im Volksleben des heutigen Orients* (Leipzig: J.C. Hinrich, 1903)

Davies, P.R., 'Ark or Ephod in 1 Sam xiv 18?', *JTS* 26 (1975), pp. 82-87.

Day, J., 'The Destruction of the Shiloh Sanctuary and Jeremiah vii 12, 14', VTSup 30 (1979), pp. 87-94.

—'The Pre-Deuteronomic Allusions to the Covenant in Hosea and Psalm lxxviii', *VT* 36 (1986), pp. 1-12.

Delitzsch, Franz, *Pentateuch-kritische Studien*, reprinted from a series of twelve articles which appeared in *Zeitschrift für kirchliche Wissenschaft und kirchliches Leben* ([1880]; publisher and place of publication not given; pagination according to the articles in the reprinted volume).

Dibelius, M., *Die Lade Jahves* (FRLANT, 7; Göttingen: Vandenhoeck & Ruprecht, 1906).

Dillmann, A., *Die Bücher Numeri, Deuteronomium, und Josua* (2nd edn; Leipzig: S. Hirzel, 1886).

Duhm, B., *Die Theologie der Propheten als Grundlage für die innere Entwicklungsgeschichte der israelitischen Religion* (Bonn: Adoph Marcus, 1875).

Dus, J., 'Die Geburtslegende Samuels 1 Sam. 1 (Eine traditionsgeschichtliche Untersuchung zu 1 Sam. 1-3)', *Revista Degli Studia Orientali* 43 (1968), pp. 163-94.

Dussaud, R., *Le sacrifice en Israel et chez les Phéniciens* (Paris: E. Leroux, 1914).

—*Les origines canaanéenes du sacrifice israélite* (Paris: E. Leroux, 1921).

—*Les découvertes de Ras Shamra et l'Ancien Testament* (2nd edn; Paris: P. Geuthner, 1941).

Eissfeldt, O., *Hexateuch-Synopse* (Leipzig: J.C. Hinrich, 1922).

—'Silo und Jerusalem', *VTSup* 4 (1956), pp. 138-47.

Emerton, J.A., 'Some Difficult Words in Genesis 49', in *Words and Meanings. Essays presented to David Winton Thomas* (ed. Peter R. Ackroyd and Barnabas Lindars; Cambridge: Cambridge University Press, 1968).

Ewald, H., *Geschichte des Volkes Israel* (8 vols.; 3rd edn; Göttingen: Dietrichsche Buchhandlung, 1864-1866).

Finkelstein, I., 'Shiloh, 1981', *IEJ* 32 (1982), pp. 148-50.

—'Shiloh, 1982', *IEJ* 33 (1983), pp. 123-26.

—'Shiloh Yields Some, but not All, of its Secrets', *BAR* 12 (1986), pp. 22-41.

—*The Archaeology of the Israelite Settlement* (IES: Jerusalem, 1988).

Fretheim, T.E., 'The Priestly Documents: Anti-Temple?', *VT* 18 (1968), pp. 313-29.

Gaster, T., *Myth, Legend, and Custom in the Old Testament* (New York/Evanston: Harper & Row, 1969.

Glueck, N. 'Shiloh', *AJA* 37 (1933), pp. 166-67.

—'Shiloh', *BASOR* 52 (1933), pp. 30-31.

—'Shiloh', *QDAP* 3 (1934), pp. 180.

Gnuse, R.K., *The Dream and Theophany of Samuel: Its Structure in Relation to Ancient Near Eastern Dreams and its Theological Significance* (Lanham, MD: University Press of America, 1984).

Graf, K.H., *De Templo Silonensi commentatio ad illustrandum locum Iud. xviii 30, 31* (1855).

—*Die geschichtlichen Bücher des Alten Testaments* (Leipzig: T.O. Weizel, 1866).

—'Zur Geschichte des Stammes Levi', in *Archiv für wissenschaftliche Erforschung des Alten Testaments* (ed. Adalbert Merx; 2 vols; Halle: Buchhandlung des Waisenhauses, 1867, 1869), I, pp. 68-106.

Gramberg, C.P.W., *Kritische Geschichte der Religionsideen des Alten Testaments* (2 vols.; Berlin: Duncker & Humblot, 1829, 1830).

Gressmann, H. *et al.*, *Die Schriften des Alten Testaments* (7 vols.; Göttingen: Vandenhoeck & Ruprecht, 1910-1915).

—*Die Lade Jahwes und das Allerheiligste des salomonischen Tempels* (Berlin: W. Kohlhammer, 1920).

Gunkel, H., *Die Urgeschichte und die Patriarchen* (SAT, I/1; Göttingen: Vandenhoeck & Ruprecht, 1911).

—*Die Psalmen* (HKAT, II/2; Göttingen: Vandenhoeck & Ruprecht, 1926).

Gunn, D.M., 'Narrative Patterns and Oral Tradition in Judges and Samuel', *VT* 24 (1974), pp. 286-317.

—*The Story of King David* (JSOTS, 6; Sheffield: JSOT, 1978).

Gunneweg, A.H., *Geschichte Israels bis Bar Kochba* (Stuttgart: W. Kohlhammer, 1972).

Guthe, H. *Geschichte des Volkes Israel* (Tübingen/Leipzig: J.C.B. Mohr [Paul Siebeck], 1904).

Hallo, W.H., and W.K. Simpson, *The Ancient Near East; A History* (New York: Harcourt Brace Jovanovich, 1971).

Haneberg, D.B. von, *Das Handbuch der biblischen Alterthumskunde = Die religiösen Alterthümer der Bibel* (2nd edn; München: J.G. Cotta, 1869).

Haran, M., 'The Ark of the Covenant and the Cherubs', *EI* 5 (1958), pp. 83-89

—'The Ark and the Cherubim. Their Symbolic Significance in Biblical Ritual', *IEJ* 9 (1959), pp. 30-38.

—'The Nature of the *'Ohel Mo'edh* in Pentateuchal Studies', *JSS* 5 (1960), pp. 50-65.

—'Studies in the Account of the Levitical Cities', *JBL* 89 (1961), pp. 45-54, 156-65.

—'Shiloh and Jerusalem. The Origin of the Priestly Tradition in the Pentateuch', *JBL* 81 (1962), pp. 14-24.

—'The Priestly Image of the Tabernacle', *HUCA* 36 (1965), pp. 191-226.

—'Holiness Code', *EncJud* 8 (1971), pp. 820-25.

—*Temples and Temple Service in Ancient Israel* (Oxford: Clarendon, 1978).

—'Behind the Scenes of History: Determining the Date of the Priestly Source', *JBL* 100 (1981), pp. 321-33.

Hayes, J.H., and J.M. Miller (eds.), *Israelite and Judean History* (Philadelphia: Westminster, 1977).

—and F. Prussner, *Old Testament Theology: Its History and Development* (Atlanta: John Knox, 1985).

Hengstenberg, E.W., *Die Authentie des Pentateuches* (Berlin: Ludwig Oehmigke, 1839).

Holzinger, H. *Einleitung in den Hexateuch* (Freiburg/Tübingen: J.C.B. Mohr [Paul Siebeck], 1893).

Hupfeldt, H. *Die Quellen der Genesis und die Art ihrer Zusammensetzung* (Berlin: Wiegandt & Grieben, 1853).

Hylander, I., *Die literarische Samuel–Saul Komplex (1 Sam. 1–15) traditionsgeschichtlich untersucht* (Uppsala: Almquist & Wiksell, 1932).

Ibrahim, M.M., 'The Collared-Rim Jar of the Early Iron Age', in *Archaeology in the Levant. Essays for Kathleen Kenyon* (ed. R. Moorey and P. Parr; Westminster, England: Aris & Phillips, 1978), pp. 116-26.

Kampinski, A., 'Shilo', *EAEHL* (1970), pp. 546-48 (Hebrew).

Karge, P., *Geschichte des Bundesgedankens im Alten Testament* (Münster i.W.: Aschendorfsche Buchhandlung, 1910).

Kaufmann, Y., *The Religion of Israel: From the Beginnings to the Babylonian Exile* (Chicago/London: University of Chicago Press/George Allen & Unwin, 1960).

Kayser, A., *Das vorexilische Buch der Urgeschichte Israels und seine Erweiterungen* (Strasbourg: Schmidt, 1874).

Keil, K.F., *Handbuch der biblischen Archaeologie* (2 vols.; Frankfurt am Main/Erlangen: Heyder & Zimmer, 1858, 1859).

Kittel, R., *Geschichte der Hebräer* (2 vols.; Gotha: Friedrich Andreas Perthes, 1888, 1892); republished as *Geschichte des Volkes Israel* (2nd edn; 2 vols.; Gotha: Friedrich Andreas Perthes, 1909, 1912).

Kjaer, H., 'The Danish Excavations at Shiloh. Preliminary Report', *PEFQS* 59 (1927), pp. 202-13.

—'Shiloh. A Summary Report of the Second Danish Expedition, 1929', *PEQ* 63 (1931), pp. 71-88.

—'The Excavation of Shiloh, 1929. Preliminary Report', *JPOS* 10 (1930), pp. 87-174.

Kleinert, P., *Deuteronomium und der Deuteronomiker* (Bielefeld/Leipzig: Velhagen & Klasing, 1872).

Knierim, R. 'The Composition of the Pentateuch', in *SBL 1985 Seminar Papers* (ed. Kent Harold Richards; Atlanta: Scholars Press, 1985), pp. 393-415.

Knobel, A. *Die Bücher Exodus und Leviticus* (ed. A. Dillmann; 2nd edn; Leipzig: S. Hirzel, 1880).

Koch, K., ''Ohel' in *TWAT* I, pp. 127-42.

Köhler, A., *Lehrbuch der biblischen Geschichte Alten Testamentes* (2 vols.; Erlangen; Andreas Deichert, 1875, 1884).

Kraus, H.J., *Psalmen* (BKAT, 15; 2 vols.; Neukirchen-Vluyn: Neukirchener Verlag, 1966).

Kuenen, A., *Historisch-kritisch Onderzoek naar het onstaan en Boeken des Ouden Verbonds* (3 vols.; Leiden: P. Engels, 1861-1865).

—*De Godsdienst van Israel* (2 vols.; Haarlem: A.C. Krusemann, 1869, 1870) = *The Religion of Israel* (London: Williams & Norgate, 1882).

—'Critische Bijtragen tot de Geschiednis van den Israelitischen Godsdienst, IV: Zadok en de Zadokieten', *Theologisch Tijschrift* 3 (1869), pp. 463-509; 'VII: De Stam Levi', 5 (1872), pp. 628-70.

Küper, C., *Das Priesterthum des Alten Bundes* (Berlin: Wilhelm Herz, 1866).

Lapp, N.L., 'Shiloh', *HBD* (1985), pp. 943-44.

Levine, B.A., 'Priestly Writers', *IDBSup*, pp. 683-87.

Lindblom, H., 'The Political Background of the Shiloh Oracle', *VTSup* 1 (1953), pp. 73-87.

Lods, A., *Israel, des origines au milieu du VIII^c siècle* (Paris: Renaissance du livre, 1930) = *Israel, from its Beginnings to the Middle of the Eighth Century* (trans. S.H. Hooke; New York: Alfred A. Knopf, 1932).

Maier, J., *Das altisraelitische Ladeheiligtun* (BZAW, 93; Berlin; Alfred Töpelmann, 1965)

Margolis, M.L., *The Book of Joshua in Greek* (Paris: Librarie Orientaliste Paul Guethner, 1931).

McCarter, P.K., *I Samuel* (AB, 8; Garden City: Doubleday, 1980)

—*II Samuel* (AB, 9; Garden City: Doubleday, 1984).

McCown, C.C., 'Seilun', *AJA* 34 (1930), pp. 95-96.

Mendenhall, G.E., 'Law and Covenant in Israel and the Ancient Near East', *BA* 17 (1954), pp. 26-46, and 'Covenant Forms in the Israelite Tradition', *BA* 17 (1954), pp. 50-76; reprinted as *Law and Covenant in Israel and the Ancient Near East* (Pittsburg: Biblical Colloquium, 1955).

Mettinger, T.N.D., *The Dethronement of Sabaoth. Studies in the Shem and Kabod Theologies* (CB OTS, 18; Lund: CWK Gleerup, 1982).

—'YHWH SABAOTH: The Heavenly King on the Cherubim Throne', in *Studies in the Period of David and Solomon* (ed. Tomoo Ishida; Winona Lake: Eisenbrauns, 1982), pp. 109-38.

Meyer, E., *Die Israeliten und ihre Nachbarstämme* (Halle: Max Niemeyer, 1906).

Milgrom, J., 'Leviticus, Book of', *EncJud* 11 (1971), pp. 138-47.

Miller, J.M., 'Jebus and Jerusalem: A Case of Mistaken Identity', *ZDPV* 90 (1974), pp. 115-27.

—'Geba/Gibeah of Benjamin', *VT* 25 (1975), pp. 145-66.

—and J.H. Hayes, *A History of Ancient Israel and Judah* (Philadelphia: Westminster, 1986).

Mowinckel, S., *Psalmenstudien* (6 vols.; Oslo: Jacob Dybwad, 1921-1924; reprinted 2 vols.; Amsterdam: P. Schippers, 1961).

—*Zur Frage nach dokumentarischen Quellen in Josua 13-19* (Oslo: Jacob Dybwad, 1946).

—*The Psalms in Israel's Worship* (Oxford: Basil Blackwell, 1962).

—*Tetrateuch-Pentateuch-Hexateuch: Die Berichte über die Landnahme in den drei altisraelitischen Geschichtswerken* (BZAW, 90; Berlin: Alfred Töpelmann, 1964).

—*Erwägungen zur Pentateuch Quellenfrage* (Trondheim: Universitetsvorlaget, 1964).

Nöldeke, T., *Die alttestamentliche Literatur in einer Reihe von Aufsätzen dargestellt* (Leipzig: Quand & Handel, 1868).

—*Untersuchungen zur Kritik des Alten Testaments* (Kiel: Schwer'sche Buchhandlung, 1869).

Noth, M., *Die israelitischen Personnamen im Rahmen der gemeinsemitischen Namengebung* (Stuttgart: W. Kohlhammer, 1928; reprinted Hildesheim: Georg Olms, 1980).

—*Das System der zwölf Stämme Israels* (Stuttgart: W. Kohlhammer, 1930).

—*Überlieferungsgeschichtliche Studien* (Tübingen: Max Niemeyer, 1943) = *The Deuteronomistic History* (JSOTS, 15; Sheffield: JSOT Press, 1981).

—'Jerusalem und die israelitische Tradition', *OTS* 8 (1950), pp. 28-46.

—*Das Buch Josua* (HAT, 7; Tübingen: J.C.B. Mohr [Paul Siebeck], 1953).

—'The Background of Judges 17-18', in *Israel's Prophetic Heritage: Essays in Honor of James Muilenburg* (ed. B.W. Anderson and Walter Harrelson; New York: Harper & Brothers, 1962), pp. 68-85.

—'Samuel und Silo', *VT* 13 (1963), pp. 390-400.

—*Geschichte Israels* (6th edn; Göttingen: Vandenhoeck & Ruprecht, 1966).

Oehler, G.F. *Theologie des Alten Testaments* (2 vols.; Tübingen: J.J. Heckenhauer, 1873, 1874).

Otto, E., *Das Mazzotfest zu Gilgal* (BWANT, 6/7; Stuttgart: W. Kohlhammer, 1975).

Pearce, R.A., 'Shiloh and Jer. vii 12, 14 & 15', *VT* 23 (1973), pp. 105-108.

Pritchard, J.B. (ed.), *Ancient Near Eastern Texts Relating to the Old Testament* (3rd edn; Princeton: Princeton University Press, 1969).

Procksch, O., *Das nordhebräische Sagenbuch: Die Elohimquelle* (Leipzig: J.C. Hinrich, 1906).

—*Die Genesis* (KAT, 1; Leipzig: A. Deichert, 1913).

—*Theologie des Alten Testaments* (Gütersloh: C. Bertelmann, 1950).

Rabe, V.W., 'The Identity of the Priestly Tabernacle', *JNES* 25 (1966), pp. 132-34.

Rad, G. von, 'Zelt und Lade', *NKZ* 42 (1931), pp. 476-98; reprinted in *Gesammelte Studien zum Alten Testament* (2 vols.; München: Chr. Kaiser, 1958), II, pp. 109-29.

—*Das formgeschichtliche Problem des Hexateuch* (BWANT, 6/26; Stuttgart; W. Kohlhammer, 1938) = *The Problem of the Hexateuch and Other Essays* (New York: McGraw-Hill, 1966), pp. 1-78.

Reuss, E., *Geschichte der heiligen Schriften Alten Testaments* (Braunschweig: C.A. Schwetschke & Sohn, 1881).

Richardson, A.T., 'The Site of Shiloh', *PEFQS* 57 (1925), pp. 162-63.

—'The Site of Shiloh', *PEFQS* 59 (1927), pp. 85-88.

Riehm, E., *Die Gesetzgebung Mosis im lande Moab* (Gotha: Friedrich Andreas Perthes, 1854).

—*Handwörterbuch des biblischen Alterthums* (2 vols.; Bielefeld/Leipzig: Velhagen & Klasing, 1884).

—*Einleitung in das Alte Testament* (Halle: Eugen Strien, 1889).

Riis, P.J., 'Discussion Remarks to the Jubilee Congress of the German Palestine Society in Tübingen' (unpublished, 1977)

Robinson, E., and E. Smith, *Biblical Researches in Palestine, and in the Adjacent Regions: A Journal of Travels in the Year 1838* (2 vols.; 11th edn; London: John Murray, 1874).

Rofé, A., 'The End of the Book of Joshua According to the Septuagint', *Henoch* 4 (1982), pp. 17-36.

Rogerson, J., *Old Testament Criticism in the Nineteenth Century: England and Germany* (London: SPCK, 1985).

Rossum, J. van, 'Waneer is Silo verwoest?', *NedTT* 24 (1970), pp. 321-32.

Rudolph, W., *Der 'Elohist' von Exodus bis Josua* (Berlin: Alfred Töpelmann, 1938).

Saalschütz, J.L., *Das mosäische Recht* (2nd edn; Berlin: Carl Heymann, 1853).

—*Archaeologie der Hebräer* (Königsberg: Bornträger, 1855).

Schmitt, R., *Zelt und Lade* (Gütersloh: Gerd Mohn, 1972).

Schrader, E., *Studien zur Kritik und Erklärung der biblischen Urgeschichte. Gen. Kap. I-XI* (Zürich: Meyer & Zeller, 1863).

—*Die Keilinschriften und das Alte Testament* (Giessen: J. Ricker, 1872; 2nd edn; Giessen: J. Ricker, 1883; 3rd edn; Berlin: Reuther und Reichard, 1903).

Shiloh, Y., Review of Marie-Louis Buhl and Svend Holm-Nielsen, *Shiloh. The Danish Excavations at Tall Sailun, Palestine, in 1926, 1929, 1932, and 1963: The Pre-Hellenistic Remains* (Copenhagen: The National Museum of Denmark, 1969), in *IEJ* 21 (1971), pp. 67-69.

—'The Camp at Shiloh' in *Eretz Shomron* (Jerusalem: IES, 1973), pp. xi-xii, 10-19 (Hebrew).

Smend, R., Sr, *Lehrbuch der alttestamentlichen Religionsgeschichte* (2nd edn; Freiburg: J.C.B. Mohr [Paul Siebeck], 1899).

—*Die Erzählung des Hexateuch* (Berlin: G. Reimer, 1912).

Smend, R., *Wilhelm Martin Leberecht de Wettes Arbeit am Alten und am Neuen Testament* (Basel: Helbing & Lichtenbahn, 1958).

Stade, B., *Geschichte des Volkes Israel* (2 vols.; Berlin: G. Grote, 1887).

Tsevat, M., 'Studies in the Book of Samuel. IV: Yahweh Seba'ot', *HUCA* 36 (1965), pp. 49-58.

Vatke, W., *Biblische Theologie* (Berlin: G. Bethge, 1835).

—*Historisch-kritische Einleitung in das Alte Tstament* (Bonn: Emil Strauss, 1886).

Vaux, R. de, *Les institutions de l'Ancien Testament* (Paris: Les Editions du Cerf, 1957) = *Ancient Israel* (2 vols.; London-New York: Longman & Todd/Doubleday, 1961).

—*Histoire ancienne d'Israel: Des origines à l'installation en Canaan* (Paris: J. Gabalda, 1971), and *Histoire ancienne d'Israel: La période des Juges* (Paris: J. Gabalda, 1973) = *The Early History of Israel* (Philadelphia: Westminster, 1978).

Vink, J.G., 'The Date and Origin of the Priestly Code in the Old Testament', *OTS* 15 (1969), pp. 1-144.

Weinfeld, M., *Getting at the Roots of Wellhausen's Understanding of the Law of Israel on the 100th Anniversary of the Prolegomena* (Jerusalem: Institute for Advanced Studies of the Hebrew University, 1978).

—'The Extent of the Promised Land—The Status of Transjordan', in *Das Land Israel in biblischer Zeit* (ed. G. Strecker; Göttingen: Vandenhoeck & Ruprecht, 1983), pp. 59-75.

Wellhausen, J., *Der text der Bücher Samuelis* (Göttingen: Vandenhoeck & Ruprecht, 1871.

—*Geschichte Israels* (Berlin: G. Reimer, 1878), reprinted as the *Prolegomena zur Geschichte Israels* (Berlin: G. Reimer, 1883).

—*Israelitische und jüdische Geschichte* (Berlin: G. Reimer, 1897).

—*Die Composition des Hexateuchs und der historischen Bücher des Alten Testaments* (3rd edn; Berlin: Walter de Gruyter, 1963); reprinted from the articles in *JbDT* 21 (1876), pp. 392-450; 531-602; 22 (1877) 407-79, and Wellhausen's excursus in the fourth edition of Bleek's *Einleitung* (1878), pp. 181-207.

Westermann, C., *Praise and Lament in the Psalms* (Atlanta: John Knox, 1981).

Wette, W.M.L. de, *Beiträge zur Einleitung in das Alte Testament* (2 vols.; Halle: ben Schimmelpfennig, 1806, 1807).

—*Lehrbuch der hebräisch-jüdischen Archaeologie* (3rd edn; Leipzig: Wilhelm Vogel, 1842).

Winer, G.B., *Biblisches Realwörterbuch* (Leipzig: Carl Heinrich, 1820).

Yadin, Y., *Hazor I. An Account of the First Season of Excavations, 1955* (Jerusalem: Magnes Press, 1958).

—*Hazor II. An Account of the Second Season of Excavations, 1956* (Jerusalem: Magnes Press, 1960).

—*Hazor III-IV. An Account of the Third and Fourth Seasons of Excavations, 1957-1958* (Jerusalem: Magnes Press, 1961).

Zayadine, F., Review of M.L. Buhl and S. Holm-Nielsen, *Shiloh. The Danish Excavations of Tall Sailun, Palestine* (Copenhagen: The Danish National Museum, 1969) in *Berytus* 19 (1970), pp. 159-61.

INDEXES

INDEX OF BIBLICAL REFERENCES

INDEX OF AUTHORS

DATE DUE